T0305164

DECOLONIZING DEVELOPMENT

Food, Heritage and Trade in
Post-Authoritarian Environments

Jennifer Keahey

BRISTOL
UNIVERSITY
PRESS

First published in Great Britain in 2024 by

Bristol University Press
University of Bristol
1–9 Old Park Hill
Bristol
BS2 8BB
UK
t: +44 (0)117 374 6645
e: bup-info@bristol.ac.uk

Details of international sales and distribution partners are available at bristoluniversitypress.co.uk

© Bristol University Press 2024

British Library Cataloguing in Publication Data
A catalogue record for this book is available from the British Library

ISBN 978-1-5292-2436-8 hardcover
ISBN 978-1-5292-2437-5 ePub
ISBN 978-1-5292-2438-2 ePdf

The right of Jennifer Keahey to be identified as author of this work has been asserted by her in accordance with the Copyright, Designs and Patents Act 1988.

Cover design: Hayes Design and Advertising
Front cover image: Duncan Hilton
Bristol University Press use environmentally responsible print partners.
Printed and bound in Great Britain by CPI Group (UK) Ltd, Croydon, CR0 4YY

FSC
www.fsc.org
MIX
Paper | Supporting
responsible forestry
FSC® C013604

For my mother, Shaunna Jensen Sandersfeld,
the sun of my heart

Contents

List of Figures

List of Abbreviations

ANC	African National Congress
APO	African Political Organization
ATO	alternative trade organization
EU	European Union
FAO	Food and Agriculture Organization
FDI	foreign direct investment
FTI	Fairtrade International
FTT	fair Trade Tourism
GI	geographic indication
GCBC	Greater Cederberg Biodiversity Corridor
GMO	genetically modified organism
IGO	international governance organization
IFOAM	International Federation of Organic Agriculture Movements
KGB	Committee for State Security (Soviet secret police and foreign intelligence)
LBLA	Association of Latvian Organic Agriculture Organizations
LGBTQ+	Lesbian, Gay, Bisexual, Trans, Queer, and beyond
LLKC	Latvian Rural Advisory and Training Centre
LSDSP	Latvian Social Democratic Workers' Party
LZS	Latvian Farmer's Union
NIC	Natal Indian Congress
NP	National Party
PAR	participatory action research
PFAS	Per- and polyfluorinated alkyl substances
SDGs	Sustainable Development Goals
SACP	South African Communist Party
SSR	Soviet Socialist Republic
TRC	Truth and Reconciliation Commission
WNC	South African Women's National Coalition
UNESCO	United Nations Education, Science, and Culture Organization
WFTO	World Fair Trade Organization

Glossary

Abya Yala: the Indigenous name ascribed to the Americas, deriving from the Guna people of Panama and Colombia, and reclaimed within decolonial science as part of the discursive process of naming and recognizing precolonial histories, languages and lands.

anomie: the collective malady of derangement that occurs when established social norms, bonds, and values are uprooted due to modernizing influences and social upheaval.

Anthropocene: our current geological epoch; an extensive interval of time measured by chronologically dating our planetary rock record and identifying key features that indicate major events over the course of Earth's history.

apartheid: an institutionalized system of racial segregation and discrimination; deriving from the South African language of Afrikaans, this term signifies an existential state of separateness.

authoritarian monocultures: a term introduced in this book to describe a colonizing mode of existence grounded in the imperial logic of categorical separateness and marked by hierarchy, uniformity and warfare.

Axial Age: an historic period of religious and philosophical development that roughly occurred between 900 and 300 BCE within the ancient Afro-Eurasian world-system.

axiology: the philosophical study of the nature of ethics, moral values and value judgements.

biodynamic: a holistic approach to food production that goes beyond organic agriculture by generating on-farm fertility through such practices as composting, crop rotation, cover cropping, animal integration and the diversification of plant species and varieties.

bourgeoisie: the mercantilist and financial classes; those who own the means of production and control most of the wealth in modern capitalist societies; in contrast to the proletariat who sell their labour power on the market.

Daina: quatrain-based poems comprising the Latvian folk song tradition. These four-line songs are a living repository of ancient oral knowledge and the basis of Latvian moral philosophy.

Digital Age: an historic period of development within the globalized terrain of the twenty-first century and marked by rapid technological change.

ecofeminism: a transnational movement and body of theory that combines feminist and ecological precepts to identify the relationship between patriarchal oppression and environmental degradation.

ecojustice: an Indigenous practice that considers the rights of human beings in relation to those of other species. An ecojustice approach to development asks us to construct caring and mutually beneficial relationships with all peoples and species.

ecologies of knowledge: a decolonial term that expresses an ecological approach to knowledge development; one that is committed to preserving intellectual diversity and bringing different knowledge systems into dialogue in social and scientific practice.

egalitarian ecocultures: a term introduced in this book to describe an emancipatory mode of existence grounded in the interconnected logic of Indigenous cosmovisions and marked by regenerative nature–society partnerships that value the diversity of life.

epistemicide: the destruction of knowledge through colonization and agricultural modernization, accompanied by the loss of biodiversity and other forms of genocidal violence.

epistemology: the philosophical study of the nature of knowledge, especially concerning methods, validity and scope.

epistemic disobedience: a decolonial term for cognitive revolution, or the praxis of delinking from the imperialist logic of either/or thinking and zero-sum relationships to advance both/and epistemologies and reciprocal relationships that support mutual learning and growth.

fair trade: a transnational social movement comprised of a wide array of actors, initiatives and certification systems that are working to institute just and sustainable alternatives to economic development.

Fairtrade: a branch of the fair trade movement governed by Fairtrade International, which employs a product certification system to support small-scale producers and workers.

foodways: the intersection of food with culture and history; a set of social practices relating to food production, distribution, and consumption; intergenerational culinary traditions.

heterotopia: a counterhegemonic space, or imperfectly realized utopia; as cultural and institutional counter-worlds, these spaces reside at the margins of the hegemonic world in which they are situated, both challenging and reproducing hegemony in practice.

Industrial Revolution: a modernizing wave of development marked by a shift from an agrarian to an industrial mode of production and the rise of secular nation states.

longue durée: deriving from the French Annales School of history and denoting the study of slowly evolving structures over extended periods of time.

more-than-representational: a social theory and movement that unpacks the embodied and multi-sensual dynamics giving meaning to everyday life; more-than-representational studies move beyond the limited sense of empirical sight to consider information obtained through sound, taste, touch, smell, memory and emotion.

neoliberal: a set of political and economic policies with origins in eighteenth-century European philosophy; extolling private property, deregulated markets and limited government.

ontology: the philosophical study of the nature of reality, being and existence.

organic: food and farming methods that do not use petrochemical fertilizers, pesticides or other industrial inputs.

perestroika: a policy of social reconstruction implemented by Mikhail Gorbachev in the 1980s, in a bid to decentralize and democratize the Soviet political economy.

praxis: a mode of knowledge production that joins theory and practice, through the practical application of theory and the advancement of theory through practice.

psychosocial: an analytical framework that sits at the junction of psychology and sociology, where it examines the social dynamics of mental health.

radical openness: a critical pedagogy with multi-situated roots in Black feminist theory; it denotes both a liberating space at the margins of society and a psychosocial attitude; the latter of which both indicates a willingness to sit with discomfort and the cognitive ability to recognize the existence of multiple truths.

rationalization: a sociological term that signifies the replacement of traditional motivators for social development – such as those pertaining to values, culture and emotions – with modern motivators like calculability, efficiency and predictability.

Russification: a policy of assimilation enacted by the Soviet Union to subdue resistance in occupied territories; it involved moving Russian-speaking peoples into these areas, deporting conquered peoples to Siberia and banning Indigenous languages and cultural traditions.

Saeima: Parliament of Latvia

social imaginary: a creative and symbolic dimension of social reality; an ideal set of social values, practices and institutions in which people revisit their social existence and imagine new ways of living.

spacetime: a physics term and mathematical model that treats three-dimensional space and one-dimensional time as a manifold four-dimensional system.

terroir: a term of French origin that denotes the biosocial relationship between a cultural commodity and the land upon which it is produced.

Third World: a geopolitical term with roots in Cold War politics; in the global North, the capitalist and the socialist spheres of power that emerged after the Second World War became the First and Second Worlds, while non-aligned territories in the global South comprised the Third World.

transmodern: a philosophical concept deriving from Spanish feminist philosophy and incorporated into the Latin American decoloniality movement; it denotes a third way between modernity and tradition, inspiring cultural movements to envision more egalitarian futures that incorporate elements of both.

Turtle Island: the name ascribed to North America by many of the Indigenous peoples of this region and reclaimed within decolonial science as part of the discursive process of reclaiming histories, languages and lands.

worldsense: In line with more-than-representational theory, this term extends the concept of worldview beyond the single sense of sight.

Comparative Timeline

Latvia	South Africa
	500–1600 (approximate) Bantu-speaking peoples enter South Africa,
1186 The German monk, Meinhard of Segeberg, establishes a Livonian colony in Baltics	intermingling with the Khoe-Sān and forming chiefdoms in the east while the Khoe-Sān retain control over the west
1195 Pope Celestine III authorizes Northern Crusades to convert Baltics to Christianity	
1201 Albert of Livonia founds city of Rīga, establishes Catholic military order	
1206 Livonian Sword Brothers embark upon campaign of ethnic cleansing	
1236 Sword Brothers defeated at Battle of Saule	
1237 German Teutonic Order sends knights to the Baltics to subdue resistance	
end of 1200s Teutonic Order subdues Latvian tribes and awards land to knights	
end of 1400s German Baltic feudalism formalized, with Indigenous Latvians locked into serfdom	**1488** Portuguese explorer, Bartolemeu Dias, lands in South African Cape
1562 Russia invades and dissolves Livonian Order but allows German Balts to retain ownership of land and serfs	
1629 Latvia absorbed into Swedish Empire	**1652** Dutch East India Company establishes
1700 Russia invades, starting Great Northern War	colonial outpost in South African Cape

Latvia	South Africa
1710 Russia secures control of Baltics	
1721 Treaty of Nystad allows German Balts to retain control over feudal estates	**1795** British Empire invades South Africa **1806** British conquer Cape Colony and outlaw use of the Dutch language **1835–1846** Afrikaners make Great Trek into interior, establish Boer Republics
1850s–1880s Young Latvians intellectual movement: first wave of national awakening	**1838** British Empire abolishes slavery
1861 Russia abolishes serfdom	**1880–1881** First Anglo-Boer War
1881 Ascension of Alexander III and reversal of liberal reforms	**1886** Afrikaners discover gold in the Transvaal
1890s–1918 New Current left political movement: second wave of national awakening	**1899–1902** Second Anglo-Boer war
	1910 South Africa becomes self-governing union within the British Commonwealth **1911** First racial census **1913** Natives Land Act institutionalizes colonial land theft
1914–1918 World War I	**1914** Formation of Afrikaner Nationalist Party
1918 People's Council of Latvia declares independence, sparking civil war	
1920 Latvia secures independence and passes Agrarian Reform Act	
1922 Kārlis Ulmanis becomes first president of the Republic of Latvia	
1939–1945 World War II	**1948** National Party wins election restricted to white voters
1949 Stalin orders mass deportations to quell opposition to collectivization of farms	**1950** National Party begins constructing apartheid state via a series of legislative acts

Latvia	South Africa

1953
Nikita Khrushchev assumes power, relaxes political repression
1957
Krushchev Thaw ends with Anti-Party Group Purge

1958
Hendrik Voerwoerd removes South Africa from the British Commonwealth
1960
Sharpeville Massacre
1960s-1970s
Black Consciousness youth movement
1976
Soweto Uprising
1984
New constitution grants limited rights to Indian and coloured South Africans

1985
Mikhail Gorbachev comes into power
1986
Chernobyl nuclear disaster
1987-1991
Baltic Singing Revolution: third wave of national awakening

1990
Frederik Willem de Klerk releases Nelson Rolihlahla Mandela from prison

1991
Latvia declares independence, reinstates inter-war constitution
1994
Soviet troops depart from Latvia

1994
Mandela becomes first Black president
1995-2002
Truth and Reconciliation Commission investigates crimes against humanity
1996
New constitution enshrines commitments to democracy and social equality

1999
Vaira Vīķe-Freiberga becomes first woman president of Latvia

2004
Latvia joins NATO and the EU
2005
Latvia pre-emptively bans same-sex marriage

2004
South Africa becomes first African nation to legalise same-sex marriage

Acknowledgements

When looking back on the writing of this book, I am astonished that I managed to finish it. I began working on this project in 2020 during the outbreak of a global pandemic and at a time of personal crisis, and I continued writing it as both predicaments deepened. These crises played a role in shaping the tone of the book, as my shock and grief over the events occurring in my world compelled me to reflect more deeply on the nature and meaning of oppression. Either through acts of cruelty or compassion, the people involved in my world at this time served to remind me that the political is personal.

First, I thank my ancestors and the many species of the American West who provided me with shelter during this storm. I include my javelina neighbours, whose playful games in the arroyo behind my home never fail to make me laugh, the coyotes whose raucous howls kept me company during late-night writing sessions, and the white-winged dove who hatched a baby on the ledge outside of my window, enabling me to witness their first flight. I also wish to acknowledge the Akimel O'odham (Pima) and Piipaash (Maricopa) peoples, upon whose ancestral homelands I work and live. I am deeply grateful for your strength and resilience in protecting the cultural and biological diversity of the Salt River Valley, and the Sonoran Desert more broadly. I aspire to uphold my responsibilities according to your example.

Second, I am grateful to close friends and family for their loving kindness and support. My mother, Shaunna Jensen Sandersfeld, took the time to listen to me read each chapter upon its completion, helping me to improve the clarity of the content from the perspective of a non-academic reader. Duncan Hilton – the founder of *The Paper Toadstool*, a queer art collective to which I belong – gifted me with the use of one of his glorious abstracts for the book cover. Frédérique Autret Leballeur organized a beachside writing retreat so that I could breathe fresh air and embrace the shifting light as I wrote the cultural chapters in this book.

My professorial friends Devparna Roy and Majia Nadesan spent countless hours talking theory with me, but it was fellow development sociologist Sam Cohn who started me down this long road by telling me that I knew more than I thought I did and to write it all down in a book. My graduate student, Cailan Cordwell played an instrumental role as well, in providing an initial edit of the book, and in drafting the comparative historical timeline.

Third, I am grateful to Bristol University Press for bringing this book to fruition and for its broader commitment to publishing transformative social research that does not shy away from big topics. My initial editor, Philippa Grand, played an instrumental role in bringing me into the press and fielding peer reviews. After her departure, my editor Stephen Wenham and assistant editor Zoë Forbes worked closely with me to bring the book to completion ahead of schedule. I also found a delightful colleague in Phylicia Ulibarri-Eglite, who provided marketing assistance and with whom I discovered a shared connection to Latvia.

Fourth, this book would not exist as it does today without the invaluable guidance of five anonymous peer reviewers. I am particularly grateful to two of these reviewers, who in their reading of my initial chapters encouraged me to focus more deeply on the question of Indigenous knowledge by developing a more complete analysis of Latvian and South African philosophies. This feedback provided me with the courage to leave my social science safe-space and return to my humanities roots, where I located appropriate methods for documenting the cultural knowledge that I informally had absorbed while living in these two countries.

Finally, I wish to thank all the scholars, farmers, poets and activists whose voices have been included in this book. Some of you I have never met, but you nevertheless have shaped my existential awareness through the outstanding quality of your work. More specifically, I wish to recognize the people listed below for playing a key role in this research and for teaching me something of your languages and cultures. While I alone am responsible for any errors in cultural interpretation, I am deeply privileged to have the opportunity to reflect deeply upon our meeting.

Aivars and Lilija Ansoni
Silvija Andernovics
Pierre Apollis
Malcolm Baard
Craig Bantom
Irēna Baraškina
Laila and Raitis Dronka
Elize Farmer
Agrita Folkmane
Anda Getliņa
Regīna Grīnblate
Indra Halvorsone
Adam Hoorns
Pieter Jafthas

Deneen Jefthas
Ilona Kiukucane
Ināra Krumiņa
Rohan Kruger
Sandra Kruger
Sharmaine Kupido
Mary A. Littrell
Eunice Marais
Sandris Mūriņš
Douglas L. Murray
Elizabeth van Neel
Lori Peek
Ligita Plate
Laura T. Raynolds
Noleen Rose
Zaitun Rosenberg
Andries du Toit
Gunita Ūdre
Silvija Vecumniece
Berna-Leigh Veloen
Ināra Vimba
Hennie van der Westhuizen
Jonene van der Westhuizen
Rodger Witbooi
Paul Zimri

Preface

This is a comparative historical tale of agrarian resistance and change, as it has occurred over the **longue durée** in two lands situated at opposite ends of Earth. In the deep forests of Northern Europe, ancestral Latvian tribes lived in egalitarian societies far from the slave-owning empires of the ancient Afro-Eurasian world-system. This changed when German crusaders invaded the Baltics in 1195, beginning a period of colonization and imperial rule that would culminate in the Soviet occupation of the twentieth century. In sun-baked Southern Africa, South African tribes likewise maintained egalitarian societies apart from the ancient imperial world. Dutch merchants invaded the Western Cape in 1652, engendering a trajectory of colonialism that would result in the formation of a White supremacist **apartheid** state in 1948.

In both countries, peasants resisted the alienating yoke of authoritarian rule by maintaining Indigenous knowledge systems grounded in social and ecological connection. Imparting life-affirming values, these intellectual and cultural currents succoured communities through desperate times, empowering people to mount collective resistance to state repression. When the Soviet and apartheid regimes collapsed at the end of the twentieth century, farmers took advantage of democratic reforms by investing in organic production technologies and establishing alternative trade networks. In Latvia, farmers have established a vibrant local and slow food movement to restore small-scale production and revitalize this nation's precolonial agrarian heritage. In the Cederberg Mountains of Western South Africa, small-scale farmers have worked to secure their heritage as artisanal producers of Rooibos tea by establishing **fair trade** partnerships with international buyers at the heart of its geographical origin.

Their efforts join a broader global justice movement that is constructing bottom-up approaches to development and social change; and, within this manifold movement, food and trade justice activists are confronting a global agro-food regime dominated by large multinational firms whose interests are backed by powerful states. While the **rationalization** of agriculture has enabled the capitalist world-system to produce cheap food at an industrial scale, the exploitative production and trade systems that rationalism has produced are a key driver of the current existential crisis in development.

The converging catastrophes of climate change and mass species extinction on the one hand, and resurgent ethnonationalism and rising class inequity on the other are threatening the survival of peoples around the world (Chase-Dunn, 2013).

This book rethinks development from the decolonizing lenses of Indigenous and global South feminist logic. My comparative case study analysis draws from Vandana Shiva's (1993) thesis on 'monocultures of the mind', to identify two existential types of development that have shaped world history.

- As a colonizing mode of existence, **authoritarian monocultures** assume different ideological forms across **spacetime** but enact analogous practices that result in similar lived experiences. Grounded in the modern-imperial logic of categorical separateness, this modality engages in endless warfare with social and biological difference to ensure uniformity and hierarchical control.
- As a decolonizing mode of existence, **egalitarian ecocultures** are rooted in Indigenous cosmovisions and cultures of resistance that recognize the interconnected nature of reality. This modality is situated at the imaginative and revolutionary fringes of the world-system, where grassroots actors are working to heal the wounds of the past by establishing regenerative nature–society partnerships that respect and restore the integral diversity of life.

While my ideal typology provides an analytical framework for troubling the existential dimension of development and social change, the empirical story that the book tells is rather more complex. My agrarian case studies show how these modes of being paradoxically co-exist in societies where farmers, environmental activists, and cultural creatives secured liberty from state tyranny only to find their efforts threatened by a neoliberal world-system that sold their countries the promise of freedom while reifying authoritarian production and trade relations in de-facto practice. Rather than concretizing outcomes, I have allowed the paradoxes of my tale to remain. I encourage the reader to explore the contradictions of decolonizing development on a divided planet, where nothing is pure, and everything is sacred.

Jennifer Keahey
Phoenix, AZ, 11 May 2023

1

Transformative Societies

Meditation

How unprepared we can be
for the silent edges of our land
for the simplicity of the wind
for spaces unbroken
by the hands of urbanisation.

How impoverished we are
By the many, many things that bind us.

If only we could remember
how to flow like the hills
to bend like a tree
to surrender to love
like earth to sky
would we know freedom then?
— Shelley Barry, South African poet

Winds of change

On a cool and cloudy evening in the late Baltic summer of 1989, a northern wind was blowing. Protesting the Soviet occupation of formerly sovereign lands, two million people peacefully joined hands on 23 August to form the Baltic Way to independence. Flowing unbroken for 675 kilometres through the capital cities of Estonia, Latvia, and Lithuania, this human chain occurred as part of a Singing Revolution that had been shaped by a series of environmental protests (Darst, 2001). Baltic insurrection generated rapid social change. Alongside its sister states, the Republic of Latvia regained its independence in 1991, enabling Latvians to embark upon a massive project of national reconstruction.

1

An equally powerful wind was blowing at the southern tip of Africa. Less than two weeks after Latvians participated in the Baltic Way, South Africans converged in Cape Town on 2 September 1989. Demanding an end to White supremacist rule, thousands of activists took to the streets in a peaceful demonstration of civil disobedience that soon became known as the Purple Rain Protest (Smuts and Westcott, 1991). The police sprayed a volley of purple water onto protestors to mark people for arrest, and so the following day, graffiti sprung up around Cape Town stating 'The Purple Shall Govern'. In less than a year, South Africa began transitioning to multiracial democracy, with the anti-apartheid movement's revolutionary leader, Nelson Rolihlahla Mandela, assuming the presidency in 1994 (Kök Arslan and Turhan, 2016).

The state apparatus was powerless to halt these winds of change. The final Soviet president, Mikhail Gorbachev, had opened the door to democracy by embarking upon **perestroika** in the wake of the Chernobyl nuclear disaster of 1986, but his plan to reform the Soviet Union was overwhelmed by populist demands for more revolutionary change (MacKinnon, 2008). Likewise, the final apartheid president, Frederik Willem de Klerk, had attempted to avert civil war by releasing Mandela from prison in February 1990, but his plans for incremental reform failed to stem the tide of populist revolution.

In the wake of national independence, Latvian and South African farmers quickly moved to invest in **organic** and fair trade initiatives. These initiatives aligned local agendas with a global justice movement that was working with small-scale producers to establish alternative food networks and green local economies. Like other agrarian movements around the world, however, Latvian and South African farmers soon found themselves confronting an expansionist global agro-food system (Goodman et al, 2012). When the Soviet bloc collapsed, Anglo-American interests proclaimed private capital as the bearer of freedom and prosperity, engendering a period of free-market triumphalism that empowered multinational corporations to consolidate control over commercial markets (Spechler et al, 2017). Yielding to international pressure, Latvian and South African policy makers aligned their nations' development agendas in accordance with **neoliberal** ideology, hindering grassroots efforts to decolonize production and trade.

Latvians and South Africans faced somewhat different political opportunities and threats. Latvia had first achieved nationhood in 1918 after 700 centuries of occupation under German and Russian rule. The First Republic immediately moved to convert Baltic German estates into small-scale farms for Latvian peasants, revitalizing an ancient cultural tradition of ecological farming on solitary homesteads. When the Baltics were annexed into the Soviet Union in 1944, Stalin crushed opposition to the Soviet collectivization of farms by removing peasants from their own land (Strods,

2005). On four bleak days in March 1949, the Soviet Union deported more than 42,000 Latvians to Siberia where most perished in labour camps. Setting the imperial constellation of Soviet Socialist Republics on the fast track to modernization, Stalin used displaced labour to institute an industrialized agricultural system that would turn Latvia into a Soviet breadbasket for the next 40 years.

In 1991, Latvia reinstated the land reforms of the First Republic, enabling a new generation of farmers to return to the land (Aistara, 2018). Yet the nation lacked the finance to convert national industry to a market economy, essentially facing 'the problem of building capitalism without capital' (Nissinen, 1999, p 65). The post-Soviet state responded to this crisis by deploying an economic programme of rapid external liberalization that involved 'decentralizing foreign trade, reducing trade protection and establishing currency convertibility' (p 63). This move enabled Latvia to secure foreign direct investment (FDI), but regional free trade agreements came with these monies, and the subsequent influx of Western European goods into Latvian markets hindered Latvian efforts to establish their own national processing and trade channels.

At the southern tip of Africa, the apartheid state had expanded the colonial estate system of agricultural production by dispossessing the majority non-White population of holdings and removing people to racially designated areas where arable terrain was in short supply. Under apartheid, Black and coloured[1] farmers migrated between impoverished homelands and large estates, where they toiled for racially privileged farmers who secured state subsidies to modernize agricultural production (Keahey and Murray, 2017). In a nation where White commerce owned most of the land and wealth, the post-apartheid state faced the problem of building a more egalitarian society. However, the incoming government failed to legislate significant land reforms during the pivotal transition to democracy, structurally obstructing the ability of small-scale farmers from developing commercial production capacity.

Fearing civil unrest, and hopeful of establishing a peaceful multicultural society, the incoming government of 1994 carved a middle path that combined laissez-faire economic policies with the apparatus of a social welfare state (Ferguson, 2010). While state funds delivered basic support to people in need and have improved national access to schooling, neoliberal policies have served to consolidate elite White power in agriculture and industry (Greenberg, 2015). Two decades into the post-apartheid era, a small number of very large estates had come to dominate domestic and international markets alike.

Within the broader world-system, the forces of neoliberal globalization have reified global production and trade imbalances whose origins may be traced to the sixteenth-century Conquest of the Americas and the subsequent racialization of labour (Fenelon, 2021). The consolidation of wealth has hollowed out the global working classes, fuelling a resurgence in ethnonationalist politics in societies around the world, as people compete against one another in a race to the bottom. Fomenting what Heller (2020) calls a politics of 'retrenchment populism', ethnonationalist politicians with ties to global capital have shifted blame for economic insecurity onto historically oppressed peoples who are struggling to reclaim their cultures and identities. As powerful corporate and state interests vie for access to diminishing natural resources, such as the fossil fuels and rare earths used in energy development, the spectre of imperial warfare is once again haunting the blue planet we all call home (Nadesan and Keahey, 2022).

Emancipatory contribution

This book decolonizes development studies in three interrelated ways. First, it disrupts a polarized political discourse by exposing the similar impulses of command and capitalist economies. The Soviet and apartheid regimes may have espoused oppositional ideologies, but these systems modernized in remarkably similar ways. Consider the following points:

- The Soviet Union presented itself as a union of federal socialist republics committed to freeing workers from the shackles of imperialist capitalism (David-Fox, 2015). Yet this regime invaded sovereign nations like Latvia, where it forcibly dispossessed peasants of their holdings and installed a collectivized agricultural sector comprised of hyper-industrialized farms. These were worked by displaced people who had been moved into Latvia under a Soviet policy of Baltic **Russification** (Darst, 2001; Schwartz, 2006).
- Apartheid South Africa presented itself as a parliamentary republic committed to nationalist capitalism (Legassick, 1974). Yet this regime modernized by subsidizing the industrialization of a colonial agriculture system worked by internally displaced people who had been stripped of their humanity under a policy of racial categorization and forced segregation (Barry, 2004; Waetjen, 2004).

In psychosocial terms, both states reproduced the violence of earlier waves of colonial rule by rationalizing pathological acts of cruelty as the necessary means for development.

Second, this book brings Indigenous and mixed-Indigenous voices from the margins to the centre of development, providing a foundation for examining the values shaping alternatives in practice. Given the inverse ideologies informing their experiences with oppression, the Latvian resistance extolled anti-communist and nationalist politics while South Africans revolted from a socialist and multicultural position. However, in both nations, small-scale farmers proclaimed similar values that were grounded in lived experience and in direct relationship with the land. Unlike many histories of revolution, both societies realized sweeping political change without descending into a period of civil war. If Latvians resisted German colonization and Soviet rule by engaging **Daina** philosophy to cultivate inward relations with land and culture, South Africans resisted European colonization and apartheid rule by employing Ubuntu philosophy to cultivate outward connections with social difference. These commonalities and differences provide a critical opportunity for identifying crosscutting currents of otherwise knowledges and practices that may be used to decolonize development.

Only recently made available to the English reader, Latvian Dainas are one of the largest recorded oral bodies of knowledge in the world. These cultural texts espouse an ecocultural ethic that situates the basis for wellbeing in the quality of nature–society relationships. Latvian farmers have enacted the wisdom of the Dainas by developing localized agro-food systems that combine traditional horticultural and modern organic science to preserve the diversity of biological life. In contrast, Ubuntu philosophy is present in the accounts of anti-apartheid activists who published numerous books, poems, and plays to inform South Africa's transition to multiracial democracy. As a humanist ethic, Ubuntu situates the basis for individual wellbeing in community wellbeing. In the artisanal Rooibos tea sector, coloured farmers have enacted Ubuntu philosophy by forming small-scale cooperatives that support community development. While production is rooted in the heritage of a mixed-Indigenous society located in the mountain *fynbos* ecology of the Cederberg region, this cooperative-based system is outward looking and actively engaged with international buyers.

By showing how producers are creatively engaging with tradition and modernity to revitalize ancestral **foodways**, I challenge conventional depictions of Indigenous heritage that ignore the existence of social and ethnic diversity, modern-colonial power relations and sociocultural shifts through time. Consequently, I use the concept of egalitarian ecocultures to explicate an interrelational mode of existence that resists the destructive impulses of authoritarian monocultures. Examining agriculture and forestry in rural India, Vandana Shiva (1993) found that industrial agriculture and its underlying system of monocultural **praxis** has been a key driver in the co-erasure of biodiversity and Indigenous knowledge. My differently situated case studies support Shiva's thesis while also illustrating the presence of other cultural alternatives that share cognitive similarities with Indian peasant tradition and knowledge.

Third, this book concludes with a decolonial theory of development. Depicted by the conceptual gears in Figure 1.1, my multi-paradigmatic framework enacts the multidimensional **epistemology** of Indigenous

Figure 1.1: Theoretical framework

science, enabling me to unpack complex forces at various scales of analysis (Kealiikanakaoleohaililani and Giardina, 2016). These interrelated knowledge systems provide the scaffolding for troubling the relationship between structure and agency, materiality and idealism and modernity and tradition in development. While my analysis is an initial step into the broader project of theory building, the information that I share offers critical insight into transformative food systems at a time when global climate change, mass species extinction and the COVID-19 pandemic are threatening food systems around the world (Altieri and Nicholls, 2020).

Eras of great transformation

Three eras in world history have changed social orders on a grand scale. To begin, the classical sociologist Max Weber (1978 [1922]) described the first era of great transformation as an age of philosophical advances that stimulated moral reforms in the ancient empires of China, Greece, India, Iran, and

Israel-Palestine. The origins of the **Axial Age** may be traced to the shift from stone-based to bronze-based technologies, a process that began approximately 5,000 years ago (Bellah and Joas, 2012). While scholars have questioned the geographic and temporal scope of the Axial Age, the evidence broadly suggests that the first historical movement toward Euro-Western modernity occurred in the ancient empires of Afro-Eurasia (Mullins et al, 2018). If Weber's initial analysis illustrates the role of religion and philosophy in social change, the records of ancient empires provide historical documentation of religious and secular movements that came into being at varying points in the Axial Age to contest the injustice wrought by imperial rule.

The empires that formed the core of the ancient world-system emerged around the same time as an initial wave of colonization that decimated prehistoric societies in Europe, the Middle East, and South Asia. At the cusp of the Early Bronze Age, between 4000 and 3000 BCE, Indo-European tribes spread outward from the central Eurasian steppes, giving rise to Indo-European languages and civilizations across the continent (Haak et al, 2015). In contrast to these patriarchal tribes, whose linguistic and cultural artefacts depict a linear logic and warlike culture, the Neolithic societies of Old Europe appear to have been matriarchal, egalitarian, and peaceful (Gimbutas, 1991; Mallory, 2006). The thousands of artefacts uncovered from Old European societies not only indicate the presence of concentric logic and sophisticated cultural expression but, as Gimbutas notes, they are entirely lacking in depictions of violence and warfare.

In a more recent study of prehistoric civilizations around the world, Graeber and Wengrow (2021, p 4) find that the inception of agrarian production and a more sedentary way of life did not inherently result in social inequality as previously has been assumed, for 'a surprising number of the world's earliest cities were organized on robustly egalitarian lines'. In the late-Neolithic Nile valley, for example, Africa's first farmers joined agricultural, fishing and foraging practices to establish an egalitarian mixed farming economy that succoured the development of artistic expression. Their cultural artefacts remind us that in the time before pharaohs 'almost anyone could hope to be buried like one' (p 264).

The Afro-Eurasian project of empire building began when the first Egyptian pharaoh, Narmer, unified the early kingdoms of the upper and lower Nile valley in 3200 BCE (Warburton, 2009). The concept of empire eventually spread to the river peoples of Mesopotamia, where Sargon of Akkad consolidated the city states of the Tigris valley in 2334. To the east, ancient China witnessed the rise of the Xia and Shang dynasties in 2070 and 1600 while ancient Indians rejected imperial existence until 321 BCE, when it formed the Mauryan dynasty. To the west, ancient Turks formed the Hittite Empire around 1600 BCE, followed by Greece in 800, and the birth of Roman kings in 753. To the south of Egypt, the Aksum Empire emerged around 100 BCE in what is now Ethiopia. Situated on a plateau by the Red Sea, the Kingdom of Aksum seized control of Nile, Red Sea and Indian trade routes, transforming it into a wealthy and cosmopolitan empire (Rose and Allen, 2018).

Most, if not all, of these empires treated women as chattel. These patriarchal formations occurred in tandem with the development of slave-based economies and imperial knowledge systems that deified violence, with snake-oil traders selling fabulous tales of cruel and capricious gods in a spiritual bid to justify the violent acts committed by imperial masters (Diamond, 2005). These colonizing worlds stood in stark contrast to the otherwise ways of living enacted by earlier and contemporaneous societies outside of the ancient world-system, where social systems were egalitarian, and where women played a key role in developing subsistence technologies that enabled people to prosper (Blumberg, 2009).

Axial empires also experienced axial moments of existential crisis and change. If ancient masters espoused destructive ideologies and engaged in violent practices to wrest power from foes, dissident scholars and activists countered these cruel impulses by establishing regenerative countercultures, or **heterotopias** of existence that opened spacetime for healing. Independently rising throughout the Axial world-system, utopian rebels developed different spiritual and philosophical traditions that collectively encouraged people to behave toward others in more loving and compassionate ways.[2] Armstrong (2006) argues that this revolution in human consciousness enabled societies to 'pause for liberty' between 'two ages of great empire' (367).

The **Industrial Revolution** comprised the second era of great transformation. This violent shift from an agrarian to an industrial world-system began in Europe in the 1700s, spread to North America in the 1800s and expanded into Soviet and **Third World** territories in the twentieth century. Examining the social unrest occurring in England in the eighteenth century, Polanyi (1957) surmised that the displacement of feudalism by industrialism resulted in the co-emergence of the modern nation state and market economy. This revolution was rooted in the rationalist ideals of the European Enlightenment, with scholars drawing upon the imperial sciences of ancient Greece and Rome to develop modern disciplines, and with practitioners institutionalizing national republics. In material terms, industrialization was driven by the replacement of a feudal aristocracy with a bourgeois merchant class (Marx, 2019 [1867]). Whereas the feudal system had enabled European aristocrats to amass wealth through the unfree labour of local serfs, distant colonial slaves financed, through unfree and unpaid labour, the European **bourgeoisie** who supplanted the aristocracy. Not only did merchant firms install colonies around the world and sell humans into slavery, but this modern social class secured capital for industrial growth through the procurement of slaveholding plantations. In the eighteenth century, Caribbean sugar greased the wheels of the world-system economy (Stinchcombe, 1995).

The Industrial Revolution fuelled productivity and innovation, but its monocultural and rationalizing **worldsense** also wrought social conflict and existential crisis. Studying suicide in nineteenth-century Europe, Emile Durkheim (2002 [1897]) uncovered a zeitgeist of **anomie**, or collective derangement, that he theorized had resulted from a collapse in social bonds and traditional belief systems. Centuries of warfare and revolution had convulsed Europe, causing displaced and persecuted people to flee to settler colonies, where they in turn displaced and persecuted others (Horne, 2018). By the end of the 1800s, colonial formations had morphed into land-grabbing empires that fleeced the global East and South alike, while fighting amongst themselves. As nineteenth-century German Kaisers scrambled their way into imperial globality by impoverishing occupied territories, the disillusioned offspring of an elite class of European subjects shook off the guilt by dancing with the glamour of death.

Taking the German model of modern-colonial rationality to its logical extreme, Friedrich Nietzsche (1844–1900) proclaimed *God is Dead* (2021) in a bold set of essays that paradoxically challenged authoritarian religious institutions while deifying modern rational science as the new God and the only epistemology worth knowing. His nihilistic worldsense echoed that of an earlier generation of German philosophy, where Immanuel Kant (1724–1804) sought to conceive of a modern and rational science that could reconcile a world where life had no intrinsic value or meaning (1998 [1781]). In the early twentieth century, this collective lack of regard for life caused the European core to erupt into the Great War in 1914, sparking the first of two capital-imperialist World Wars that would deeply fracture people in the core as well as the periphery of the rapidly industrializing world (Zinkina et al, 2019).

If the modern world-system was informed by the imperialist capture of Enlightenment logic, the liberating ideals of equality, democracy and justice also flowed through counter-current knowledge flows. In the 1500s, Mesoamerican scholars in colonial universities situated at the centre of **Abya Yala** delivered an Indigenous critique of the Conquest of the Americas, providing the intellectual fodder for revolutionary European scholars to theorize democracy in subsequent centuries (Chase-Dunn et al, 2020). This fusion of Indigenous and revolutionary European philosophies sparked the world's first global justice insurrection; namely the transatlantic anti-slavery movement (Hochschild, 2005; James, 1989 [1938]). After the Second World War, the democratic ideals established during previous revolutionary movements enabled European societies to develop social contracts and establish more peaceful relations (Zafirovksi, 2010). Yet the afterlife of colonialism and imperialism continued to shape social relations within the twentieth-century world-system, where they became structurally embedded in the telecommunications technologies that are driving development in the current **Digital Age**.

According to Held and colleagues (1999), the process of globalization is marked by a 'widening, deepening and speeding up of worldwide interconnectedness in all aspects of contemporary social life' (p 2). Globalization has enabled people to consume goods produced all over the world, empowering global corporations and neoliberal markets. However, as control over production practices has shifted from producers to buyers, worker rights and environmental protections have eroded, with nations currying the favour of financially empowered elites (Gereffi, 1994). Pointing to a small group of proprietors who now control most planetary resources, Rita Segato (2016) argues that the world-system is entering into a neo-feudal phase of domination. Due to their purchasing power and ability to circulate offshore, global corporate overlords have freed themselves from institutional controls, 'rendering fictional all ideals of democracy and the republic' (p 621).

The Digital Age is driven by surges of technological rationalization that destabilize eco-social cohesion. Examining the prevalence of risk in modern societies, Beck (1992) finds that intensive periods of rationalization occur when complex scientific knowledge is reduced into technocratic practices, or bureaucratic efficiencies, that often engender irrational outcomes and exacerbate risks. By standardizing development practices across geographies, rationalized management systems are harming the integrity of agrarian ecosystems around the world. Consider, for example, the following realities:

- The destruction of traditional agrarian cultures has resulted in high rates of farmer suicide in nations as differently situated as India and the United States (Shiva and Jafri, 2002; Viswanathan, 2014; Bissen, 2020).
- Modern-industrial water systems are harming the eco-social integrity of waterways through the creation of risk-prone infrastructures that harm wildlife and are costly to maintain (Randle and Barnes, 2018).
- Krøijer and colleagues (2020) find that marginalized people who disconnect from their cultural systems in search of prosperity largely enter a globalized realm where a sense of economic precarity, labour disposability and perpetual crisis undergirds everyday existence.

Addressing the psychopathology of the mid-century world-system, the Martinican scholar Frantz Fanon (1967) conducted decolonizing research on the **psychosocial** consequences of cognitive violence. In subsequent decades, Boaventura de Sousa Santos (2014) has advanced decolonial scholarship by defining epistemicide as the destruction of global South and Indigenous sciences. According to this Portuguese scholar, the monocultural logic of cognitive empire has been reproduced within global academe, where elite administrators and scientists have come to perceive a singular body of rational Western knowledge to the sole source of accurate knowing.

If rigid adherence to the logic of categorical separation serves to erase the breadth of scientific traditions that societies around the world have spent millennia establishing, it also results in the various types of abstraction that produce undesirable outcomes. For example, digital mainstreaming has promulgated a performance-based development regime wherein standardized metrics determine who gets access to funding. A recent study by Springer (2020, p 56) finds development agencies that adopt 'quantified knowledge production' are financially rewarded, while those committed to the far more time-intensive labour of producing ecologically and culturally situated knowledges and practices are penalized.

Paradoxically speaking, the Digital Age has also supplied counterhegemonic movements with the means to develop transnational advocacy networks (Hawken, 2007). Not only are global justice movements highly networked, but according to Smith and colleagues (2018), organizational expansion is fostering participatory governance in the world-system periphery. In a separate study, Santos (2014, pp 115, 134) likewise finds that transnational social activists are participating in a subaltern politics of 'insurgent cosmopolitanism'. These movements appear to be grounding their actions in diverse '**ecologies of knowledge**' that resonate with the construction of otherwise worlds, rather than in monocultural ideologies that reproduce warring worlds. Rather than assuming a hyper-localist position that rejects cosmopolitanism, decoloniality is a manifold praxis that involves delinking from hegemonic knowledge systems that hinder the creative construction of intercultural relationships and transmodern futures (Mignolo and Walsh, 2018). As the following section illustrates, other possible worlds – or realms of existence that support the subaltern project of global peacebuilding – have opened culturally diverse vistas for social change.

Indigenous knowledge and transmodern resistance

Ecofeminism in France and India

The French feminist Françoise d'Eaubonne (1974) coined the term **ecofeminism** to explain the co-constituted reality of violence against women and Earth. Joining deep ecology with radical feminism, d'Eaubonne more broadly founded France's ecology and feminism movement. In a subsequent fertile article, d'Eaubonne and Paisain (1999) defined ecofeminist society as post-revolutionary, self-managed and decentralized. To construct such societies, French ecofeminists reclaimed their bodily sovereignty in praxis. The theoretical goal was to collectively lower birth rates to reduce the production of an exploitable labour base upon which ecologically extractive economies depended. In practice, the movement secured the decriminalization of abortion in 1975 under the leadership of Simone Veil, a prominent feminist legislator and former health minister. However, the ecofeminist movement in the global North largely became assimilated into ideological feminism, where it met with criticism for producing essentializing depictions of women as vessels of care and reciprocity (Rao, 2012).

The cognitive terrain in India was less rigid, where ecofeminism spoke to the lives of peasant women. As a key founder of Indian ecofeminism, Vandana Shiva drew from the cosmovisions of Indian peasant resistance to articulate a cultural pathway to sustainability. Examining the Chipko women's movement, Shiva (2003) asked activists why they had chosen to risk their lives by using their bodies to block loggers from destroying the forests near their homes. They taught her a concept of freedom that was intertwined with the conservation of traditional sources of food, medicine and energy. As one activist stated, 'with our own food production we are prosperous – we do not need jobs from businessmen and governments – we make our own livelihood' (p 418).

Mies and Shiva (2014 [1993]) note that rural Indian women always have played a pivotal role as stewards of cultural and ecological affairs. In the traditional Indian village, gender demarks space, but the territories occupied by men and women are reciprocal and do not conform to modern public–private divisions. If men's work occurs in cultivated fields, women forage for wood, medicine, and spice, making them the frontline guardians of the goddess (*dieva*) Shakti's wild forest realm. In Hindu mythology, Shakti is the Mother Earth consort of Vishnu, the god of the universe and archetypical preserver of social order (Narayanan, 2001). The Hindi word *shakti* translates into power and strength; meaning that these qualities arise from the energetic force of creation, as denoted by the archetype of the mother. Unlike Western logic, which assumes intrinsic difference between women and men, planet and universe, chaos and order, Hindu cognition recognizes these constructs to be multiple dimensions of two diametric flows of energy. According to Hindu science, Shakti's yin and Shiva's yang are co-constituted in material life. The merger of these energetic forces sparks sentience into being, enabling all forms of life to develop of consciousness.

Hindu knowledge may be interpreted in ways both secular and divine, for in essence, it perceives a karmic world where cause and effect are manifested through the kinetic quality of social relations occurring between material beings. Simply put, the nature of the relationship between the dairy farmer and the cow shapes the consciousness of both. By returning Hinduism it its peasant roots, ecofeminists have joined Indian knowledge and tradition to the modern subject of feminism, articulating a culturally situated morality for establishing democratically organized, socially just and environmentally responsible communities.

Liberation theology in Latin America

In the 1960s, revolutionary Roman Catholic priests rose in Brazil to challenge the imperialist power of the Church by seeking to establish a 'Church of the poor' (Tombs, 2021, p 158). As part of a broader wave of anticolonial movements occurring at the time, the liberation theology movement rapidly spread throughout Latin America. Decrying the Church's role in the Conquest of the Americas, priests demanded liberation for Indigenous people who had long suffered the whip of the colonial missionary and modern master. Joining Marxist analysis with Catholic social teaching, liberation theologists published an extensive body of ecclesiastic philosophy over the following three decades. Their engagement was not simply academic, for activist priests also converted their services into spaces for raising critical consciousness (Smith, 1991). Using the pulpit to argue the moral necessity of economic redistribution and political democratization, these priests experienced repercussions for exposing the violent social order of their spacetime. During the spring of 1970, the San Salvadorian Archbishop, Oscar Romero, 'was gunned down before his congregation while celebrating mass', executed by an assassin who most likely was a member of the far right-wing White Warrior Union (Smith, 1991, p 1).

By the early 1970s, women had begun to publish scholarship on feminist liberation theology. Rosemary Radford Ruether's (2000) edited volume, *Women Healing Earth*, brought feminist writers from Latin America, Asia, and Africa to retheorize liberation theology with an ecological and feminist frame. As a K'iche' woman and traditional healer, Rigoberta Menchú (2010), played a central role in bringing the consciousness-raising praxis of liberation theology into conversation with the liberated consciousness of the 'ancestral soul' of her Mayan homeland (Alschuler, 2006, p 128). Not only was Menchú awarded a Nobel Peace Prize in 1992 for her defence of Indigenous land and rights during the genocidal Guatemalan Civil War; but Menchú (2003, p 126) also attended the 1992 Rio Earth Summit, where she argued that sustainable development could not be achieved without blending 'the ancient and the modern' to open pathways for 'living together' in peace. Menchú's articulation of interconnection resonated with concurrent social movements in France and India, where counterhegemonic scholars and activists were writing similar philosophies of integral development.[3]

Indigenous sovereignty on Turtle Island

The American Indian Movement (AIM) has prioritized sovereignty as the locus of social transformation. Like liberation theology, AIM articulates freedom from oppression as its primary goal. However, it differs along theological lines, as its conceptualization of sovereignty draws from precolonial cosmologies instead of from Christian doctrine (Tinker, 2020).

In contrast to imperial Western perception, which views sovereignty in terms of having dominion over land, people, and other species, Native American philosophy articulates sovereignty as the having the ability to ensure the integrity of cosmic creation. The Indigenous concept of **ecojustice** undergirds AIM's praxis. Defined as the development of compassionate and caring relations with all forms of creation, ecojustice is a community-based approach to development that is inclusive of people and other species.

Discussing the role of spirit in Indigenous resistance to the ongoing colonization of Native lands and communities, Tinker (2004, p 45) states:

> Perhaps the most precious gift that American Indians have to share with Amer-europeans is our perspective on the interrelatedness of all creation and our deep sense of relationship to the land in particular. We are all relatives: from buffaloes and eagles to trees and rocks, mountains and lakes. Just as there is no category of the inanimate, there can be no conception of anything in the created world that does not share in the sacredness infused in the act of creation. Traditional stories relate dialogue and interaction between different animal relatives quite as if they were like us human beings. Indeed, they may have been in some earlier age – or rather we humans were like them.

The shamanic traditions of American Indian and other Indigenous societies espouse diverse mythologies, with creation stories spatially grounded within specific geographies and in relation to the other species inhabiting the ecocultural terrain. Yet in all shamanic traditions, there is no perception of inanimate existence. In a world where even the tiniest grain of sand is sacred, life cannot so readily be converted into a commodity for sale to the highest bidder, meaning that the status of sanctity can no longer be limited to the privileged few.

Socially engaged Vietnamese Buddhism

Vietnamese Thiền (Zen) Buddhism articulates a similar awareness of our interconnected cosmos. As an ordained monk trained in Mahāyāna and Zen traditions, Thich Nhất Hạnh became a peace activist during the Vietnam War. In 1966, Nhất Hạnh (2008) created the Order of Interbeing (*Tiếp Hiện*), launching what would become a global movement of socially engaged Buddhists. Forced into exile, Hạnh first taught theology at Princeton and Columbia then relocated to France, where he and Buddhist Nun Chân Không founded the Plum Village Monastery in 1982. The Order of Interbeing now has monasteries in several countries, along with a grassroots network of thousands of *sanghas* (chapters) around the world. According to Sullivan and Arat (2018, p 339) this movement across borders has been possible through a 'post-secular' ethical foundation that is 'neither secular nor religious' in orientation. When creating the Order of Interbeing, Nhất Hạnh constructed the Five Mindfulness Trainings, an interrelational code of ethics that has made Zen philosophy accessible to secular and religious people alike. These trainings ask practitioners to cultivate: (1) reverence for life; (2) true happiness; (3) true love; (4) loving speech and deep listening; and (5) nourishment and healing in their daily practices and social relationships. According to Nhất Hạnh (2013, p 193), 'it is the insight of interbeing that leads to compassion, and that insight comes from the practice of looking deeply, without wavering, in meditation'.

The Five Mindfulness Trainings are adaptable to diverse cultural contexts. During his time in the United States, Nhất Hạnh became friends with Martin Luther King Jr, and his support of the US struggle for civil rights has brought Western activists into the Order of Interbeing. These include Zen teacher and racial justice scholar Larry Ward (2020), who has written about breaking the cycle of racial karma. Ward is part of a broader community of US-based practitioners that are joining Vietnamese Buddhist philosophy with Black feminist theory. For example, the ARISE Sangha has revisited Nhất Hạnh's Five Mindfulness Trainings through the lens of intersectionality to deliver a socially engaged Buddhist paradigm for racial justice and collective healing (Gomez and Brown, 2020). As the *sangha* custom of mindful tea ceremony suggests, refreshment has an important role to play in establishing restorative communities, and food is the focus of the final theoretical framework to which I now turn.

Critical perspectives on food, heritage and trade

Critical agrarian and food studies complement critical heritage and alternative trade studies. Collectively, these offer a multifaceted foundation for analysing foodways in decolonial contexts. To begin, critical agrarian scholarship has been informed by Marxist, anticolonial, and feminist theories of development and change, with its origins in the peasant resistance movements of the 1960s and 1970s. This body of knowledge provides a holistic lens for examining 'the ways in which agrarian life and livelihoods shape and are shaped by the politics, economics, and social worlds of modernity' (Edelman and Wolford, 2017, p 960). While some studies engage a structural interpretation of political economy, others employ poststructural and decolonial logic to rethink human–nature relations. These regenerative frames are enabling scholars to interrogate the human/non-human relations of production, the intersections of nature and national development and the hidden costs involved in appropriating natural resources for economic growth.

Alternative food studies likewise focus on unpacking conventional assumptions about the nature and meaning of development. According to Goodman (1999), mainstream agro-food studies draw from a Western knowledge tradition that views nature as separate from society. By treating interconnected material phenomena as detached subjects and objects, modern science constructs dualistic oppositions or falsely divided parts of one whole, generating mechanistic development policies and practices that harm land and people. In the industrial agro-food sector, the objectification of nature and social labour are co-constituted through rationalized technologies that sever eco-social connections. To address this gap, critical food scholars employ the postmodern concept of 'shared corporeality', defined as interconnected material existence, to examine the eco-social relationships occurring within alternative agro-food systems (Goodman, 1999, p 17). This material and relational framing enables scholars to unpack the structural and agentic forces informing agrarian change.

Critical food and agrarian studies also intersect with scholarship that examines food justice and sovereignty movements. Food justice movements have been working with marginalized communities to create local food systems that improve access to 'healthy, nutritious, environmentally sustainable, and culturally appropriate food' (Gonzalez, 2021, p 133). The food sovereignty movement broadens the scope of resistance. Within this movement, the international peasants' organization *La Via Campesina*[4] has played an important role in establishing transnational activist networks. During a 2007 forum in Mali, it brought together 500 delegates who represented peasant, artisanal, and Indigenous producers from more than 80 countries to clarify the meaning of food sovereignty. Published in La Via Campesina's (2007) Declaration of Nyéléni, the delegates in attendance arrived at a multi-pronged definition that illustrates this movement's commitment to holistic thinking:

> Food sovereignty is the right of peoples to healthy and culturally appropriate food produced through ecologically sound and sustainable methods, and their right to define their own food and agriculture systems ... food sovereignty prioritizes local and national economies and markets ... [and] promotes transparent trade that guarantees just income to all peoples and the rights of consumers to control their food and nutrition. It ensures that the rights to use and manage our lands, territories, waters, seeds, livestock and biodiversity are in the hands of those of us who produce food. Food sovereignty implies new social relations free of oppression and inequality between men and women, peoples, racial groups, social classes and generations.

Food sovereignty may be a big-tent philosophy, but as a global justice movement, it challenges the economistic discourse of conventional development (Patel, 2009). Whereas the Food and Agricultural Organization

(FAO) engages the individualistic lens of food security to inform development in practice, the food sovereignty movement is pressuring the United Nations to develop a more comprehensive understanding of food and society. As a new category of human rights, food sovereignty denotes the collective right of peasants and small-scale producers to live and produce in accordance with the socio-ecological traditions of their heritage and in relation to the cosmovisions of their ancestors (Claeys, 2015).

Despite these multifaceted contributions, cultural histories remain under-theorized in agro-food scholarship. Critical heritage studies address this gap by offering a poststructural lens for examining the relationship between culture, identity and power. Defining heritage development as a multi-sensual, politically contingent and contested process, this body of scholarship asks scholars to generate '**more-than-representational** understanding' of the power dynamics shaping heritage arenas and investments (Waterton, 2014, p 823). Work in this area has begun to inform local and slow food studies, where scholars are examining the embodied and affective dimensions of food politics in the United States and Western Europe (Carolan, 2011; Bowen and De Master, 2011) However, critical heritage studies on global South food politics is underdeveloped. There is a need to redress this, as the European system for protecting the production of culturally distinctive goods at their geographic origin has moved into global South landscapes, calling into question the relationship between coloniality and terroir (Besky, 2013; Ives, 2017).

Agro-food activists have tackled the related issue of trade justice by developing alternative trade organizations (ATOs). These include formal organic and fair trade certification systems, somewhat less-formalized local and slow food networks, and informal barter and trade networks (Goodman et al, 2012). First, organic and fair trade ATOs promote sustainability through a practice of third-party monitoring and certification. In the case of Fairtrade International's (FTI) certification system, member producer organizations access minimum pricing guarantees and support for community development (Raynolds and Greenfield, 2015). Second, local and slow food networks seek to revitalize agrarian economies by encouraging people to become 'sensually engaged with regional, traditional foods' (Nabhan, 2002, p 312). Not all local food producers embrace organic production practices; indeed, some favour conventional methods, but ultra-localized **biodynamic** and regenerative farming models increasingly are informing production practices. These beyond-organic approaches merge scientific and Indigenous philosophies by viewing each farm as an embodied system comprised of interrelated humans, plants, animals and soils that can be rehabilitated to conserve broader ecosystems (Reed, 2010).

Finally, Raynolds (2004) provides a poststructural foundation for studying the political economy of alternative trade networks. Merging actor-network analysis with convention theory, she clarifies the social conventions undergirding the development of sustainable economies. If conventional agro-food prioritizes industrial and market conventions that promote industrial production by equating product value with efficiency, standardization and competitive pricing standards, alternative agro-food systems redefine quality in terms of: (1) domestic conventions that appeal to nature and locality; (2) civic conventions that promote fairness and health; and (3) reputation conventions that value artisanal production practices (Evans and Mylan, 2019). Efforts to redefine product quality have garnered commercial success, for sustainability standards and certifications now inform the buying practices of global corporations (Conroy, 2007). However, this success has not translated into systemic agrarian reform. As large agribusinesses have entered sustainability markets, industrial and market conventions are resuming a position of dominance in global sales, hindering the ability of small-scale farmers to compete in commercial networks that they worked to establish (Jaffee and Howard, 2010; Raynolds and Bennett, 2015).

Methods and positionality

This book uses inductive reasoning to ground theory in lived knowledge and experience. Figure 1.2 presents the methodological framework informing this process. If my theoretical toolbox joins complementary knowledge systems to unpack research findings, my methodological toolbox includes multiple methods that I have engaged in a series of related studies conducted over the past two decades. The seminal knowledges that Latvian and South African producers imparted to me during two periods of intensive fieldwork have closely informed the more recent comparative historical and textual studies that structure several book chapters.

First, I engage comparative historical methods to develop a material understanding of development and change, with specific focus on Latvia and South Africa over the longue durée. Next, I conduct a comparative textual analysis of Indigenous Latvian and South African sciences, interpreting the moral philosophies embedded within key cultural texts through autoethnographic reflections that impart my acculturation into these ways of being. I subsequently bring the ideal into conversation with the material via two producer case studies. The Latvian case draws from a multi-method qualitative field study that I conducted in 2005. Situated at a national level of analysis, this study encompasses the breadth of product sectors and local regions involved in Latvia's organic farming and slow food movements at a time when the nation was assimilating into the European Union (EU). The South African case study is situated within the racialized terrain of Rooibos tea terroir. It engages research findings from a participatory action

Figure 1.2: Methodological framework

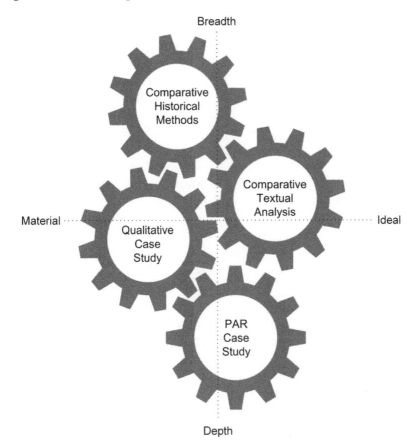

research (PAR) study that I conducted with a team of community-based farmer leaders in 2010, at a time of certification crisis, economic turmoil and livelihood diversification.

As a multi-methodological study, *Decolonizing Development* gives voice to agents of change, complexifying insight into the forces shaping alternatives to development. Given their differing positions in terms of scale and logic, each chapter in this book has a distinct voice, texture, and feel. Viewing my role as that of interpreter, my purpose is to bring different knowledges into dialogue by identifying crosscutting patterns and interweaving voices across chapters. Consequently, this book imparts an interdisciplinary articulation of decolonial development, one that joins the Western knowledge traditions of the humanities and social sciences as well as the diverse knowledge systems informing global Indigenous science. While I allow each chapter to stand in its own cultural and disciplinary voice, my decolonial framing of the topic brings intellectual cohesion to the study.

In 1989, when the winds of change were blowing in Europe and Africa, I was a White teenager growing up on a third continent, in the wide open but colonized and racially troubled landscape of the American West. At the time, I had no personal connection to either Latvia or South Africa, nor was I aware that these two countries would figure so largely in my future. My life experience was almost entirely limited to northern Utah, where my summers were spent fishing and camping, buying food from roadside produce stalls, attending the annual peach festival in my mother's hometown and eating traditional meals with extended family. Nevertheless, two events occurred during my early teenage years that made me aware of the monumental shifts occurring in the world beyond the mountains protecting my home.

The first event involved a trip to Europe with my father during the summer of 1987. While in Germany, we took a day trip to West Berlin, and I boarded the bus curious about the Iron Curtain, or the world within the Soviet sphere of influence. The crossing into East Germany was uneventful, but the atmosphere on the bus became tense as we approached West Berlin.

When I handed my passport to the border guard, he barked a command that I did not understand. A young man seated in front of me whispered that I should look directly at the guard so that he could see my face. That moment of eye-to-eye contact with a verbally hostile armed man frightened me, for I had been shielded from subjection by parents who encouraged me to roam with limited supervision. Several years later, as I watched people scrambling over the Berlin Wall on television, I was so overcome with emotion that I struggled to breathe. I subsequently spent four years living in post-Soviet Latvia, first as a Peace Corps volunteer then as a Fulbright scholar; and it was in the lush landscape of rural Latvia that my interest in sustainable food and agriculture crystallized.

The second event was a more violent awakening. By 1989, I had begun moving through the queer fringes of Salt Lake City's punk scene where I joined in the rebellion against the social mores of a conservative US state. The punk spaces that my friends and I frequented were fraught with racial tension, but as a naive White teenager, I thought I was immune to this reality. One evening, I was walking alone to a music venue when I was cornered, beaten and robbed by skinheads who decided I did not look White enough. I later stumbled into the bathroom of a fast food restaurant where I asked an Asian woman for money to make a phone call. She did not speak English but took me out to meet her husband who insisted on driving me home. As I sat quietly bleeding in the backseat next to a sleeping infant, I could not help but consider the cruelty of White supremacy in relation to the kindness of an immigrant family who took the time to care for a stranger in need.

The following year, I awoke to South Africa's anti-apartheid movement and the common thread of settler colonial racism that ran through our societies when a bisexual White friend of mine – who was wearing a Free Mandela!

t-shirt – was attacked by a skinhead while walking through a park at dawn. These formative exposures awakened me to the brutal reality of racism that led me, many years later, to conduct fieldwork with small-scale farmers in post-apartheid South Africa.

My critique of development is grounded in more than 20 years of experience working as a scholar, teacher and alternative development practitioner in Africa, Europe, Asia, and North America. Over the course of these years, I have strived to cultivate radical openness to social and intellectual difference by positioning myself as a learner – particularly when confronted with ideas that challenge my own. Defined by bell hooks (1989) as a space of resistance situated at the risky margins and open edges of possibility, **radical openness** is an essential component of relational praxis in communities of resistance. My unconventional education has supported my cultivation of openness to difference. Not only do I possess BA degrees in French and anthropology, an interdisciplinary MA in development and change, and a PhD in sociology, but I also have studied five foreign languages and continue to speak two of these fairly well. In short, my intellectual journey has been one of transgressing borders.

Given my linguistic training, I neither perceive European knowledge as a singular epistemology, nor do I reject European contributions to emancipatory science. If my worldsense has been informed by decolonial scholars like Frantz Fanon, it also is enriched by the medieval feminist scholarship of Marie de France (1983) and Marguerite de Navarre (1982), who – in delightfully different ways – examined the deeply embodied, mutually entangled and queerly transcendent gender relations of feudal Europe. If my praxis is guided by the intersectional pedagogy of bell hooks, it also aligns with the compassionate humanism of Victor Hugo (1985), whose novels shed light on the systemic violence structuring social existence in nineteenth-century France. My education has taught me that there is as much diversity within global South and European epistemologies as there are outside them. While this book critiques conventional perspectives on development and change, it follows a both/and feminist tradition by bringing the Indigenous and mixed-Indigenous sciences of Latvia and South Africa into conversation with the global South and Indigenous discourses on development and social change, and more broadly with critical Western bodies of knowledge.

Chapter overview

Chapter 2 weaves a comparative history of Latvia and South Africa over the longue durée. In the north-eastern reaches of Europe, German knights of the Teutonic Order conquered Latvian lands during the thirteenth century, leading to 700 years of occupation by German and Russian lords who relegated Indigenous Latvians to serfdom (Plakans, 1995). In South Africa, Indigenous Khoekhoe[5] pastoralists and Sān hunter-gatherers first encountered Bantu farmers around 500 CE, and these groups were met by Dutch colonizers about a thousand years later (Mlambo and Parsons, 2019). If the commonalities of these cases support a comparative decolonial analysis of Southern African and Eastern European struggles for self-determination, their differences provide a cross-cultural lens for analysing the role that local knowledge systems have played in challenging hegemonic power. Chapter 2 lays the foundation for a deeper examination of the cultural knowledges informing post-authoritarian transitions to sustainability.

Chapters 3 and 4 use textual analysis and autoethnographic reflection to document the Indigenous moral philosophies of Latvia and South Africa. Chapter 3 brings Daina philosophy to a global audience. Traditionally transmitted through folk songs, Dainas are a recorded body of quatrain-based texts that teach intergenerational wisdom and ecocultural values (Vīķis-Freibergs,[6] 1999). Chapter 4 engages literature produced by anti-apartheid activists who brought Ubuntu philosophy to an English-speaking audience. Deriving from the Xhosa and Zulu languages, this term denotes 'being-with-others', as it perceives individuals to be part of the greater whole of interdependent existence (Okoro, 2015, p 3). My comparative analysis illustrates a common awareness of the relational dynamics shaping our collective existence within a participatory universe. It also identifies differing cultural expressions of relationality. As complementary knowledge systems, Daina and Ubuntu philosophies clarify the inner and outer work of sustainability.

Chapter 5 delivers an in-depth study of Latvia's organic farming movement.[7] Conducted over a 10-month period in 2005, it captures the dynamics shaping the movement at the end of the first decade of democratic transition and during a period of EU accession. I found that land reforms had enabled a generation of farmers to return to small-scale production during the first decade of democratization. These farms reinvented the matriarchal horticultural model of ancient Latvian tradition by combining organic or biodynamic production technologies with the gathering of seasonal forest foods. Farm economies depended upon a mix of commercial sales, bartered food exchanges with other farms and the reciprocal custom of food gifts. EU entry sparked a nationwide shift to organic farming, as it provided conventional farms with state funds to undergo conversion. This resulted in a market glut that was exacerbated by the influx of organic goods from Western Europe and the underdevelopment of a national food processing sector. In response to market turmoil, the organic movement invested in slow food campaigns, marketing Latvian foodways to draw attention to this nation's rich ecocultural heritage.

Chapter 6 focuses on the case of **Fairtrade** certified Rooibos tea in southwestern South Africa.[8] This study draws from 10 months of PAR fieldwork conducted in 2010 with small-scale farmers in the Cederberg region of Wupperthal. Employing a critical heritage lens, I interweave a broader analysis of the racialized political economy informing Rooibos **terroir** with the cultural knowledges of coloured farmers whose ancestors harvested and first cultivated this product. I show how Wupperthal formed as a colonial mission station where Indigenous Khoe-Sān, ex-slave and European influences converged to create a distinctive cultural identity. Under apartheid, Wupperthal became designated as a rural coloured area, and the state barred coloured farmers from commercial production. In the post-apartheid era, Wupperthalers became the first small-scale farmers in South Africa to enter global organic and Fairtrade certified networks. Experiencing market volatility, farmers began diversifying into related heritage enterprises ranging from ecotourism to the artisanal production of Rooibos body care products. My analysis of Rooibos terroir and coloured identity confronts an idealized food and heritage discourse that fails to acknowledge the reality of racial mixing and cultural fusion.

Chapter 7 articulates a decolonial theory of development and change. I begin by delivering a decolonial critique of modern rationalism. I then lay out the three features of authoritarian monocultures and egalitarian ecocultures. As an ideal type, authoritarian monocultures are constructed through rationalized knowledge and top-down practices, resulting in warring monocultures that dichotomize and subjugate life in service to the master. Egalitarian ecocultures invert this modality by using Indigenous and counterhegemonic knowledges to construct more egalitarian political economies that support the rise of regenerative ecocultures. Like organic farmers who depend upon interspecies relationships to develop robust and resilient production practices, democracy relies upon multi-ethnic engagement, and diverse ecologies of knowledge are needed to solve complex problems. I conclude the book by arguing that the solution to the challenge of sustainability lies not in choosing sides between warring visions that promulgate either/or solutions. If societies are to survive the converging catastrophes of the **Anthropocene**, we must learn how to work in collaboration with our differences by cultivating caring and multi-sensual relationships with the rich tapestry of life on Earth.

2

A Comparative History of Latvia and South Africa

Latvian hymn

Through a hundred years of moaning,

under the pressure of the abusers

on this radiant day, our tongue still rings clear.

This land is ours. From God and Fortune

a dowry brought ancient Latvians together.

This land is ours.

It will no longer be given to strangers.

Latvju himna

Caur simtgadu vaidiem,

zem varmāku spaidiem

šo baltdien vēl dzidri mūsu mēle te skan.

Tā zeme ir mūsu. Tā Dieva un Laimas

latvju tautai sensenis līdzdotais pūrs.

Tā zeme ir mūsu.

To nedos vairs svešiem.

— Latvian freedom song, penned by Vilis Plūdons in 1922 and translated by author

Ancestral origins

South Africa

In 1999, UNESCO added three paleo-archaeological sites to its World Heritage list. Situated in South Africa, these offer crucial evidence into the origins of our species, for their artefacts show that early hominids began living in Southern Africa more than three million years ago and that human ancestors domesticated fire more than a million years in our past (UNESCO, 1999). In northwest South Africa, the Cradle of Humankind World Heritage Site (2020) claims that our 'collective umbilical cord lies buried' in Africa, where the earliest hominids emerged about seven million years ago, invented stone tools more than two million years ago, and evolved into modern humans around 200000 BCE. Although archaic humans, such as the Neanderthal, have been found in other parts of the world, the genetic and fossil evidence points to an African genesis of anatomically modern humans (Relethford 2008). As genetic findings indicate a degree of inter-hominin mixing, modern human ancestry is mostly, although not entirely, African in origin.

Given its placement at the confluence of two oceans, Southern Africa is a biodiverse and heterogeneous land. Khoekhoe and Sān peoples comprise its original inhabitants (Besten, 2009). Among the most diverse peoples on earth, the gather-hunter Sān historically lived in ethnically defined areas, where they moved according to the seasons in symbiosis with water, plant, and animal life. Sān societies spoke numerous unrelated languages, some of which remain in use (Barnard, 2019). Khoekhoe societies either displaced or broke away from the Sān around 2,300 years ago when these peoples accepted animal husbandry as a way of life (Smith, 2009). From the *fynbos* biome of the southwestern Cape to the semi-desert karoo of the north and into what is now the nation of Namibia, pastoral Khoekhoe societies tended sheep and cattle. Kinship ties informed the relations of production, but the means for making a living were secured through tribute to leaders (Penn, 1986).

Originating in West Africa, Bantu peoples now cover a third of the African continent. These Black African tribes began domesticating crops in 8000 BCE; and over the centuries diverged into two migratory streams, with one moving southward and the other eastward then south along the Indian coast. As tribes settled along the way, communities practiced swidden agriculture and adopted Iron Age technology (Mlambo and Parsons, 2019). Filtering into Southern Africa as early as 300 CE, small Bantu groups mingled with the Khoe-Sān, incorporating clique consonants from their tongues to form southern Bantu languages such as Xhosa and Zulu.

Whereas the Khoe-Sān occupied the arid lands of the west, the Bantu inhabited the sub-tropical east, where they employed a mixed farming system that combined crop cultivation with pastoralism (Thompson, 2014). Bantu ethnic groups formed chiefdoms, and leaders governed in tandem with councillors. Cattle symbolized wealth and were the purview of men; yet women owned and cultivated agricultural fields. Artisanal blacksmiths produced jewellery; and metal production fuelled Bantu trade, with iron, copper, tin, and gold flowing through networks that reached East African ports where they connected to Arabia and Southeast Asia (Miller, 2002).

Latvia

In contrast to the rugged terrain of South Africa, Latvia is a land of deep forest, situated along the amber-strewn coast of the Baltic Sea. During the Last Glacial Period, the Baltics rested under a great ice sheet. Once the ice had retreated around 11000 BCE, fisher-hunters followed reindeer into the region (Kasekamp, 2018). Settling alongside rivers and lakes during the Early Neolithic Age, small bands of people developed a material culture based on bone and antler industry (Zagorska, 2019). Over time, these Finno-Ugric tribes moved northward into Estonia, Finland, and Russia leaving behind Livs who inhabited the northern Latvian coast. Around 2500 BCE, the rest of the Baltics were settled by tribes originating from the proto-Indo-European Yamna cultural complex bordering the Black Sea (Gimbutas, 1963). In what is now Latvia, Baltic Indo-Europeans mingled with Finno-Ugric Livs. If these ethnic tribes shared certain features of pagan belief in common, including a reverence for nature, ancient Latvians and Lithuanians differed from Livs and Estonians on linguistic grounds. Retaining archaic Indo-European features, Lithuanian, Latvian, and the Latvian dialect of Latgalian have become the sole survivors of an ancient Baltic language family (Fortson, 2010).

During the Neolithic age, the Baltic mode of production shifted from one of foraging to nomadic pastoralism and sedentary farming. Given its impenetrable forests and long winters, Latvia was never assimilated by the ancient empires of the Afro-Eurasian world-system, but its main river – the Daugava – joined the Baltic and Black Seas in trade. Known as 'the gold of the north', Baltic amber was highly coveted in the ancient empires of Egypt, Assyria, Greece, and Rome (Kalnins, 2015, p 7).

At the time of the Middle Iron Age, between 400 and 800 CE, proto-Latvians consisted of five tribes who maintained close ties with other Baltic peoples and traded with Scandinavians and Slavs (Buceniece, 1997). The Finno-Ugric Livs retained control of the northern coast, where they warred with Scandinavian Vikings from the eighth to eleventh centuries. In the southwest, the seafaring Curonians likewise repelled and traded with Vikings. Semigallians farmed the fertile lowlands of southcentral Latvia and traded along the Daugava. The Selonians occupied the uplands of southwestern Latvia, where they farmed and specialized in various crafts. Latgalians comprised the largest chiefdom and were located to the northeast (Kasekamp, 2018). As relative latecomers to the area, this eastern Baltic tribe likely was pushed westward by Slavic peoples who settled Belarus. All these groups established wooden hill forts along trade routes, providing a place of refuge for farmers to retreat to in times of attack (Mägi, 2018).

Located near the estuary of the Daugava, the Liv hill fort of Daugmale had become established as a trade centre by the tenth century (Mägi, 2018). While most Balts continued to live freely as mixed farmers, tribes had begun transitioning to a class society during the Early Medieval Age, when land gradually shifted from communal to private ownership. Examining evidence from eastern Latvia, Šnē (2006) found that this change was accompanied by the transition of hill forts into proto-urban specialized craft centres that supported a merchant class. Yet Šnē also found that political ideology remained egalitarian, with chiefs redistributing wealth garnered from tributes to all social classes. For precolonial Latvians, all life was animate and deserving of care. Not only were the Baltics the last seat of pagan power in Europe, but Balts fiercely resisted Christianity when Northern Crusaders arrived in the region.

Two colonial frontiers

Latvia

Near the end of the twelfth century, the German monk Meinhard of Segeberg established a mission station near the Daugmale hill fort. In service to the Holy Roman Empire, Meinhard became the first bishop of the Baltic German colony of Livonia in 1186. This ailing bishop called for military support when the Indigenous Livs of the region resisted conversion to Christianity (O'Connor, 2019). Pope Celestine III authorized a Livonian Crusade in 1195 and shortly thereafter, the second bishop, Berthold, died in battle. The third bishop, Albert of Livonia, founded the city of Rīga at the mouth of the Daugava in 1201 and formed a Catholic military order. Its ranks filled by German and Danish warrior monks who were promised riches, the Livonian Sword Brothers embarked upon a campaign of ethnic cleansing, subduing the Livs in 1206 (Murray, 2001). Latgalian chiefs capitulated to Livonian rule by the end of the decade, enabling the Sword Brothers to conquer Estonian tribes further to the north.

The other Latvian chiefdoms joined their related Lithuanian tribes in resistance (Lettus, 2003). Together with the Samogitians, the Semigallians decimated the warrior monks at the Battle of Saule in 1236 (Mugurēvičs, 2016). The few German survivors were incorporated into the Knights of the Teutonic Order in 1237. This Order subsequently conquered the Curonians in 1267 and the Semigallians and Selonians by 1290, with many survivors fleeing into Lithuania where tribes had united into a pagan kingdom to repel the crusaders (Rowell, 1994). In Latvia and Estonia, the Teutonic Order awarded land to its knights, establishing the conditions for German colonial rule.

The victorious Germans brought Rīga into the Hanseatic League, a confederation of merchant guilds that joined market towns along the coasts of Northern Europe (O'Connor, 2019). In a struggle for control over this key trading port, the Teutonic Order vied with Rīga's bishop for power, causing burghers to develop an alliance with the pagan Lithuanian Grand Duchy which warred with the Teutonic knights well into the fourteenth century. Yet German control was consolidated over the course of the following two centuries, as the knights built fortressed castles throughout the region (Turnbull, 2004). Indigenous Latvians initially retained a measure of freedom in the new social order: peasants were only required to work for brief periods on feudal estates, and some tribal chiefs secured positions of nobility (Kalnins, 2015). By the end of the 1400s, however, Latvian lords and farmers alike had 'lost their lands and their descendants were reduced to serfdom' (p 52). Imposing high taxes and harsh working conditions, the Baltic German nobility forbade Latvians from leaving the estates of their masters. Latvians responded by retreating into an inner ecocultural world, where they kept their language and customs alive through the singing of Dainas, poetic folk songs that imparted Indigenous knowledge.

In 1562, Russians invaded Latvia and dissolved the Teutonic Order, causing Protestant Scandinavia, Catholic Poland-Lithuania, and Orthodox Russia to struggle for control of the region over the next 20 years (Kasekamp, 2018). After a period of Polish-Lithuanian rule at the turn of the seventeenth century, Sweden absorbed the now Lutheran colony of Livonia into its empire in 1629. The religious struggle of these decades helped keep the peasant languages of Latvia and Estonia alive (Taagepera, 2011). During the brief period of Polish-Lithuanian rule, Jesuit missionaries used local languages to bring peasants back into the Catholic fold; and under Swedish rule, the empire subsidized scholars to translate the bible into various Baltic languages. Inspired by Martin Luther's call to make religion more accessible to the masses, a German pastor published a Latvian language bible in 1694. The conversion of Latvian from several oral dialects into one written language enabled the various Latvian tribes to unite as one people. While this 'dawn of Latvian poetics' would later inspire a national awakening, Indigenous Latvians did not experience meaningful change under Swedish rule, for Baltic Germans retained ownership of vast agricultural estates and the Liv and Latvian serfs who worked the land (Grudule, 2013, p 149).

Northern Europe erupted into the Great Northern War in 1700. Coveting the ice-free ports of the Baltics, the Russian Tsar, Peter the Great, seized control of Rīga in 1710; and after two decades of warfare and plague that decimated much of the population, expelled the Swedes from the region (Tucker, 2015). The 1721 Treaty of Nystad enshrined the privileges of German Baltic nobility, enabling this ethnic class to retain its control over Indigenous peasants (Bagger, 1993). However, in the early 1800s, the Tsarist regime began dismantling feudalism by passing a series of laws that secured the passage of peasants to emancipation.

Latvians took advantage of these reforms by achieving near universal literacy during the second half of the nineteenth century. The emergence of a rural Latvian bourgeoisie supported a generation of Young Latvians who began publishing Latvian folk songs and cultural histories (Page, 2018). This poetic moment of national awakening conflicted with ruling interests. While Latvians resisted German attempts to regain cultural influence, they met with a powerful Russian foe when Alexander III ascended the throne in 1881. Instituting a policy of Russification, this Tsar reduced the authority of Baltic Germans and halted Latvian aspirations. Latvians would not secure their independence until the end of the First World War. Nevertheless, the idea of Latvian statehood had been firmly established in the poetic renderings of a people living in exile on their own land.

South Africa

During the Late Medieval Age, the Portuguese monarchy funded Atlantic exploration, enabling Bartolomeu Dias to arrive at the South African Cape in 1488. However, Europeans rarely set foot in the Cape until 1652, when the Dutch established a colonial outpost to provide refreshment to traders (Thompson, 2014). As the Dutch West and East India Companies established colonies around the world, the Netherlands formed into a global empire. The flood of overseas goods into European markets disrupted the feudal social order, and Protestant dissidents challenged the authority of Rome (Brook, 2008). Refugees fled to the Netherlands, and from there to its colonial territories where the nexus of slavery and settler colonialism replaced religion with race as a key dimension of oppression (Chaplin, 2020).

As the ancestors of modern Afrikaners, Protestant settlers became established as Boers, or farmers, in the Dutch Cape colony during the 1600s and 1700s. Influenced by the doctrine of predestination, Boer society was devoutly religious, but unlike European Protestants, 'it was in the passages of the Old Testament that the Afrikaners found God' (Olivier, 2009, p 1473). The colonial regime instituted a policy of ethnic cleansing, meaning that Boer acquisition of Khoe-Sān lands occurred through a process of genocide (Adhikari, 2015). While Boer settlers invested in livestock and built agricultural estates on seized lands, colonial officials imported slaves from Indonesia, India, Sri Lanka, Madagascar and Mozambique to supply settlers with low-cost labour (Fourie, 2013). The subsequent mixing of African, Asian and European ancestries generated an ethnically heterogeneous creole population that would later become designated as coloured (Adhikari, 2009). Merging their languages with the Dutch spoken by the master, Cape coloured people produced a Kaapse Afrikaans dialect that Afrikaners later assumed and standardized (van der Waal, 2012, p 448).

In the late eighteenth century, Boer settlers began moving into the Eastern Cape. This region was occupied by the powerful Xhosa Kingdom whose chiefs would fight nine wars against Dutch and British invaders over the next hundred years (Mostert, 1992). Indeed, the British Empire invaded the Cape in 1795 and conquered the Dutch in 1806, outlawing the Dutch language. Viewing themselves as a tribe of White Africans who – like the Israelites of the Old Testament – were subject to the tyranny of pharaohs and beset on all sides by heathens, the Boer embarked upon an exodus into the wilderness in a voyage known as the Great Trek (Feder, 2012). Thus, while the British and Xhosa battled, Afrikaners largely left the colony behind, with a second wave of exodus occurring after the British ended slavery in 1838.

Initially travelling as nomadic pastoralists, Trekboers settled the most arable plains of the interior and established several Boer Republics. Along the way, slaves left their masters to settle in less desirable zones, where they mingled with displaced Khoe-Sān peoples. German and Dutch missionaries soon followed these coloured homesteaders into the hinterlands (Penn, 2005). Although settler colonial mission stations developed through the seizure of land and the imposition of paternalistic rule, these soon became spaces of refuge for people seeking to escape systemic violence and the 'quasi-bondage imposed on many rural ex-slaves after emancipation' (Elbourne and Ross, 1997, p 46).

In 1853, the Cape became a British Crown colony and formed a parliamentary government. The new constitution enabled adult men of all races to vote if they owned property, introducing a liberal British tradition that subdued resistance by affording racially marginalized people technical equality before the law (Bickford-Smith, 2002). At the same time, the British continued to conquer Black territories, fighting the last Xhosa war, battling the Zulu Kingdom and annexing Lesotho in the 1870s alone. As the British expanded, they came into conflict with the Boer Republics of the interior, where diamonds recently had been found.

The First Anglo-Boer War began in 1880 in response to the British seizure of the South African Republic of the Transvaal (Thompson, 2014). Delivering a sharp blow to imperial troops, the Boer quickly secured a peace treaty. Yet relations remained tense, particularly once Transvaal gold was discovered in 1886. The second war erupted in 1899, after Cecil Rhodes, the Prime Minister of the Cape Colony, attempted to overthrow Paul Kruger, the President of the South African Republic. During this war, the British held Afrikaners – most of whom were women and children – in concentration camps alongside Black captives. Nearly 28,000 Boer and untold numbers of Africans perished (Coetzer, 2000). When the British won the war in 1902, relations were superficially restored, but this holocaust was never addressed (Tutu, 1999). The formation of the Afrikaner National Party (NP) in 1914 recast this conflict as a political division between liberal British and conservative Afrikaner factions (de Gruchy and de Gruchy, 2005).

National formations

South Africa

By the turn of the twentieth century, Herbert Spencer's theory of Social Darwinism had become fashionable across Europe and its diaspora. This White supremacist ideology sparked a transnational eugenics movement that promoted Jim Crow segregation in the United States and the Nazi movement in Europe. In South Africa, the British-dominated Native Affairs Commission likewise used Social Darwinism to justify racist legislation. In a 1903 debate on native affairs, an Anglophone member of parliament stated: 'Let us keep the two races separate, and let us govern the Black races to the best of our ability because ... the negro races occupy the lowest position in the evolutionary scale' (Fredrickson, 1981, p 196). In 1910, South Africa became a self-governing union under the British Commonwealth. Although English- and Afrikaans-speaking Whites ideologically were divided, they nevertheless colluded in legalizing racial discrimination throughout South Africa, largely eradicating the limited political rights that marginalized racial groups had achieved (More, 2004).

In 1911, the Union of South Africa conducted its first census, developing a modern classification system that determined racial identity based on a combined assessment of ancestry and skin colour. This first census employed three racial categories: (1) Bantu, renamed Native, African, and Black in subsequent iterations; (2) European/White; and (3) mixed and other coloured, which encompassed mixed-race people as well as anyone who did not fit into the first two categories, including the Indigenous Khoe-Sān and East Asians. This move was soon followed by the passage of the Natives Land Act in 1913 (Everingham and Jannecke, 2006). Institutionalizing land theft, this piece of legislation placed 90 per cent of South Africa's landmass under White control, designating barren and unproductive zones as racial homelands, in effect creating impoverished labour reserves to service White capital (Penn, 2005; Waetjen, 2004).

Although sidelined in the nation-building process, racially marginalized South Africans remained active in union politics (Thompson, 2014). In the southeast, Indian activists developed passive resistance campaigns in connection with Mohandas Gandhi, a young civil rights lawyer from India who helped form the Natal Indian Congress (NIC) in 1894. In the Cape, coloured activists formed the African Political Organization (APO) in 1902 to address racial segregation in the Western Cape, where they were the majority population. As the dominant racial group in the eastern two-thirds of the union, Black activists united into one political block in 1912. Later renamed the African National Congress (ANC), this party sought full voting rights for all South Africans. In response to perceived threat, the NP formed a coalition government with the Labour Party in 1924 at which time British and Afrikaner legislators halted African social mobility while granting welfare to poor Whites (Seekings, 2007).

During both World Wars, South Africa sided with Great Britain and fought with Allied forces. Yet Afrikaners were divided in their support. In the early 1940s, thousands of Afrikaners joined a pro-Nazi movement that attempted to subvert the war effort, including John Vorster, a future apartheid head of state (Fokkens, 2012). Far from declining in influence, pro-Nazi sentiment expanded after the Second World War ended, in response to perceived racial threat. Having organized into trade unions, 74,000 impoverished mine workers went on strike in 1946, stopping production in eight gold mines (Thompson, 2014). Fearing the potential strength of well-organized workers, the government deployed police who opened fire on peaceful demonstrators, killing several workers and wounding more than a thousand. Stoking White racial anxiety by reframing the strikes as violent harbingers of Black peril, the NP turned on its more moderate members, claiming them to be closet liberals. In an election limited to White voters, Afrikaner nationalists came into power in 1948, at which time the Dutch Reformed church cleric cum, Prime Minister Daniel François Malan, began constructing a one-party police state (Dubow, 2014).

Latvia

In contrast to South Africa, the Baltic states secured their independence from colonial rule at the end of the First World War. Inspired by the poetics of National Awakening, which had identified 'closeness to nature' as a core aspect of Latvian ethnic identity, early twentieth-century nationalists imagined a 'nation of farmers' joined through cultural connection to a land that countless generations had worked and cherished (Schwartz, 2007, p 261). Taking advantage of the collapse in law and order at the end of the First World War, Latvians mobilized by merging two political parties to establish the People's Council of Latvia. When this body declared national independence in 1918, Latvian Bolsheviks and Baltic Germans formed counter governments. The three governments each had loyal armed forces, thrusting Latvia into civil war (Minins, 2015, p 50). Having overthrown the Tsar in 1917, Russian revolutionaries backed the Bolsheviks, invading the Baltics in a wave of red terror. Germany then sent military volunteer units to support Baltic Germans in a counterwave of white terror. As Latvians, Lithuanians, Estonians, and Finns had all declared liberty at the same time, these Baltic states collectively turned to the British Empire for military support. Recognizing the value in establishing a buffer zone between Germany and Russia, the British sent aircraft and weaponry, and the British navy remained in the region until 1920, when the four states formally secured their independence (Fletcher, 1976).

The multi-party Constitutional Assembly of Latvia was elected in 1920 and immediately passed the Agrarian Reform Law, transferring land ownership from the Baltic German nobility – who were less than four per cent of the population – to Latvian peasants. The Assembly then developed a national constitution, enabling the young Republic to hold its first parliamentary election in 1922 (Plakans, 1995). During the next 12 years, civil society actively participated in national politics, with four elections experiencing high voter turnout. The parliament, or **Saeima**, involved multiple parties, but two dominated the political scene: the left-leaning socialist Social Democratic Workers' Party (LSDSP) and the right-leaning Farmer's Union (LZS). These parties collaborated in transitioning 'from warfare to welfare' by instituting social spending policies to build housing, improve access to education and support the development of small- and medium-scale enterprise (Norkus et al, 2020, p 1).

By 1930, Latvia had attained a national literacy rate of 80 per cent, with ethnic Jews, Latvians, and Germans achieving literacy rates between 89 and 97 per cent. Nor were Slavic-speaking minority groups left behind, for Latvian educational policy engaged the principle of 'ethnic cultural autonomy'. As the Latvian state financed minority language schools alongside Latvian language schools, it enabled ethnic Russians and Belarusians to increase their literacy rates by more than 20 points in 10 years, with around 63 per cent of Slavic speakers literate by 1930 (Silova, 2006, p 27). By 1931, however, the national economy was reeling from a global depression, and unemployment was rising, causing the young Republic to falter in its commitment to ethnic autonomy and multicultural democracy.

In 1934, Kārlis Ulmanis staged a bloodless coup d'état to seize control of the struggling state (Plakans, 1995). As the nationalist leader of Latvian independence, Ulmanis had co-established the People's Council, founded the Farmers' Union, and presided as the nation's first prime minister, eventually serving four terms in this capacity. This reputation enabled him to secure the backing of the military and reinstall himself in power. Ulmanis quickly moved to outlaw all political parties and suspend the constitution and, disproportionately targeting social democrats for removal, he sent hundreds of party members to prison camps. Rejecting the principle of ethnic cultural autonomy, Ulmanis cut spending for minority schools and banned all but a few minority news outlets.

Unlike other European dictators of his time, Ulmanis sought to maintain an aura of legitimacy during the six years of his dictatorship. He constantly promised to return to democratic rule at some unspecified future date, and he projected a false image of support to minorities, for example by making displays of respect to right-wing Jewish groups while repressing left-wing Jewish organizations. He also performed festivity instead of militancy, hosting mass festivals that celebrated Latvian culture, while also obscuring his moves to dismantle democracy (Hanovs and Tēraudkalns, 2014).

Soviet and apartheid rule

Latvia

The Second World War moved into Latvia in June 1940, when Soviet commando units entered the nation through three remote outposts in the fog of early dawn (Feldmanis, 2002). The Soviet Union had coordinated this invasion in secret with Kārlis Ulmanis the previous autumn, and he instructed the Latvian Army to stand down at the last moment (Lumans, 2006). Watching Soviet tanks roll toward Rīga, and told not to resist, some Latvian officers shot themselves in humiliation. By the end of the month, a new government had been installed, formally joining Latvia to the Soviet Union as the Latvian Soviet Socialist Republic (SSR).

Although Ulmanis capitulated to Stalin's demands under the threat of widespread massacre, he prevented Latvians from determining their own destiny, for he alone decided the fate of the nation (Lumans, 2006). Nor did his decision protect civilians. Over the course of the following year, Stalin unleashed Baigais Gads, a Year of Terror in which up to 34,000 people were either executed or deported. During this time, the Red Army conscripted the entirety of Latvia's military, hunting down and executing deserters.

Prior to the Soviet invasion, Stalin and Hitler had negotiated a secretive non-aggression pact wherein they planned to cleave Europe into two spheres of power. This Molotov-Ribbentrop pact enabled Nazi Germany to seize Poland without Soviet opposition in 1939. Once this domain was secured, Hitler broke the terms of the pact by invading the Baltics in 1941. Given the unbridled violence of the Soviet occupation, many Latvians initially welcomed German forces as liberators; indeed, many men volunteered to join the fight against the Soviet Union, with Hitler approving the formation of a Latvian Legion in 1943 (Mangulis, 1983). Yet 80 per cent of the Latvians serving in the Waffen-SS Legion were drafted, and those who refused to fight for the Nazis were sent to German labour camps or local concentration camps.

The general populace struggled to survive the brutality of a second invading army, one bent on slaughtering Jewish and Romani people as well as people with disabilities and anyone suspected of homosexuality. After embarking upon a series of Jewish massacres, the Nazis herded survivors and other undesirable social and ethnic groups into Jewish ghettos and concentration camps where they were enslaved, malnourished and murdered (Ezergailis, 1996).

When the Red Army regained control of Latvia in 1944, 66,000 Jewish people had perished. Less is known about the Gypsy Holocaust; but drawing from reports of massacres, Ezergailis has estimated the decimation of one-half of Latvia's ethnic Romani population. By the end of the Second World War, Latvia had lost one-third of its population through mass killings, deportations and flight. In the immediate aftermath of the war, 120,000 people fled to Western Europe (Plakans, 1995). Most ended up at refugee camps in war-torn Germany and eventually were resettled around the world.

Those who did not flee prayed for the arrival of Allied forces. During the war, tens of thousands of Baltic men and women had hidden in the forests where they formed guerrilla warfare units. Establishing forest bunkers throughout the Baltics, these *meža brāļi* (forest brothers) and *meža meitas* (forest daughters) mounted sustained resistance to the Soviet occupation (Reinsone, 2016). Despite their hope for ongoing British support of their independence, the Allies did not arrive. Winston Churchill – who oversaw the British war effort – had initially ordered plans for a surprise attack on the Red Army in Eastern Europe, but Operation Unthinkable was never put into action due to the potential for a Soviet counterattack on Western Europe (Richardson, 2018). Thus, the Iron Curtain descended, cutting Europe in half.

In 1949, Stalin ordered another round of mass deportation. Apart from quelling resistance to Soviet farm policy, this move was part of a broader stratagem of Russification that involved relocating ethnic groups around the Soviet Empire to remove the threat of revolt in occupied regions (Strods, 2005). Latvian families were pulled out of their homes in the middle of the night, people were arrested at work, and thousands of children were placed on trains to Siberia, sometimes with families but also in groups of unaccompanied children.

Over the course of four days, Latvia lost more than two per cent of its total pre-war population and a third of its rural inhabitants. Nearly 73 per cent of the people deported in 1949 were women and young children who were deemed by the Soviets to be such a threat to security that they required immediate removal to labour camps in Siberia (Strods and Kott, 2002). By the early 1950s, Soviet troops had flushed out most of the forest partisans (Kalnins, 2015).[1]

Upon Stalin's death in 1953, Nikita Khrushchev assumed control of the regime. During the Khrushchev Thaw, the Soviets instituted a policy of de-Stalinization that involved releasing political prisoners, relaxing censorship and rebuilding international relations (Jones, 2006). In the Latvian SSR, a reformist wing of national communists responded by to the Thaw by protesting Russification policies to protect the Latvian language (Michael, 2018). Experiencing broader threats from Soviet Communist Party members who challenged his leadership, Khrushchev halted de-Stalinization in 1957 and instituted an Anti-Party Group Purge that mimicked Stalin's Great Purge conducted 20 years earlier. Latvian national communists were expelled in 1959 through a multi-step process of demotion and exile. Installing servile Latvian or ethnic Russian Communist Party members in positions of Soviet Latvian leadership, Khrushchev intensified Russification.

By the early 1960s, the Soviet Union experienced a scientific-technological revolution. If Stalin had drawn from massive oil and gas reserves to rapidly transition the Soviet Union from an agrarian to an industrial society, it was Khrushchev who launched Soviet satellites and astronauts into space, setting off the US–Soviet Space Race (Lashendock, 2019). This technological revolution shifted the political economy of Estonia and Latvia, and to a lesser degree, Lithuania. Designating the Baltics as a key site for industrial development, the Soviet Union opened massive factories 'across a wide variety of sectors, including heavy industry, the automotive and chemical industries, the military industrial complex, and more' (Purs, 2013, p 73).

As the demand for labour far outpaced the diminutive local population, not yet recovered from losses incurred during the war, tens of thousands of Russians and other Soviet citizens were relocated to Estonian and Latvian towns. Before the Second World War, ethnic Latvians had been more than three-quarters of the population; by 1989 this number had tumbled to nearly 50 per cent, making Latvians a scant majority on their own land.

In addition to linguistic repression, the Soviet Union strove to eliminate religion and culture, elevating authoritarian rulers as the sole sources of moral authority. Operating under Marxist-Leninist ideology, the Communist Party replaced religious doctrine with scientific atheism to establish social control (Van den Bercken, 1989). Churches were converted into secular spaces, and the KGB, or Soviet secret police, placed religious and cultural communities under close surveillance. The Soviet Academy of Sciences in Rīga censored scholarship and tasked historians with rewriting Latvian history while schools and *Komsomol* Communist Youth groups indoctrinated children (Kalnins, 2015).

To preserve their ethnic identity, Latvians again retreated into an inner world of cultural expression. In addition to developing a robust underground press, Latvian dissidents engaged in 'non-aggressive, coded forms of protest', for example, by decorating cultural food items with folk symbols for international visitors (Šmidchens, 2014, p 171). As the state funded art that adhered to the rule of Soviet realism, artists took advantage of this cultural space to disseminate coded messages of resistance. By hiding cultural symbols in outward depictions of Soviet workers and peasants, dissident artists passed under the radar of censors, and some Latvian SSR officials who outwardly complied with the dictates of the Communist Party, chose not to see these coded messages in tacit support of the resistance.

The Chernobyl nuclear disaster occurred in 1986, one year after Mikhail Gorbachev had come into power. An ardent environmentalist and democratic reformer, Gorbachev responded to this crisis by instituting a policy of perestroika, an ambitious plan to systematically restructure the Soviet political economy (Gorbachev, 2006). In Latvia, resentment over Soviet rule had reached a boiling point, not simply because people could no longer tolerate social and cultural repression, but also because Latvians were infuriated by the violence inflicted upon the Baltic ecology. Soviet agriculture and forestry had flooded waterways with toxic chemicals, causing two-thirds of the Baltic Sea to become de-oxygenated dead zones (Darst 2001). Contaminated drinking water and the lack of wastewater treatment facilities had engendered a series of health crises, including a 1988 Cholera outbreak in Latvia's capital city, Rīga (Auers, 2012) Soviet dams had flooded places of cultural import, and agricultural policies had devastated Latvia's rural farm culture (Schwartz, 2006). By the 1980s, only 16 per cent of the labour force worked in agriculture and 70 per cent of the population resided in urban areas (Purs and Plakans, 2017). Thus, Latvians took advantage of Gorbachev's reforms to demand the reinstatement of national independence.

South Africa

While Latvians experienced Soviet occupation, South Africans confronted an apartheid state. After securing power in 1948, the NP instituted a socio-legal system of racial separateness that would dictate all aspects of human life. It began by prohibiting mixed marriages in 1949 and banning interracial sexual intercourse in 1950, at which time the regime consolidated racist land laws by passing the first Group Areas Act (Thompson, 2014). Over the next three decades, the apartheid regime expropriated holdings through forced removals, sending 3.5 million people to overpopulated townships or homelands where the intensified pressure on natural resources degraded environments (Fabricius and de Wet, 2002).

These laws were accompanied by the Population Registration Act of 1950 and the Pass Laws Act of 1952, which required South Africans who were not registered as White to carry *dompas*, or passbooks. Functioning as an internal passport, these passbooks included precise employment details. Adverse reports submitted by White employers went on the passbooks and resulted in internal deportation to racially designated homelands. The movement of Black women was even more strictly curtailed: those not working as domestic servants largely were confined to homelands, fulfilling the task of reproduction to maintain a ready supply of cheap labour (Barchiesi, 2011). If apartheid policies resembled the Jim Crow policies enacted in the United States, the ultra-rationalized South African model extended well beyond 'the Jim Crow system in its rigor and comprehensiveness' (Fredrickson, 1981, p 269).

When the government banned the South African Communist Party (SACP) in 1950, the Black-led ANC became the primary party of resistance (Ellis and Tsepo, 1992). Within the ANC, a Xhosa lawyer by the name of Nelson Rolihlahla Mandela became a key political leader. Together with Oliver Tambo, Mandela opened one of the first Black legal firms in South Africa in 1952, delivering low-cost legal counsel for people suffering from racial injustice. This firm provided a critical space of hope for South Africans who suddenly found themselves evicted from ancestral lands and barred from walking through White-only doors; using water fountains; going to the beach; participating in commerce; not being employed; being employed in the wrong place; living in the wrong place; and having no place to live, in a flood of new laws that collectively implied the illegality of African existence (Mandela, 2008).

State violence intensified under the leadership of Hendrik Verwoerd, a Dutch-born Afrikaner. Having obtained a doctoral degree in 1928, Verwoerd had served as chair of Applied Psychology at the University of Stellenbosch, where he also was a member of the Afrikaner Broederbond (Brotherhood), an extremist group that supported Nazi Germany (Kenney, 2016 [1980]). It was at Stellenbosch that Verwoerd developed the ideological foundation for apartheid, which combined the Calvinist principles of Christian Nationalism with the modern rational doctrine of Social Darwinism. In 1950, Verwoerd was appointed Minister of Native Affairs in 1950 and he became prime minister in 1958. Removing South Africa from the Commonwealth, Verwoerd established the Republic of South Africa in 1961 and set about constructing a managerial police state staffed with 'apartheid intellectuals, social engineers, and bureaucrats' (Louw, 2004, p 63). Verwoerd also expanded national military and police forces until his assassination in 1966, at the hands of Dimitri Tsafendas – a communist sympathizer officially classified as Greek/White. Tsafendas believed social conditions would improve by removing a key architect of apartheid (Posel, 2009). Yet his action had negligible impact, for Verwoerd's police state would expand into a military industrial complex in which government, military, and capitalist elites colluded in an international arms money laundering scheme (Van Vuuren, 2018).

The Sharpeville Massacre was an early signpost of the growing brutality. In March 1960, Black people residing in the township of Sharpeville participated in an act of civil disobedience with approximately 5,000 people gathering in front of a newly installed police station to protest the racist pass law system. Without warning, the police opened fire on the unarmed and singing crowd, killing 69 people and wounding 180 more (Parker and Mokhesi-Parker, 1998). In the aftermath, the state banned African political organizations and responded to civil claims filed by Sharpeville victims by introducing legislation to indemnify the police and government from legal responsibility for violence. Mandela and other activists reacted to the escalation of state brutality by organizing *Umkhonto we Sizwe* (Spear of the Nation) as a military wing of the ANC, causing the anti-apartheid movement to branch into non-violent and armed factions (Seidman, 2001). In early 1962, Mandela travelled to Ethiopia where he met with African nationalist leaders and secured access to guerrilla training. Upon his return in August, Mandela (2008) was captured during a police raid and eventually sentenced to life in prison for attempted sabotage. Several other activists stood trial with him, including Denis Goldberg, a communist of Lithuanian Jewish origin.

During the 1970s, a new generation of activists entered the struggle. The Black Consciousness movement included student leaders like Steve Biko who wrote prolifically on the subject, as well as leaders of the Christian resistance such as Desmond Tutu, who drew from Black theology and African humanist philosophy to articulate ideals for social change (Magaziner, 2010). If the movement motivated Black people to recognize their self-worth, it also encouraged members of all races to join the resistance, for Biko (1978b) encouraged people to view Black as a mindset rather than a colour. Inspired by the ideals flowing through the underground press, school children formed a civil disobedience campaign that became known as the Soweto Uprising (Switzer, 2000). This revolt began with a march in June 1976 in protest of Bantu education laws that required students to learn in the foreign tongue of Afrikaans. Security forces opened fire, killing at least 176 unarmed children, causing civil disobedience to spread like wildfire to Black and coloured communities across the nation. Over the course of one and a half years, more than 600 people were killed, 3,000 more were wounded, and 2,000 were arrested (Switzer, 2000). To stifle rebellion, the police arrested Biko in 1977 and beat him to death in custody. Activists went underground; and in a state of paranoia, a segment of ANC leadership murdered township inhabitants accused of collaboration, in acts of violence that were 'used to very good effect as Nationalist Party propaganda' (Tutu, 1999, p 141). Yet Black Consciousness continued to sweep the nation and, in the final decades of apartheid, coloured South Africans assumed Black identity in a mass demonstration of interracial solidarity (Adhikari, 2006).

The apartheid regime was as patriarchal as it was racist. Extolling intrinsic difference, the state indoctrinated children into a complex and rigid hierarchy of power that ranked people according to their race/class, ethnicity/culture, and gender/sexuality. School children were formally and informally segregated from one another, and the apartheid educational system groomed them for distinct types of work (Baatjes, 2003). Taught to discipline and punish subordinate social groups, White South Africans paid 'a psychological price of constant fear, anxiety, guilt, and uncertainty' and suffered from high rates of alcoholism, suicide, child abuse, and familicide (Pretorius-Heuchert, 1992, p 407).

The regime socialized White boys to kill or be killed. Having invaded Angola in an imperialist manoeuvre, the NP instituted universal military conscription in 1967 and established social structures to militarize White children. It deployed 600,000 males to fight a border war that raged for a quarter century (Symons, 2020). If White men were traumatized by a culture of toxic masculinity, women of all races endured domestic abuse: studies conducted at the end of apartheid found that one in three women were battered by intimate partners (Andrews, 1998). The LGBTQ+ population suffered as well. Within the military, doctors screened conscripts for gays and lesbians, sending those identified to psychiatric wards where they were subjected to aversion shock therapy and chemical castration (Belkin and Canaday, 2010).

Facing economic stagnation, international trade sanctions, and worldwide condemnation, South Africa reluctantly drafted a new constitution in 1984 as part of an initial thaw in race relations (Thompson, 2014). While the

NP allowed for the limited participation of coloured people and Indians in politics, it excluded Black people. Activists responded by protesting around the nation, generating a sustained Mass Democracy movement. Threatened by this expression of civil power, the regime declared a state of emergency and placed townships under military occupation (Switzer, 2000). Yet massive worker and rent strikes continued to rollick the nation, and White support for the NP eroded.

Frederik Willem de Klerk assumed the presidency in 1989, shortly before the Purple Rain Protest. Although a conservative Afrikaner, he realized the nation was headed toward civil war. Like Mikhail Gorbachev, de Klerk thought he could blend the old system with the new but encountered a revolutionary force of change that could not be contained (MacKinnon, 2008). De Klerk legalized African political parties and the right to protest. He released Mandela and other activists from prison in 1990 then worked with the ANC to establish universal suffrage and hold general elections. When South Africans voted the ANC into power in 1994, the National Assembly elected Nelson Rolihlahla Mandela to serve as the first Black president of the democratic Republic of South Africa. After 27 years of incarceration, in one of the world's most infamous prisons, Mandela had chosen to walk into freedom with love in his heart. Committed to the prevention of civil war, he enacted forgiveness by including NP representatives in his government and appointing de Klerk to serve as his deputy (Mandela, 2008).

Democratic transitions

When the ANC came into power, it abolished the Group Areas Act, affirming South African citizenship for the inhabitants of former racial and ethnic homelands. The national population in 1996 was more than three-quarters Black; thus, most South Africans lived in overcrowded rural homelands (Lehohla, 1998). South Africa's transition to democratic rule thereby occurred under conditions of racialized economic inequality: 71 per cent of Blacks and 30 per cent of coloureds were living in extreme poverty in comparison with 2 per cent of Whites (Gradín, 2012).[2] Only 50 per cent of the national population was literate, and Black women – who were the majority of rural homeland inhabitants – were less literate than their male and urban peers (Malik, 2014). Life expectancy fell below the global median as well. In 1996, South African men lived an average of 52 years and women a decade longer. Life expectancy rates varied significantly across race and geographic location, with Black infant mortality rates more than four times higher than White rates due to poverty, hunger and lack of available health care (Chopra and Sanders, 2004).

Despite these disparities, the public mood was optimistic. In the 1990s, South Africans were eager to develop an interracial national identity.

Although people continued to experience de-facto segregation, more than 90 per cent of the population was proud to be South African and wanted their children to have a unified South African identity (Seekings, 2011). In 1995, the government established a Truth and Reconciliation Commission (TRC) to prosecute human rights violations committed by the previous regime. Desmond Mpilo Tutu, an anti-apartheid activist and Anglican Archbishop, was appointed to chair the TRC, and he drew from Christian theology and the African humanist philosophy of Ubuntu to develop proceedings. If Tutu's (1999) African worldsense comprehended the relational interdependence of life, his faith was grounded in the notion that suffering can be transformed through acts of loving compassion. Recognizing that the humanity of apartheid perpetrators and their victims were mutually entangled through acts of aggression that dehumanized the oppressor as well as the oppressed, the TRC sought to break the cycle of racial hatred and violence by uncovering the truth in a caring and compassionate way. Via a series of hearings conducted between 1996 and 2003, it provided the families of apartheid victims with an opportunity to face those who had caused them harm. During this deeply emotional moment in time, thousands of criminals and tens of thousands of victims told their stories; and in return for their testimony, 849 perpetrators received amnesty from the court (Gibson, 2002).

The new constitution of 1996 enshrined South African commitments to democracy and equality. It prohibited unfair discrimination on a wide range of grounds, including those related to race/ethnicity, culture/language, gender/sexual orientation, and age/disability (Gutto, 2001). Not only had feminists played a strong role in the anti-apartheid movement, but in 1992 thousands of women formed the Women's National Coalition (WNC) to demand equal rights in the post-apartheid social order (Cock and Bernstein, 2001). As a result of their influence, South Africa's constitution was heralded as one of the world's most progressive and, in 2004, South Africa became the fifth country in the world to legalize same-sex marriage (Mwaba, 2009).

Confronting a vast and secretive bureaucracy, Mandela's government also restructured public institutions. First, it eliminated inefficient departments by shifting redundant personnel to essential services and creating thousands of affirmative action positions to bring marginalized groups into public work (Thompson, 2014). Second, having ended universal military conscription in 1993, the government merged the apartheid defence force with resistance and homeland units to create a multiracial national defence force. Third, it introduced structural and legal reforms to convert the police from a militarized White supremacist institution to a publicly accountable community policing model (Pruitt, 2010). However, it failed to reform the existing judicial system: in the early 2000s, nearly all South African judges were White men who had been installed under apartheid, and a number of these remained unsupportive of social justice.

The post-apartheid economy remained under White control as well. Having compromised to secure a peaceful transition to democracy, the ANC carved out a middle path between socialist and neoliberal interests when it came into power. Facing a stagnant economy and needing to rebuild trade relations at a time of globalization, Mandela's government instituted a development approach that combined laissez-faire economic policies with the apparatus of a social welfare state (Ferguson, 2010). In 1994, the ANC passed the Black Economic Empowerment Act (BEE) to encourage racially marginalized groups to enter commerce, and it subsequently introduced Agri BEE policies to encourage private capital to invest in Black and coloured farmers.

South Africans have continued to vote for the ANC, but this party has failed to deliver meaningful land reforms despite decades in power (Aliber and Cousins, 2013). Eighty per cent of South Africa's agricultural lands remain under White ownership and four-fifths of the rural population continue live in overcrowded former homelands where they struggle to access markets as small-scale farmers (Keahey, 2018). Corporate interests have continued to ignore the material legacy of 'colonial conquest, land dispossession, and the triumph of commercial farming through the naked exploitation of Black labour' making it difficult to see how land reform and rural development can be realized within a neoliberal framework (Ntsebeza, 2011, p 306).

Post-apartheid South Africa has been at the forefront of developing welfare technologies that have provided essential funds to people in need, for example through the Child Support Grant, a non-conditional cash allocation system that has reduced food insecurity and enabled poor children of all races to attend school, particularly in rural areas where students must pay to lodge at school during the week (Triegaardt, 2005). However, the evidence presented in Chapter 6 suggests that neoliberal policies have served to further consolidate power within the White-owned corporate agro-food sector, making alternatives to economic development a priority for small-scale producers (Greenberg, 2015).

Latvian farmers have experienced similar economic barriers to agrarian development, but from the different context of post-Soviet transition. During the first election for a new Saeima in 1993, people voted the reinstated Farmers' Union into power, with Guntis Ulmanis, the great nephew of Kārlis Ulmanis, becoming the fifth president of the Republic of Latvia. Unlike Mandela's government, the Farmers' Union immediately instituted sweeping agrarian reform. Having reinstated the land reforms of 1920, the Saeima passed a series of laws in the 1990s to decollectivize land and holdings, resulting in the dissolution of 200 *sovkhoz* (state) and 400 *Kolkhoz* (peasant cooperative) farms (Žakevičiūtė, 2016). The state converted large industrial holdings into smaller commercial farms and hundreds of thousands of family farms that were returned to the original owners or any person with a rightful claim (Žakevičiūtė, 2016). Although Latvia's nascent organic farming movement lacked capital and was unable to secure the state support needed to develop commercial production, it took advantage of land reforms by securing farms, converting to organic or biodynamic production and introducing the nation's first organic food labels (Zobena, 1998).

More broadly, however, Latvia lacked the finance needed to convert its national industry to a market economy. While the nationalist Farmers' Union was aligned with the Latvian Green Party and committed to environmental restoration, it also readily embraced the neoliberal growth policies recommended by the World Bank (Žakevičiūtė, 2016). Having seized control of British and US politics during the Thatcher–Reagan revolution in the 1980s, neoliberal interests rode into the crumbling Soviet sphere on a wave of free-market triumphalism in the 1990s, with the UK and the US currying Baltic favour by sending cultural ambassadors to 'introduce English as a foreign language' (Uysal et al, 2007, p 198).[3]

Buoyed by this revolutionary zeitgeist, Estonia and Latvia chose to deploy an economic programme of rapid external liberalization that involved 'decentralizing foreign trade, reducing trade protection and establishing currency convertibility' (Nissinen, 1999, p 63). Unlike South Africa, where capitalist production was entrenched, these nations were 'faced with the problem of building capitalism without capital' (p 65). Thus, the acquisition of foreign direct investment was imperative. While rapid liberalization engendered an economic freefall in the early 1990s, Estonia and Latvia began to experience robust market growth in the late 1990s, causing Western economists to laud these national economies as Baltic tigers (Pabriks and Purs, 2001). At the same time, extreme market openness fragmented social solidarity and placed these nations in a heightened state of vulnerability to global market flux (Sommers, 2009).

Within the cultural domain, post-Soviet Latvia immediately reinstated the interwar Republic principle of ethnic cultural autonomy. This move signalled the right of Latvians to national autonomy and recognized the right of Russians and other ethnic groups to attend school in their native language (Silova, 2006). Whereas the Latvians involved in the Singing Revolution prevented civil war through non-violent resistance (Šmidchens, 2014), Russians who desired democracy averted bloodshed by supporting Latvian independence, with 38 per cent of the Russians inhabiting the Latvian SSR voting for freedom (Smith et al, 2002).

Notwithstanding these displays of multicultural amity, Latvia has experienced significant ethnic tensions. At the time of independence, the vast majority of Russophones knew little about the local culture and could not speak the language, as the Soviet Union discouraged them from learning it (Ginkel, 2018). The urgent question at hand was whether Russians would be granted Latvian citizenship. This was answered in 1994, when the newly elected Saeima introduced the Citizenship Law. For anyone who was a Latvian citizen or a descendant of a citizen during the interwar Republic, it awarded automatic citizenship.[4] For those whose families entered during the Soviet era, the law initially stipulated a three-part naturalization process that later was reduced to two requirements: passage of a Latvian language test and a Latvian history test (Ginkel, 2018). Implemented as a form of historic redress, these requirements sought to restore Latvian history and language after nearly 50 years of Soviet erasure. However, the language and history tests also generated an ageing body of stateless persons who either refused or were unable to learn the material needed to secure citizenship, stoking international concerns regarding Latvia's commitment to minority rights.

In 1999, Vaira Vīķe-Freiberga became the first woman president of the nation. As a member of the Second World War diaspora, she returned to her homeland in 1998 when the prime minister appointed her to promote recognition of Latvian culture abroad (Eglitis and Ardava, 2017). Vīķe-Freiberga was not affiliated with a Latvian party, nor did she run for office, but the Saeima recruited her to the position after failing to garner a majority vote on the existing list of candidates. Hugely popular among the people, Vīķe-Freiberga served two terms where she advanced Latvian foreign policy by bringing Latvia into NATO and the EU in 2004. While this move helped ensure financial investment and enhance national security, the evidence that I present in Chapter 5 shows how accession into the EU trading bloc created new pressures for Latvian farmers.

The following two chapters shift focus by documenting Indigenous Latvian and South African knowledge systems. My coverage of Daina and Ubuntu philosophies complements the historical material information presented in this chapter by providing critical insight into the cultural ideals shaping agrarian resistance in two post-authoritarian environments.

3

Indigenous Baltic
Knowledge: Daina Philosophy

Latvian folk song

As I watch the weather turn,   Kadu laiku redzēdama,
So I choose which shawl to wear;   Tādu sedzu villainīti;
To the people and their ways   Kādus ļaudis zinādama,
I adjust my language.   Tādu laidu valondiņu

— Translated by Latvian poet, Velta Sniķere

Latvia's cultural and linguistic heritage

Baltic moral philosophies perceive a participatory universe where dynamic flows of energy interweave material existence. Drawing from archaeological and linguistic sources, Endre Bojtár (2000) finds that ancient Baltic societies developed in accordance with an animist **ontology** and a matriarchal **axiology**. Like many other Indigenous societies around the world, precolonial Balts inhabited a cosmological realm where humans, trees, and animals transmuted into one another through cycles of reincarnation. Not only did people worship sacred forests and make daily offerings to Mother Earth, but they also maintained intimate bonds with all living beings, from flora and fauna to hills, rivers and stones. Cultural customs, such as seasonal festivals, encouraged people to view non-human forms of life as kin, and to nurture biodiversity as one would care for children.

When German crusaders colonized the Baltics, proto-Latvians responded by enfolding their pagan spirituality into Christianity. Although colonizing forces have fragmented Indigenous Baltic knowledge systems, obscuring their contributions to global science, their lessons are encoded in linguistic and oral traditions, as well as in folk symbols that transmit the wisdom of an archaic Baltic science.

Song is central to cultural identity across the three Baltic sister states, where Latvian Dainas, Lithuanian Dainos, and Estonian Runo song traditions house ancient moral philosophies. Latvian Dainas are quatrain-based poems, composed of four lines that alternately rhyme and typically are sung at gatherings. There are more than 1.2 million poems in existence – many of which are more than a thousand years old – making Dainas one of the largest recorded bodies of oral knowledge in the world (Bula, 2017). Dainas share linguistic ties to Lithuania's non-rhyming songs, but they employ a similar rhythm as ancient Liv and Estonian songs; indeed, Latvian Dainas are culturally unique (Stepanova and Stepanova, 2011).

Akin to the Japanese Haiku in their brevity, Latvian Dainas teach relational lessons in an easily memorizable format that leaves room to ponder. Using 'similarity and contrast as structuring principles', Dainas condense great intellectual complexity into rhythmic stanzas that are notable for their natural simplicity (Vīķis-Freibergs, 1999, p 201). When Latvian children sing folk songs with their families and communities, this next generation becomes socialized into an archaic knowledge system that teaches people how to establish harmonious self-other relationships.

Not only do Latvians come together to sing Dainas during seasonal festivals like Jāņi, the summer solstice, but choirs also sing these sacred poems at song and dance festivals. Latvia's ethnocultural regions host annual events, and every five years, all regional choirs – now including diasporic groups from around the world – join in Rīga for a national festival. These song and dance festivals have played a critical role in affirming cultural identity among the Latvian diaspora as well as in facilitating collective healing during the post-Soviet era. When Latvia began transitioning to democracy in 1990, the song and dance custom brought exiled Latvians home for the first time in nearly 50 years, enabling families who had been torn apart by the Cold War to reconnect and share their memories (Carpenter, 1996; Skultans, 1998).

If the spirit of the Daina is embodied through the regenerative breath of song and dance, its ethos is rooted in the archaic linguistic forms that the Latvian language has stubbornly retained. Neither Germanic nor Slavic in origin, Latvian is a member of a small language family that includes Lithuanian and Old Prussian, the latter of which is no longer spoken (Dini, 2014). These Baltic languages preserve proto-Indo-European linguistic forms that are only otherwise found in Sanskrit, a classical language in South Asia. In fact, Dainas share social concepts and spiritual values in common with the pre-Vedic verses that gave rise to the Vedic and Hindu religions of South Asia. According to Chatterji (1968), the Dainas have retained a natural simplicity that is lacking in the heavily modified Vedas, as 'the quiet romance and love of Nature flows through them, like brooks in a forest glade' (p 63).

Although Dainas have retained the archaic ethos of natural knowing, this body of knowledge is by no means static, for numerous Dainas came into being during the colonial era. These songs not only describe the torment of serfdom, but they also draw from ancient wisdom to articulate cultural resistance to Baltic German landowners.

During the National Awakening Movement of the late nineteenth century, a newly literate generation of Latvians sought to preserve this oral record of Indigenous Latvian knowledge. Alongside other Young Latvians who led this cultural revolution, Krišjānis Barons (1835–1923) translated nearly 182,000 Dainas into written form (Vīķe-Freibergs, 1989). While the Soviet Union occupied Latvia in the twentieth century, folk-song symbology served as coded messages of resistance to a subjugated people (Šmidchens, 2014).

Feminist interpretive methods

In this chapter, I engage the feminist 'speaking with' model for social research to interpret Latvian cosmology for the global reader (Nagar and Geiger, 2007, p 268; Chilisa, 2020). Specifically, I combine a textual analysis of the Dainas with autoethnographic reflections of my acculturation into Latvian cosmology. To bring my subjective self into dialogue with Latvian moral philosophy, I engage the method of Indigenous storytelling, using the combination of text and story to situate epistemic solidarities. I first arrived in Latvia as a US Peace Corps volunteer, where I worked with the Latvian Association of Teachers of English to develop a nationally accredited teacher training programme from 1999 until 2002. I later returned to Latvia in 2005, when I secured Fulbright funding to develop a qualitative study of Latvia's organic farming movement, during which time I spent nearly a year in the field.

Given the subjectivities involved in speaking with difference, feminist ethics call for researchers to disclose their positionality in relation to the topic when publishing research. In terms of my own moral philosophy, I identify as a multi-paradigmatic and interdisciplinary sociologist, with cognitive training in the social sciences, humanities, and Zen Buddhism. I am religiously agnostic but in ontological agreement with Indigenous spiritual traditions that teach the sacredness of Nature, as inscribed in capital form. In my worldsense, the separation between science and religion is a false dichotomy, for I recognize that literal and fluid interpretations of reality are present in all knowledge systems, whether these are secular or divine.

My textual analysis engages recently published English translations of Dainas, with the recognition that I – who speak Latvian as a second language – am not qualified to translate the hidden complexities of these archaic verses. However, my interpretation is enhanced by my own reading of the source material, and I include the original Latvian versions of selected Dainas alongside English translations for the multi-linguistic reader. The Dainas that I examine derive from two translated volumes: (1) *Dainas*, published in 2019 by the formerly exiled Latvian poet, Velta Sniķere; and (2) *Dainas: Wit and Wisdom of Ancient Latvian Poetry*, published in 2018 by the Latvian American linguist, Auzina Szentivanyi. Their linguistic approaches differ. Sniķere's verses are sparse and lyrical, shifting the original tune of the Dainas into a rhythm conducive to English words. In contrast, Auziņa Szentivanyi's verses retain diminutive forms of address that are awkward in the English tongue, but that operate as symbolic reminders of the underlying Daina ethic of gentle love.

The teachings of the Dainas

During my years in Latvia, women often told me that their society was a matriarchy disguised as a patriarchy. Upon my initial arrival in 1999, I was met by a group of women who had taken charge of acculturating American volunteers into Latvian language, history, nature and culture. I soon discovered their perception of womanhood markedly differed from mine. Having grown up in Utah, where I ran wild in the mountains with two older brothers and several male cousins, I had been socialized into a world of men. I had no interest in women's roles, for my encounters with patriarchy had taught me that to be a woman was to be less than a man. In Latvia, however, I was struck by the powerful stature of women who were active at all levels of society. As I awakened to the experience of no longer being subjected to misogyny at work and in public, I found myself becoming comfortable in my own skin for the first time in my life.

Latvian mythology played an important role in my gender re-socialization. My cultural instructors, both formal and informal, orally communicated this body of knowledge from the varying positionalities of their subjective selves; however, all my teachers emphasized the matriarchal values embedded within Latvian gnosis. During my time in Latvia, I learned that Baltic goddesses had retained the original features of Old Europe, unlike in ancient Greece and Rome whose prehistoric goddesses either were militarized or married off to gods when these regions transitioned to Indo-European logic and imperial development (Gimbutas, 1985, p 19). In *Civilization of the Goddess*, the Lithuanian American archaeologist Marija Gimbutas (1991) conducted an extensive analysis of Old European artefacts in relation with those of invading Indo-European civilizations. She found that the Old European evidence was replete with the matriarchal imagery of life-giving gods, cyclical logic and egalitarian social systems. In stark contrast, Indo-European artefacts conveyed the imagery of warlike societies grounded in the patriarchal worship of vengeful gods, linear thinking and hierarchical organization.

Latvian mythology is a living body of archaic knowledge that has remained closely aligned with proto-Indo-European and Old European cosmovisions (Beldavs, 1977). A brief introduction into Latvian goddesses offers clear

Figure 3.1: Major Latvian goddesses

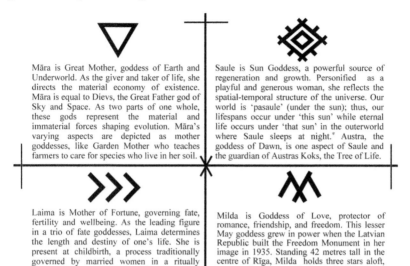

Māra is Great Mother, goddess of Earth and Underworld. As the giver and taker of life, she directs the material economy of existence. Māra is equal to Dievs, the Great Father god of Sky and Space. As two parts of one whole, these gods represent the material and immaterial forces shaping evolution. Māra's varying aspects are depicted as mother goddesses, like Garden Mother who teaches farmers to care for species who live in her soil.

Saule is Sun Goddess, a powerful source of regeneration and growth. Personified as a playful and generous woman, she reflects the spatial-temporal structure of the universe. Our world is 'pasaule' (under the sun); thus, our lifespans occur under 'this sun' while eternal life occurs under 'that sun' in the outerworld where Saule sleeps at night.* Austra, the goddess of Dawn, is one aspect of Saule and the guardian of Austras Koks, the Tree of Life.

Laima is Mother of Fortune, governing fate, fertility and wellbeing. As the leading figure in a trio of fate goddesses, Laima determines the length and destiny of one's life. She is present at childbirth, a process traditionally governed by married women in a ritually cleansed sauna. Laima's intentions are never cruel, but in the vast scope of existence, suffering is inevitable; thus, when one suffers a cruel fate, it is said that Laima suffers as well.

Milda is Goddess of Love, protector of romance, friendship, and freedom. This lesser May goddess grew in power when the Latvian Republic built the Freedom Monument in her image in 1935. Standing 42 metres tall in the centre of Rīga, Milda holds three stars aloft, representing the constitutional districts of the first Latvian republic. Protected by a national Guard of Honour, the Freedom Monument overflows with flowers on important dates.

* Vīķe-Freiberga (1997, 1999, 2002) has produced three volumes on Latvian sun Dainas, identifying these cosmological, chronological, and meteorological themes.

insight into a matriarchal worldsense that has resisted centuries of patriarchal invasion and systemic erasure. Figure 3.1 details the qualities of four Latvian goddesses who figure largely in post-Soviet Latvian culture and displays their individual signs. These signs are part of a symbolic language system that is recorded in art, clothing, and jewellery. Individual signs often are interwoven into complex geometrical patterns that illustrate the relationship between cosmogenic forces shaping the evolution of life in a participatory universe (Ozola, 2021). As moral allegories, Latvian gods and goddesses teach us that the material economy of our individual and collective existence shapes and is shaped by the psychosocial quality of our self-other relationships. The goddesses illustrate this karmic mindset.

Ancient Latvian science co-exists with the modern knowing of a postcolonial and post-Soviet nation, resulting in what my Latvian informants have described as a system of soft patriarchy. Several women told me that men hold symbolic power as the formal heads of households, schools, farms and towns, but that women often direct affairs in practice. These gendered relations are grounded in a cultural ethos that centres the family in society, for as Mole (2011) notes, this social institution was the sole space where Latvians could retain their independence under foreign rule. Latvian women have secured power as the guardians of a minority language and culture repeatedly threatened with extinction; yet fundamentalist interpretations of this guardian role have hindered progress toward gender equity in the post-Soviet era.[1] For example, Mole's study finds that sexual minorities are struggling for acceptance in a society where nationalist politics have framed any deviation from gender tradition as an existential threat to Latvian culture.

In Latvia, the cultural past is very much alive in the present moment. While my reading of the Dainas recognizes the ongoing presence of gender-based inequities, it also records the relationship between my individual experience of empowerment and a matriarchal knowledge system that recognizes women to be powerful beings. In accordance with Latvian quatrain logic, I separate my coverage of the Dainas into four alternating themes: Mother, Master, Song, and Kin. Visually depicted in Figure 3.2, each of these themes includes four Dainas that teach relational lessons on social and ecological wellbeing. As a methodological device, the quatrain structure has helped me systematically narrow my inquiry into the Dainas, for it provided me with an alternating rhythm to identify themes. After presenting each Daina, I bring it into conversation with an autoethnographic reflection that flows in four brief paragraphs. By maintaining the quatrain rhythm in my own voice, I seek to retain the natural simplicity of Latvian logic in my interpretation of the source material.

Mother

I. Light

I light a taper, candles burn,	Dedzu skalu, dedzu sveci,
Dark is my room and dark remains;	Tumša mana istabiņa;
My mother enters, instantly	Ienāk mana māmuliņa,
Light floods the room. Bright is my room.	Tūdaļ gaiša istabiņa

(Sniķere, 2019, pp 64–65)

In Latvian mythology, the powerful sun goddess, Saule, provides the warmth of light to all who inhabit her realm. Saule displays her full radiance during the short-lived summer months, when she shines the energy of regeneration and growth upon the Baltics. The summer solstice festival of Jāņi is the most important cultural event of the year.

On the night before Jāņi – known as *līgo nakts* – Latvians of all ages remain awake, gathering around bonfires to sing and dance the night away. Like the sun, the bonfire symbolizes fertility. Couples who want children jump over the fire together before disappearing into the forest, in search of fern blossoms. These mythical flowers bloom only at midnight on Jāņi.

The word *līgo* translates into to sway, rock, or swing. It implies a playful sexuality, for people often told me that '*līgo*' is related to the Sanskrit word

Figure 3.2: Daina analysis

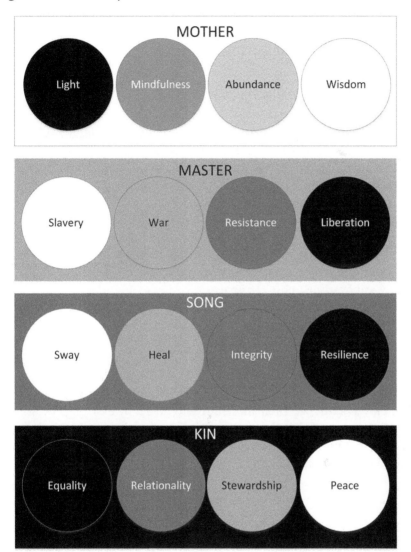

'lingam' the phallic symbol of the Indian God, Shiva, whose union with the goddess Shakti symbolizes the generative force of creation.[2] On *līgo nakts,* all women wear the floral crown of the maiden.

Latvians also invoke Saule at winter solstice by placing candles on trees and making *puzuri.*[3] Reeds are cut into even lengths and strung together. A downward pyramid connects to *Zemes Māte,* an aspect of Māra, and an upward pyramid connects to *Dievs,* the Sky God.[4] The completed rhombus illustrates equality between earth and space, women and men.[5]

II. Mindfulness

Always warm my brother's room,	Silta brāļa istabiņa
Whether heated or unheated;	Ir kurēta, nekurēta;
Pleasant are my mother's words,	Jauka mates valodiņa
Whether spoken or unspoken.	Ij runāta, nerunāta.

(Sniķere, 2019, pp 72–73)

In 1999, I attended a workshop along with a female colleague who was a Latvian English teacher. This multi-day session was conducted in English, but largely facilitated by Latvian educators. My colleague and I were asked to develop a presentation. She lacked the confidence to publicly speak; thus, I agreed to present our material.

Afterwards, I was summoned into the office, where the lead facilitator pleasantly told me to stop taking all the credit. My tendency to use 'I' rather than 'we' when speaking had silenced my colleague's expertise, inadvertently reproducing a power dynamic between a triumphalist capitalist west and the newly impoverished post-Soviet east.

That evening, my colleague and I dialogued, surmising that broader cultural and geopolitical forces had shaped our relationship in ways we had not fully recognized. We determined that I should learn from her humility and she from my confidence. The following day, my colleague began talking and I assumed a supportive role.

This lesson in relational ethics has made me cognisant of the words that I employ as a teacher. I remain sensitive to power by ensuring any critique I make supports rather than silences my students. My goal is not to force my way upon those with less power, but rather to open room for respectful dialogue and mutual growth.

III. Generosity

Four corners has this room of mine,	Isabiņai četri kakti,
Four corners, all four empty.	Visi četri tukši ira.
Were mother here, abundance would	Ja šeit būtu māmuliņa,
Be filling all the corners.	Visi četri pilni būtu.

(Sniķere, 2019, pp 66–67)

When I moved to Krustpils in 1999, I spent several months living with a family, where my host mother played a key role acculturating me into Latvian society. After I moved into Saule's[6] home, I travelled to Rīga, planning to take the last train home. Saule insisted on meeting me at the train station, as I was still unfamiliar with my surroundings.

That night, I dozed on the train, coming to wakefulness upon hearing the word Krustpils on the speaker. I leapt off the train just before the doors closed and found myself in the middle of a deep forest close to midnight. Realizing I had gotten off one stop too soon, I knew I needed to walk in the direction of the departing train.

Eventually I made my way out to a highway and later still to a gas station, closed but lighted. Shocked to find a foreigner speaking broken Latvian at her country doorstep late in the night, the proprietor called my host mother then drove me into Krustpils, where Saule stood waiting in the chill at the side of the road with a flashlight to guide me home.

Although it was nearly three in the morning, Saule insisted that I warm up with a steaming bowl of borscht before bed. My hands shook so badly that I knocked over the bowl. While I cleaned up sprays of beet froth, she dished out a new bowl from her abundant pot, commiserating with my hitherto repressed fright.

IV. Wisdom

Of small value is a belt,	Es par jostu nebēdāju,
Unless the ends fringe thickly;	Kad tik kupli jostu gali;
A husband is not my concern,	Es par vīru nebēdāju,
As long as he has a good mother.	Kad tik laba vīra māte.

(Sniķere, 2019, pp 76–77)

My mother was assaulted by a man in the US during the winter of 2002. After hearing of her ordeal, I injured my neck in sleep. A Latvian friend recommended an affordable massage therapist who collaborated with my gym trainer to develop a therapeutic programme that enabled my body and spirit to heal from this secondary trauma.[7]

In Latvian folklore, men who commit violence against women and other species are the consequence of mothers who do not raise their sons wisely. In this fourth Daina, the wise mother is invoked in relation to the belt of Latvian folk dress, for the symbology woven into belts communicate values to those who know how to read their geometric patterns.

In her translation of the thickly fringed Lielvārde belt, Ozola (2021) explains the meaning of its 22 symbols, which are woven into patterns that express the relationship between varying planes of existence. All planes are interdependent and of equal value, teaching the importance of cultivating harmonious self-other relationships.

The town of Lielvārde is situated on the right bank of the Daugava River, with whom it has evolved in ecocultural relation. If the Daugava represents the lifeblood of the land, the Lievārde belt is the symbolic belt of the nation.

This maroon and white belt is woven in the same colours as the national flag, another legendary symbol of Latvian lifeblood.

Master
I. Slavery

No one has it quite so bad,	Nevienam tā nebija
As my brother dear has had;	Kā manam bāliņam;
He was traded for a beast,	To pārmija ar lopiņu
Taken to a foreign land.	Aizved tālu svešumā.

(Auziņa Szentivanyi, 2018, p 109)

When I was conducting field research with small-scale farmers in 2005, I met a young woman who invited me to visit Jaunpils Castle where she worked as a tour guide. Built by the Livonian Order in the agrarian heartland of Zemgale, the Baltic German von der Recke family owned this estate until 1920, when Latvia first secured independence.

Showing me the wintry view from the top of the turret, my guide told me of a medieval von der Recke who liked to go there to shoot the serfs working his fields. As guns recently had been invented, the von der Recke in question saw it as an opportunity to instil the fear of God in his serfs by punishing those perceived to be lazy with inexplicable death from above.

In the 1700s, the poet, Eliza von der Recke, wrote a letter to a friend, stating that the enslaved children labouring barefoot and in rags on the Jaunpils estate were the offspring of her rapacious husband (Ray, 2003). Eliza succeeded in divorcing her husband, but the estate's children experienced the far bleaker fate of life in servitude to a violent patriarch.

II. War

Fellows young and young boars,	Puisīšam kuilīšam
They all have awful lives:	Tiem abiem grūts mūžiņš:
Autumn cometh, boars are butchered,	Nāk rudens, nokauj kuili
Fellows then must soldiers be.	Nodod puisi zaldātos.

(Auziņa Szentivanyi, 2018, p 114)

Dainas often sing of masters sending their serfs to fight in winter wars, for the Baltics were desirable to the German, Swedish, and Russian empires alike. The loss of entire families to war caused turmoil in the spring, when German lords lacked the labour needed to cultivate their estates. The colonial agrarian economy was in a constant state of crisis.

Numerous colonial Dainas situate the suffering of Latvians in relation to the suffering of other species, typically in the form of farm animals who shared in their familial life. These depictions serve as a counterpoint to older Dainas that sing of a differing set of eco-social relationships that support the awakening of one's heart to reality of true love.

While pigs continue to be slaughtered in the autumn, the Latvian method is humane. In a discussion with high school students in Krustpils in 1999, I was surprised to discover that most boys had spent the weekend killing the family pig. This custom occurs on Saint Martin's Day, typically when a son conducts the slaughter with his mother's guidance.

While talking to small-scale farmers in 2005, I further learned that women traditionally have taught boys how to kill gently and with compassion. Recognizing that any of us might experience such a sad fate, one must care for the emotional wellbeing of pigs who sacrifice their lives so that their human kin may survive the winter.

III. Resistance

I'm charged to cart a heavy load	Kundziņš man spītēdams,
By my spiteful master;	Like man lielu vez'mu vest;
In return I spite my lord:	Es, kungam spītēdams,
I labour whistling gaily.	Brauc pa ceļu svilpodams.

(Sniķere, 2019, pp 46–47)

In 2005, I had the opportunity to attend Latvia's first Pride event. Organized by the nascent group Rīga Pride, this event faced significant political opposition. Not only did the nation's prime minister publicly oppose Pride, but the deputy mayor of Rīga resigned when the Latvian court system overturned a withdrawal of the event permit.

I expected an anti-LGBTQ+ presence but thought the day would be exuberant, akin to the Pride events I previously had attended in conservative Utah. Latvia's first gay and lesbian clubs had opened in the 1990s, and I had witnessed a vibrant underground movement. Moreover, an American friend had come out to Latvian colleagues and had been embraced with love.

I was not prepared for the depth of homophobia that I witnessed that day. Flanked by the police, Latvia's LGBTQ+ community quietly walked through Rīga, followed by a massive mob that hurled insults and rotting vegetables. The police fulfilled their duty in protecting the community, but the violence in the air was palpable.

The activists were frightened but confronted the mob with quiet pride. Although Latvian nationalists had reproduced the Soviet repression of LGBTQ+ people by labelling them as a foreign entity, the quiet resistance that I witnessed was deeply Latvian. As a lesbian friend later told me, social oppression had taught her to look inward for liberation.

IV. Liberation

Masters dear, ye do by forcing	Ar varīti, jūs, kundziņi,
Brothers do by wisely thinking	Ar padomu bāleliņi;
Using force fails in defeating	Ar varīti nevarēja
What is done with thought and wisdom.	Padomiņu pievarēt.

(Auziņa Szentivanyi, 2018, p 118)

During my first year in Latvia, I struggled with the interior-ness of Latvian existence. As someone accustomed to constant movement and loud conversation, I found the quiet solitude unnerving, particularly in the winter when it seemed that an already taciturn society became even more silent than usual.

By my third year, I had developed a deep appreciation for the quietude. I enjoyed not having to speak to the store clerk, our scowls alone communicating displeasure with the slanting sleet outside. I had come to prefer slow weekends to nights out, as this unbroken stretch of time allowed me to cook, read, draw and take walks in the fleeting sunshine.

It was more difficult for me to learn how to actively listen, for Latvians do not interrupt. The conversation pauses when the speaker stops, even in large groups. This moment of silence enables those listening to process what they have heard, to consider the most thoughtful response and to allow others to respond before inserting one's own voice.

In addition to promoting active listening, the prohibition on interruption encourages people who disagree to influence conversation through reason rather than through force. Inflexible declarations hold far less weight than do responses that consider other points of view. To insist that one is right is to act like a child who has not yet learned how to reason.

Song

I. Sway

Singing spun I, singing wove I,	Dziedot vērpu, dziedot audu,
Singing did I fill my hope chest.	Dziedot pūru pielociju
Have no father, mother dearest,	Ne man tēva, ne māmiņas,
In sweet songs I solace find.	Dziesmiņas remdējos.

(Auziņa Szentivanyi, 2018, pp 20–21)

In 2001, I went with my Latvian friends to a song and dance festival that was held to commemorate the founding of Rīga, the capital city. The event was held at the Grand Bandstand of Mežaparks – an open-air ethnographic museum where artisans showcase the traditional cultural life of the nation to the forest park's visitors.

The president, Vaira Vīķe-Freiberga, came to the stage to deliver a speech. The press later referred to it as a 'mass psycho-hypnotic session' by a psychology professor who had spent most of her life in exile. Lifting her arms to the sky, Vīķe-Freiberga urged the crowd to repeat with her, "We are strong! We are powerful! We are beautiful!" (Ozoliņa, 2019; Vīķe-Freiberga, 2001).

I turned to my friends to express my joy of the moment. "No!" Usinš said to me, wide-eyed with pain. "We are not strong! We have been occupied for most of our history!" Later that night, on the drive home, Usinš amended, "I don't know, maybe it is true that we Latvians have a kind of strength, but it's not our way to speak of such things."[8]

When Vīķe-Freiberga had stepped back from the stage earlier that evening, a choir of 10,000 singers rose gently into song. As the gloaming dusk filled with harmonious notes, the crowd swayed. It was as if all our worrisome thoughts had flowed away into the forest, opening our bodies and spirits to the timeless sensation of unencumbered existence.

II. Heal

Sing to me sister,	Dzied māsiņa, tu pret mani,
Join in my yodelling;	Es pret tevi gavilēšu;
Trees will be swaying	Lai lokās koku gali,
In response to our voices.	Kad balstiņas pāri skan.

(Sniķere, 2019, pp 22–23)

Later in 2001, Vīķe-Freiberga gave a speech at the World Conference on Racism in Durban, South Africa, wherein she stated that the negative emotions of fear and distrust give rise to prejudice and "endless cycles of violence." The civilizational challenge of our era involves learning that "diversity can be a source of mutual enrichment rather than oppression … the basis of complementarity rather than confrontation" (Cimdiņa, 2003).

My coverage of eras of great transformation in Chapter 1 suggests the accuracy of this statement. From ancient agrarian empires to the modern era, colonizing forces have transmitted a systemically violent mode of existence that reproduces collective trauma. This traumatic mode of existence is reified in societies that have been colonized by a culture of fear.

If the logical fallacy of separate existence is a cognitive virus that results in oppression, what is the antidote? According to Vīķe-Freiberga, one cannot break the cycle of abuse without taking the time to heal. By learning to recognize the source of suffering, social groups may halt the reproduction of relations and structures that cause collective trauma.

The Latvian concept of *līgo* offers critical insight into collective healing. To sway not only invokes the regenerative energy of midsummer, but it also denotes the kinetic sensation of interconnectivity and belonging. To sway is to let go of fear and to open to love. The rhythm of song and dance support this, as does communion with other species.

III. Integrity

I walk along singing,	Ej pa ceļu dziedādama,
Wagtail-like dancing;	Kā cielava dancodama;
Ill-meaning gossip	Svešu ļaužu valodiņas
I toss overhead.	Pār galviņu mētādama.

(Sniķere, 2019, pp 24–25)

Latvian moral philosophy strongly discourages gossip. People are socialized to refrain from engaging in needless speech and potentially harmful speech. Apart from sharing practical details, one does not speak of those who are not present. By teaching people to speak with integrity, the Dainas cultivate a wholeness of being.

When I first arrived in Latvia in 1999, it seemed to me that women of all ages, shapes, and sizes were comfortable with their bodies. One did not have to be young or beautiful in the Western European sense to strut confidently through town in revealing clothing, and women routinely took off their shirts while walking along the beach or sitting by rivers.

I soon learned that Latvia's sauna culture encouraged women to celebrate their bodies. Although sauna parties included both men and women, the sauna itself was sex segregated. I was taught that one must enter the sauna naked so the skin may sweat out impurities. Bathers stimulated circulation by beating each other with leafy birch branches.

In 2005, women told me that the ubiquitous 'gossip' on social media was harming girls. Having come of age watching social media market idealized images of beauty, younger women had begun to feel insecure in their own skin. I no longer saw young women in public saunas, disrupting an ancient rite of sisterhood that had promoted body positivity.

IV. Resilience

Sorrow mine, great is my sorrow,	Bēdu manu, lielu bēdu,
But I do not care for sorrow;	Es par bēdu nebēdāju;

Underneath a stone I place it	Liku bēdu zem akmeņa,
And walk over sorrow singing.	Pāri gaju dziedādama.

(Sniķere, 2019, pp 20–21)

During the summer of 2005, I attended a seminar that brought Latvian agrarian agents into conversation with European peers at a time of EU accession. This event focused on EU standards for organic production, but it also enabled Latvians to introduce their food and culture to Europeans who possessed little knowledge of this new EU nation.

One session involved visiting a priestess to learn about Indigenous Latvian perspectives on nature. As a member of Latvia's neopagan revival movement, this priestess routinely performed traditional ceremonies, such as forest weddings where she asked couples to seal their vows while standing on large stones that symbolize endurance.

Guiding her bemused flock of agricultural scientists into a forest clearing, the priestess lit a bonfire, upon which she made offerings of various plants, explaining their agrarian function and spiritual meaning in turn. I learned that the differing strengths of oak and birch trees complement that of stone, whose hardness can absorb the gravest of sorrows.

For Latvians, the oak tree possesses a masculine energy, one that is stolid and unyielding. Oak remains still in light wind, neither his trunk nor spirit buffeted by the fickle moods of the day. Yet Oak cannot withstand the hurricane, for his unyielding nature causes him to become uprooted when faced with the unrelenting energy of the howling gale.

Birch's energy is feminine. Lively and flexible, she is buffeted by the slightest of winds. Yet gale force cannot uproot her, for however violently Birch may sway, her ability to bend ensures her survival. Resilience is knowing when to be an oak, when to be a birch, and how release sorrow to the stones rather than allowing it to harden the heart.

Kin

I. Equality

In this home there is no need	Šis sētiņas meitiņām
Towels fine for maids to weave:	Dvieļus aust nevajaga:
All along the walls I see	Zirneklīši sāuduši
Spiders sweet display their work.	Pa visām sienmalēm.

(Auziņa Szentivanyi, 2018, p 15)

The Soviet Union did improve the material quality of life for Russian peasants through the erasure of Tsarist capital. In Latvia, however, the First Republic already had transferred land ownership from Baltic German lords to Latvian peasants. When the Soviet Union invaded, it replaced an egalitarian peasant system with an authoritarian agrarian regime.

In the early spring of 2000, I visited the Krustpils Castle with a Latvian friend. Laima was eager to teach me the local history, sharing information alongside the tour guide. When we approached the room with Soviet memorabilia, Laima fell behind. Deep in discussion, the guide and I did not notice, but turned when she cried out in pain.

Laima had stopped just inside the door, her face blanched of colour and body shaking. "Džena!"[9] she gasped, "Do you smell it?" I inhaled, smelling something undefinable underneath the mustiness. Seeing my confusion, Laima choked out "it's the smell of the red paint! It's the smell of the lies and propaganda I had to breathe all my life!"

The room was filled with placards slathered in red paint. Laima went on, saying "they talked about equality, but we were not equal! My family was Lutheran, but we were not allowed to practice our faith. The KGB followed us everywhere. We were hungry while the leaders of the Communist Party got cars and went on spa vacations!"

Later, we stepped outside and walked through a poplar grove just starting to awaken from winter. Laima stopped to take deep breaths of the blustery air. The colour finally returning to her face, she said "I wanted to burn those signs, but it is better that they are there. Let them be a reminder that there is no equality without freedom."

II. Relationality

Tell me, speak, explain it, language,	Teici, teici, valodiņa,
What the bubbling brook is saying,	Ko upīte burbulēja,
What the bubbling brook is saying	Ko upīte burbulēja,
And what trills the nightingale.	Ko pogāja lakstīgala.

(Sniķere, 2019, pp 16–17)

Latvia is a gently rolling land whose people value the language of songbirds over the drums of war. Not only do the Dainas encourage one to take an interest in the language of other species, but given their geographical position between warring empires, Latvians often speak upwards of five human languages.

In 2001, I moved between Latvian, English, and French in my everyday life. While I primarily spoke Latvian with friends, I worked as an English teacher trainer and as a part-time high school teacher in Krustpils. I also had put my French degree to work, teaching introductory French at the Jēkabpils Language School, across the river from Krustpils.

The Jēkabpils City Council approached me to ask if I might serve as translator for a cultural exchange with a visiting French delegation. I agreed. Once on stage, however, I struggled to translate words that I understood in their own context. My rational and human-centred French lexicon was at odds with my poetic and nature-centred Latvian.

This experience taught me how deeply cultural assumptions about the nature of reality shape the languages we speak. To move between languages is to transverse dimensions of being. By learning a foreign tongue, one develops a capacity for relationality that goes beyond mere tolerance for difference, for one begins to perceive the world anew.

III. Stewardship

Everyone can live contented	Visiem labi, visiem labi
On my father's lovely land	Mana tēvi zemitē:
Hares can lope in sweeping loops,	Zaķiem labi cilpu mest
Birds can peep, chirp and trill.	Rubenim rubināt.

(Auziņa Szentivanyi, 2018, p 123)

From 2001 until 2002, I travelled all over eastern Latvia, delivering monthly seminars to teachers of English in four regional towns. Many lived in small villages where they were involved in horticulture and animal husbandry. It was through talking to these women that I first gained an interest in Latvia's organic farming movement.

During coffee breaks, Māra would often sit with me, telling of farming philosophy and the financial struggles that she and her husband faced as farmers. On one winter day, in which we had all travelled in frigid buses through a driving blizzard to attend the seminar, I was feeling frozen and disgruntled when I watched Māra get off the bus.

The exhaustion was apparent in her eyes, yet her smile was radiant. "Džena," she called out, "my cow foaled during the night!" To celebrate the coming event, Māra had killed a piglet, hanging it in the rafters to smoke while she midwifed her cow. The smoky fire had provided them both with warmth while curing the tender meat she had hung above.

Māra told me that the calf had arrived in the wee hours. She woke her husband, dressed for travel, and sliced off a hunk of smoking meat. "It may be a bit rare," she said, handing me a package, "but I wanted to share it with you." A shaft of sunlight pierced through the swirling blizzard. "Look!" Māra exclaimed, "Saule is smiling at us!"

IV. Peace

Deep in fog, deep in dew	Migliņa rasiņā
Flower golden marigolds;	Ziedēj' zelta purenītis;
A shepherdess, eyes wide, stands still:	Ganu meita ieraudzīja,
It seems to her like sunrise.	Šķiet saulīti uzlecam.

(Sniķere, 2019, pp 104–105)

In 2005, I used grounded theory to develop fieldwork with Latvia's organic movement. My goal was to understand the movement from the perspective of farmers who were using organic technologies to restore Latvian agrarian tradition; thus, I began my inquiry by working on Aivars and Lilija Ansoni's farm.[10]

This couple had embraced the beyond-organic philosophy of biodynamic farming, securing Demeter certification for their fruit and flowers. They farmed in accordance with the moon cycle, provided habitat for buzzing bees, and produced their own fertilizer from the manure of sheep who happily trimmed the orchard grass.

Aivars and Lilija traded fruit for milk with the farmer down the road, and Aivars routinely loaded his truck with produce for sell in Rīga's open-air markets. When George Bush, then US president, arrived in Latvia to meet with President Vaira Vīķe-Freiberga, the Ansoni farm provided a glorious bouquet of flowers for the presidential dinner.

I returned to Rīga to find that Old Town had been closed for the visit.[11] Many elderly people hid indoors, reliving memories as the streets filled with barricades and helicopters whirred overhead. I remember feeling sad that my president might gaze upon the Ansoni's flowers without ever knowing the peaceful quietude of the land whence they had come.

Sustainable development in the Latvian context

Latvian moral philosophy addresses a gap in sustainability studies by making 'abstract concerns about global nature … relevant in local and everyday contexts' (Vallance et al, 2011, p 347). In this section, I identify three Latvian contributions to the discourse: (1) the concept of *padoms*, or wise knowing; (2) the use of poetic 'I' as a modality for teaching relationality; and (3) a culturally situated modality of development from within.

First, Auziņa-Szentivanyi (2018) discusses the importance of *padoms* to Latvian moral philosophy. Ubiquitous within the Dainas, this term denotes 'the ideas of wisdom, common sense, and experience that was accrued over generations' (p 118). In colonial-era Dainas, the concept of *padoms* is used to contrast two ways of existence: that of the master and that of the Latvian serf. While the Dainas acknowledge the master's material power, they do not covet his way of being. Rather, the master is routinely depicted as barren of love and lurching from one violent moment to the next, without ever taking the time to understand that which he seeks to control.

Padoms indicates a wise knowing approach to development and social change that is rooted in centuries of centuries of ancestral knowledge and lived eco-social experience. It is akin to the slow knowledge tradition of Bali, where temples in service to the water goddess Dewi Danu sustainably managed agricultural production 'for more than a millennium' (Orr, 1996, p 699). This system was dismantled by the Asian Development Bank in the 1980s. Employing the fast knowledge approach that had engendered the industrialization of agriculture, the Bank spent 24 million US dollars to replace a functioning system with 'something that did not work at all'. According to Orr, the new system reduced crop yields, destroyed habitat, and poisoned waterways, causing the guardians of water temples to reject reforms and reassert control.

Second, the Dainas engage the poetic 'I' by using first person pronouns when referring to 'animals, trees, rivers' and other forms of life. In short, this linguistic tool teaches people 'to address everyone and everything" as free agents with a moral right to their own existence and opinions (Muižniece, 1989, p 145). By learning how to engage in playful dialogue with the diverse forms of life that one encounters in everyday existence, Latvian children are socialized to ascribe sentience to all that is, ever was, and will ever be. Like other Indigenous traditions that give voice to non-species kin, the Dainas teach us how to inhabit a participatory universe. By learning how to be present with the emotions that arise when we interact with ourselves (through internal dialogue), other people, and other species, we come to understand that the realities we experience are rooted in the quality of our self-other relationships.

The use of the poetic 'I' dispels the colonizing impulses of anomie and alienation by helping people become more present in their everyday lives. Within the context of sustainability, it offers a relational and psychosocial antidote to the detachment of a development regime all too dominated by 'specialists without spirit, sensualists without heart' (Weber, 2012 [1920], p 182). If the master's epistemology imposes order through force, his way of being is undergirded by fear of losing control, resulting in the Iron Cage of collective suffering and madness. In the face of a modern world-system that has alienated people from their labour and cultures to achieve the velocity of constant growth, the poetic 'I' represents a cognitive strategy for reclaiming our connection to life on Earth.

The Dainas illustrate the potential of connection by describing an idealized society of gardeners, fishers, artisans, and singers who are in active dialogue with the world around them. In teaching children to explore the language of birds by singing along with them, the Dainas socialize children to understand reality from the perspective of difference. As a cognitive mechanism for development and change, the Dainas encourage Latvians to revisit their most joyful traditions when problematizing transitions to sustainability.

Third, Latvia historically has followed an inward path to development, resistance, and transformation. If the trajectory of colonial and authoritarian rule made it impossible for generations of Latvians to influence the political economy of their society, the possibility of psychological liberation was always at hand. Like the whistling serf charted to carry a heavy load, Latvia has managed to sustain its language, knowledge and values across centuries of foreign occupation and repeated attempts at cultural genocide; and Dainas have played an important role in inspiring generations of Latvians to carve out spaces of self-determination. In a psychosocial analysis of the associative structuring of longer Latvian folksongs, where each module of the song is one quatrain poem, Vīķis-Freibergs (1997, p 303) writes:

> By playing a new variation on a common theme, each module induces a cathartic visualization of both the felt problem and of its desired solution. Long before psychotherapy was invented, the singer of old could look to her oral tradition, where she would find a plentiful supply of poetic icons to reinforce her sense of personal integrity, reassure her about the strength of her inner resources, and assure her of divine love and protection.

The psychosocial orientation of Latvian moral philosophy contributes to a growing body of Indigenous and decolonial science that is rethinking development from within. In Guatemala, for example, Indigenous communities have instituted an agroecology approach to development that is in alignment with the relational knowing of their ancestral tradition (Einbinder and Morales, 2020). Indigenous cosmovisions are multi-temporal in scope, providing critical insight into the longue durée and the interrelated material–immaterial praxis of social change. By revisiting the wisdom of the past to develop a relational science of wellbeing that opens room for agency in the present, Indigenous science is constructing **transmodern** futures. As a decolonial concept, the transmodern paradigm proposes the development of alternative modernities that are grounded in a radical sense of heritage, and thereby is capable of accounting for cultural and ecological differences (Bialostocka, 2022).

If transmodern liberation denotes a praxis of delinking from the warring epistemology of the master who can only conceive of either/or outcomes, the Latvian concept of sway offers some clarity on the praxis of delinking. Colonized by fear, the master has forgotten how to sway in rhythm with the vicissitudes of life. Like the rigid oak, the master cannot withstand the howling gale of the storm he has unleashed, thusly fated to sow the seeds of his own demise. Latvian moral philosophy teaches that both the flexible *yin* energy of the birch and solid *yang* energy of the oak are needed if we are to produce resilient societies that are capable of thriving in changeable conditions. In a universe where the dual forces of chaos and order co-constitute the complex realities of our existence, one must know what to preserve and how to bend.

When Latvia regained its independence in 1990, it swayed outward in its relations. Having returned to the global community, the post-Soviet government has aligned a national development agenda with the UN's sustainable development goals (SDGs). Yet the wisdom of the Dainas also has informed Latvia's 2030 goals, which articulate the preservation of language and ecology through the revitalization of art and culture (Latvia 2030, 2010). Calling for poets and artists to construct sustainability values that will be appreciated and known in Europe and around the world, Latvia's agenda departs from conventional sustainability approaches in that it centres creative expression as a driving force for sustainability. Offering a reflexive counterpoint, South African Ubuntu philosophy offers outward-focused lessons on community building and multicultural liberation. It is to this knowledge that I now turn.

4

Indigenous African Knowledge: Ubuntu Philosophy

A person is a person through other persons. To dehumanize another inexorably means that one is dehumanized as well.
— From *No Future Without Forgiveness*,
by Desmond Tutu (1999)

South Africa's multi-ethnic heritage

African science articulates a cosmology of interconnectedness like that of the Baltics. According to Mathias Guenther (2020), the Sān peoples of Southern Africa shared a common perception of the universe as unbounded and changeable. Roaming an arid landscape alongside the other species they depended upon for subsistence, the ancient Sān believed humans and animals flowed into one another through spacetime. These social interactions brought meaning and order to the chaotic impulses of a participatory universe. In contrast to the gather-hunter Sān, who recognized the right of all life to a free existence, the pastoral Khoekhoe possessed livestock and paid tribute to tribal leaders (Smith, 2009). While Khoekhoe societies introduced a degree of hierarchy into the self-other relationship, animal welfare was a shared value among all Indigenous Southern Africans, who often shifted between herder and hunter lifestyles and Khoe-Sān identities (Barnard, 2008).

Across Sub-Saharan Africa, Bantu-speaking societies teach a similar worldsense. Experiencing the cosmic web of life as a divine Vital Force, Bantu-speaking peoples recognized the rights of other species to wellbeing, with cultural philosophers appointing the spirits, ancestors, and living human elders as ecological guardians. During the colonial era, the Bantu concept of Vital Force merged with Christian notion of God, giving rise to African Christianity, in all its cultural, linguistic, and ethnic forms (Kaoma, 2014).

Ubuntu is a pan-African moral philosophy. Although the term derives from the Xhosa and Zulu languages of Southern Africa, Ubuntu concepts undergird moral thinking across the continent. As a distinctly African science, Ubuntu challenges the Euro-Western discourse on human rights, which places individual and collective rights into opposition rather than recognizing their interdependence. In *The Lessons of Ubuntu*, Mark Mathabane (2018) identifies the hostile and nihilistic ideologies undergirding racial and ethnic relations within the neoliberal world-system. The survival-of-the-fittest theorem buttressing modern rational discourse reduces human agency to a stark choice: 'to hate or be hated, to oppress or be oppressed, to kill or be killed' (p 9). Mathabane concludes that this line of reasoning is myopic, for history has repeatedly shown us that fear and hate result in escalating cycles of violence, militarization, and warfare. In our current global climate, individual societies cannot hope to preserve the best of their own cultures without cultivating a sense of loyalty to all people and all societies. Thus, as a socially engaged and relationally oriented praxis, Ubuntu offers a radical corrective for global development.

When South Africa transitioned to democracy in the 1990s, anti-apartheid activists sought to construct a multiracial democracy in accordance with Ubuntu principles. Presiding over South Africa's Truth and Reconciliation Commission (TRC), Anglican Archbishop Desmond Mpilo Tutu instituted an Ubuntu model of restorative justice, becoming known around the world as 'the moral conscience of South Africa' (Otieno, 2020, p 591). Tutu's articulation of Ubuntu-based governance provided the world with an alternative model for international criminal justice. Instead of replicating the post-Second World War Nuremburg model of retributive justice, which involved prosecuting and executing Nazi officials, the TRC organized its trials for the purpose of national healing, in some cases offering people who had committed crimes against humanity amnesty in return for their candid and repentant testimonies.

If South Africa's transition to democracy was marked by hopeful feelings of interracial unity, the triumphalist discourse surrounding the collapse of apartheid minimized the bitter realities facing the nation. At the time of liberation, South Africa was severed into four racially distinct nations, each ordered hierarchically in terms of access to social privileges and legal rights. White South Africa had become wealthy and empowered, Black South Africa had been systematically impoverished and illiterate, and the Indian and coloured nations were situated between these poles (Alexander, 2003). Enchanted by the neoliberal promise of racial equality through economic growth, the post-apartheid state neglected to act upon many of the TRC's recommendations, destabilizing longer-term prospects for interracial forgiveness and healing. More than thirty years have passed since the 1999 Purple Rain Protest signalled the end of apartheid, yet the multiracial democracy that South Africans so desperately have struggled to realize remains all too often the social imaginary of multiracial sitcoms that erase the ongoing reality of systemic oppression (Ives, 2007).

Troubling Indigeneity

Given its racialized history, Southern Africa has a troubled relationship with Indigeneity. According to Koot et al (2019), Namibia, Botswana, and South Africa have refused to "'recognize officially the unique status of the region's original inhabitants", via their policy position that "all of the people in their countries are indigenous'" (p 350). As a result, some of the descendants of European colonizers have mobilized claims of Indigeneity to express their belonging to the land, resulting in the capitalist appropriation of natural resources.

Steve Biko's (1978a) theory of Black Consciousness offers a more power-sensitive framework for exploring the meaning of Indigeneity in Southern African contexts. As discussed in Chapter 2, the Black Consciousness movement encouraged all racially marginalized people to assume the identity of Black as a collective statement of opposition to White supremacist rule. By centring the Ubuntu concept of unity in diversity in antiracist struggle, it provided South Africans with the means for finding common ground in their differently situated experiences with racial oppression. In the post-apartheid era, South Africans have begun unpacking their specific racialized histories (Arendse, 2020). Within South Africa's most heterogenous racial nation, people historically labelled as coloured are assuming a wide array of identities, from creolized, coloured, brown and Black affiliations to non-racial identities and reclaimed Khoe-Sān identifications that are challenging the colonial-apartheid narrative of Indigenous extinction. These developments suggest the need to problematize Indigeneity at the racial borderlands of its evolving lived existence.

My multiracial analysis of Ubuntu philosophy contributes to the global Indigenous science and the advancement of Indigenous environmental sociology more specifically. Norgaard and Fenelon (2021) define this body of knowledge as a reflexive examination into the relationship between individual and collective existence. The affective relationships that we experience – or to put it more bluntly, how we engage with ourselves, our families, communities, and members of other species – reflect the lifeways into which we have been socialized. Over the longue durée of human history, our intergenerational relationships have become fractured through modernizing movements, isolating humanity from the Indigenous sources of our collective human history and existence. Ubuntu philosophy contributes to the discourse by providing Indigenous science with a means for enacting truth and reconciliation in settler colonial and mixed Indigenous landscapes.

Antiracist interpretive methods

To culturally situate my inquiry, I employ a modified version of the interpretive methods introduced in my previous chapter on Daina philosophy. I maintain the feminist modality of dialogical inquiry by combining textual and autoethnographic methods; and I also incorporate the inclusive logic of Black Consciousness by purposely selecting a racially diverse sample of textual material for analysis. Specifically, I draw from the published memoirs and poetry of anti-apartheid activists to unpack Ubuntu in relation to my socialization into South African society. In 2010, I spent nearly a year living in the semi-rural coloured community of Pniel. I also lived with host families in more remote Rooibos farming communities while conducting fieldwork with community leaders who comprised my research team. My co-investigators did not agree on any one categorical label to describe their racial identity; thus, my analysis recognizes that the Khoekhoe and Sān are the original peoples of South Africa while embracing the multiracial threads of African humanism that have shaped national resistance to colonialism and apartheid.

To shorten the cultural distance between the Latvian and South African literature, I intersperse activist memoirs with voices from the Black Poetics Movement, steered by cultural communities like WEAVE, a multiracial collective of Black women writers that formed in 1997 (Barry et al, 2002). As in the quatrain-based Daina teachings, I ground my analysis in a multi-sensual rhythm, this time employing the polyphonic beat of pan-African song and dance tradition (Mutere, 2012). Figure 4.1 illustrates the 5:3 polyrhythm that I engage to unpack Ubuntu philosophy. The next section shares 15 testimonies across three relational-affective dimensions. Within each dimension, the fifth testimony derives from my own lived experience, bringing my voice into conversation with the literature.

The teachings of Ubuntu

Fear and hate

I. Segregate

Eddie Daniels (1928–2017) was an activist from District Six, a coloured community that free people formed by the Cape Town dockside in the 1800s after their emancipation from slavery. The apartheid state liquidated District Six through forced removals in the 1970s while Eddie was serving a 15-year term at Robben Island prison, located on a barren spit of land off the coast of Cape Town. In his autobiography, *There and Back* (1998, pp 25–26), Daniels discusses his lived experience with racial segregation, beginning with his childhood memories of the 1930s and 1940s:

From an early age, I noticed that white was associated with superiority and black with inferiority. It was the white man who drove a motor car and who was prosperous. He owned the large businesses and the houses in which we lived. He was everywhere in authority: He was the doctor, the policeman, the magistrate, the judge, the parliamentarian. He was the clerk in the post office, the inspector, the conductor or the driver on the buses and trains. He was the religious minister, the teacher, the principal, or the inspector at the school. He was in charge at the dispensary and at the hospital.

On the other hand, it was the blacks who were arrested, who were drunk in the streets, who made up the street gangs that preyed on the

Figure 4.1: Ubuntu analysis

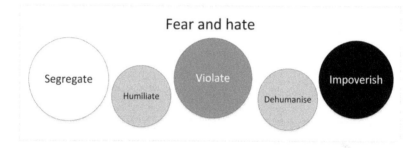

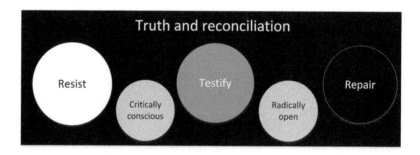

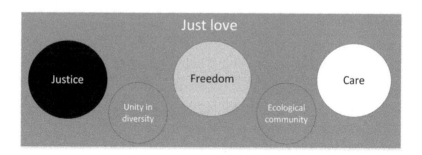

weak and the poor. They also were the many, descent, honest, and hardworking citizens of District Six who performed jobs that carried no authority. There were exceptions to the above … but they were few and far between. When one is born into such an environment, one initially accepts the status quo. Then little incidents occur which make one start to question it.

II. Humiliate

Desmond Mpilo Tutu (1931–2021) was born into a mixed-ethnic (Xhosa-Motswana) Black family in the North West Province. He served as the first Black Anglican Archbishop of Cape Town from 1986–1996, when he played a critical role in facilitating the national transition to democracy. Tutu worked with Mandela's government to establish the TRC and oversee its publicized trials, becoming the moral conscience of South Africa. He also wrote several books on Ubuntu philosophy and African theology in English, a common tongue in a polyglot nation. In *Made for Goodness*, a book that Tutu co-authored with his daughter and fellow Anglican priest, Mpho Tutu, they draw from his childhood memory to teach the Ubuntu lesson on 'The Habits of Wrongness' (2011, pp 83–84). Their account shows how children learn racism through early and constant exposure to humiliating taunts.

> 'Pik swart!' ['black pick!'], I heard them shout as my legs pumped furiously on the bicycle pedals. I was panting and sweating as I sped past the group of sneering white boys. I was afraid of that mocking little gang, but I was also angry. In a few moments I was far enough away that I judged they couldn't catch me. Only then, heart racing, did I spin around to face them. 'Graf!' ['Shovel!'], I yelled, my clever retort. I knew from their tone that they had insulted me. But I hadn't understood the insult: not a 'black pick,' a tool to break up hard ground, but 'pitch black.' They learned them so early, these insults of racism. The words of distain that adults offered at the dinner table were repeated in the sneering taunts heard on the street …

III. Violate

Ismail Vallie (1959–) is a South African man of Indian Muslim heritage. He grew up in District Six, where he attended coloured schools and participated in the student uprisings. As a boy, Vallie experienced the brutality of the South African Police (SAP), causing him to deepen his commitment to the resistance by joining the Ashley Kriel detachment of Umkhonto we Sizwe (Spear of the Nation). This paramilitary wing of the ANC had been established by Nelson Mandela in 1961, in response to the

Sharpeville Massacre of 1960. In an edited volume produced by Ashley Kriel freedom fighters, Vallie (2019, pp 206–207) describes his first arrest as an idealistic teenager. This passage exposes the unchecked power of an authoritarian police state. Akin to the KGB in the Soviet Union, the SAP routinely deployed surveillance against South Africans, using psychological and physical torture in an effort to ensure total control over the thoughts and actions of its citizens.

> It was midday. As we walked past the Castle of Good Hope, I saw a black car approaching, then two well-dressed black guys walked up to me. My first thought was that they wanted to rob me. Rudy had stopped to light a cigarette, and when he looked up he saw the men grab me and force me into the car. There was a white man behind the wheel and Rudy instantly suspected they were policemen. The railway police must have informed the SAP about students distributing pamphlets on the train. Rudy assumed I'd been arrested and immediately reported what he had seen to our friends.
>
> … A day passed. It was June and freezing cold. While I was lying on a thin foam mattress, covering my head with the thin blanket, trying to get warm enough to fall asleep, white plain-clothes policemen entered my cell. It was about three o'clock in the morning. Then another policeman entered the cell and poured a bucket of cold, dirty water over me. 'Trek jou klere uit!' they shouted. [Take off your clothes!] I was made to strip and then ordered to jump up and down and do push-ups. The place was cold and wet but my body slowly began to warm up. Then one of the policemen came with his big boots and stood on me, pressing my body against the ice-cold cell floor. It became apparent they were doing this because I was, in their words, ''n kommunis' [a communist] …

IV. Dehumanize

Winnie Madikizela-Mandela (1936–2018) was the iron-willed 'Mother' of the nation (Cropley, 2018). Born to a royal Xhosa family, she married fellow activist, Nelson, in 1958. For nearly all their marriage, Nelson was imprisoned in Robben Island, making Winnie the public face of the resistance. She too was detained and imprisoned on several occasions, and the violence that she suffered subsumed her resistance praxis. In the 1980s, Winnie's security detail committed gross violations of human rights, including acts of torture, kidnapping, and murder against people whom she suspected of collaborating with the apartheid state. Madikizela-Mandela's autobiography, *491 Days*, describes, in minute detail, the psychosocial torture of solitary confinement (2013, pp 233–234). *491 Days* does not condone her crimes against humanity, but it does shed essential light on authoritarian psychologies of dehumanization:

> When we arrived at the Pretoria Central Prison, we were all held in a certain section of the prison. Then I was removed and placed on death row, in that cell with three doors – the grille door, then the actual prison door and then another grilled door. The sound of that key when they opened the first door, the first grille door, was done in such a way that your heart missed a beat and it was such a shock. You had been all by yourself with dead silence for hours and hours and hours, and suddenly there would be this K-AT-LA, K-A-T-L-A. That alone drove you berserk; that alone was meant to emphasize the fact that 'we are in control, not only of your being, but your soul as well and we can destroy it.' Solitary confinement is worse than hard labour. When you do hard labour you are with other prisoners, you can tolerate it because you all dig together, you communicate and you are alive. Solitary confinement is meant to kill you alive. It is the most vicious punishment that you could wish on your worst enemy.
>
> You are imprisoned in this little cell. When you stretch your hands you touch the walls. You are reduced to a nobody, a non-value. It is like killing you alive. You are alive because you breathe. You are deprived of everything – your dignity, your everything. We were held incommunicado. We were not allowed to even see a lawyer. In those days we were completely at their mercy. Some families never knew that their loved ones died after they were detained. We were lucky to be alive and it was purely because of my name that I survived because the easiest thing for them at the time would have been to kill me, which they threatened every day. 'Oh you're still alive?' They would come in every day and say, 'You're still alive? We don't know if you will be alive tomorrow.'

V. Impoverish

The following passage shares my own testimony on crossing the de-facto colour line. My experience illustrates the pattern of racial segregation that I navigated when living in South Africa in 2010, and its strong correlation with social class.

I crossed the colour line approximately one month after my arrival in South Africa, moving away from a room that I initially had rented from a White woman in Stellenbosch into the coloured community of Pniel. This semi-rural area was a short drive over the Hottentots-Holland Mountain.[1] On the other side, Pniel had been established as a United Congregational Church mission during the nineteenth century. On the day that I left Stellenbosch,

I got into my ancient Volkswagen Beetle and chugged up the mountain, passing two White-owned wine estates as I began my descent into the small valley beyond. Working-class Pniel climbed the hillside at the northern end of the valley. To its immediate southwest lay the desperately impoverished farmworker village of Languedoc.

I moved into Noleen Rose's home after she agreed to rent a room to me when we discovered a shared love of hiking. In addition to working as the secretary for the Pniel Congregational Church, Noleen had organized an informal neighbourhood watch programme to address the spate of crime afflicting her community. Unlike the gated wine estates up the road, Pniel was wholly unfenced, and single women like Noleen experienced home invasions with alarming regularity. I soon learned to live behind locked doors and closed windows.

One evening, I returned home after dark. As I walked toward the front porch, a man ran at me from behind a tree. He was masked, had a knife, and told me to give him my computer bag. I did not make a conscious decision to attack: it was as if my mind and body abruptly detached from one another. While my body fought in what felt like slow motion, my mind briskly catalogued every detail: my attacker clearly was a teenager whose body appeared stunted from malnutrition; he was scantily clothed for such a cold night; and there was fear and desperation in his eyes when they met mine. My racing mind wondered whether his parents were farmworkers who had been paid in *dops* (standard portions) of cheap wine, and if he might be suffering from foetal alcohol syndrome. My mind screamed at me to call a truce and invite him in for a hot dinner, but my body continued fighting until he ran off and I ran into the house.

Later that night as I lay in bed with a switchblade under my pillow for comfort, I remember thinking that this is what structural inequity does: it produces desperate circumstances that detach us from our basic humanity. When there is no opportunity for friendship and love, the inverse qualities of estrangement and fear come to dominate our psychosocial existence, impoverishing us all.

Truth and reconciliation

I. Resist

Gertrude Fester (1952–) is a poet, activist, and member of the Black women's writing collective, WEAVE. Born in Cape Town, she founded several women's organizations in the early 1980s and was arrested in 1988. While in solitary confinement, Fester (2000) composed a now famous one-woman play, *The Spirit Shall Not Be Caged*, in her head 'as a survival mechanism' (p 79). The following 'A Plea to Poetry' (Figure 4.2) expresses her cognitive resistance to dehumanization.

Figure 4.2: A Plea to Poetry

```
                          hold     in this hell hole of hostility
              hold onto your mind            this cell
      do not let dumb fascists taunt you     claustrophobically covering you
      psychologically terrorize you          closing in on you
                  pulverize you              overwhelming you
      do not let them break you              the powerful over the powerless
              crumble you
                  bit                                your soul
                  by bit                             your spirit
      into a seething mass                           slouches inside yourself
      of unbridled emotions                          your pent up frustrations
  random pieces of yourself                          cloud your brain
              your soul                              imprison your soul
          flung furiously                            like they imprison your body
      scattered sporadically                         your hands shiver
              like bits                              vibrating with impotence
              of shit
          on to cell walls                           though your mind cannot
      hold onto your anger                           form clear thoughts
              contain it                             systematize them
          do not let it                              though your hands cannot
      like a malignant cell                          produce polished letters
          spread insidiously                         go on
      throughout your body                           write on
              your soul                              contain your mind
          eating it up                               hold
  devouring your very self                           hold onto your thoughts
          your very soul                             write them down
          consuming all
      consuming the residue                          you
          of your humanity                           paralysed
              your dignity                           powerless in prison
  do not let them dehumanize you further             hold onto life
                                                     to sanity
                                                     soothe your tormented soul
                                                     push
                                                     prod on to pusillanimity pusillanimous
```

Source: Gertrude Fester (2000, pp 82–83)

II. Critically conscious

Fatima Meer (1928–2010) was born in Durban to a Muslim father who had immigrated from India and an orphaned mother of Portuguese Jewish heritage. In 1950, Meer was one of the first two women to be elected to an executive position within the Natal Indian Congress (NIC). In the 1970s, she collaborated with Winnie Mandela to form the Black Women's Federation (BWF). Alongside 11 other women from the BWF, Meer was arrested in 1976, where she spent time in solitary confinement. After her release, she survived an assassination attempt, an account vividly described in her memoir of love and struggle. Although she turned down a parliamentary seat when the ANC assumed power in 1994, she remained active in charity work and retained a sense of critical consciousness, becoming a powerful voice against political corruption in the post-apartheid era. In her memoire, Meer (2017) called for the nation to commit to 'perpetual revolution' by giving direct voice and power to the poorest and most marginalized segments of society:

Many things have improved since 1994. For one thing racial laws have disappeared. However, the aspirations of the Freedom Charter – the only historic document that we have registering people's voices and dreams – have not been realized. By the year 2000 we do not have a leadership committed to fighting poverty – we have a corrupt leadership. That is our tragedy.

If resources are reserved only for the wealthy, if government shows a commitment only to the middle class then all I can say is 'cry the beloved country, and cry and cry and cry'! And those of us who can shout no matter how many years we have lived on this earth, we must get up and shout.

I have always stood for the poor and the rights of the poor and though I and all my friends have been in the ANC for over 60 years, if I have to stand against the organization to address the needs of the vast majority of South African citizens then I will unhappily do so. We have to be in the process of perpetual revolution to progress and guarantee the rights of people.

There can be no peacetime so long as there is poverty and hunger and so long as basic human rights are trodden. The cause of rampant crime in our country is inequality. We are the second most unequal country in the world.[2] More than half the population lives in poverty. Can we call this living in peace? The definition of peace is equity, harmony, not starvation.

III. Testify

Ruth First (1925–1982) was a White anti-apartheid activist. The Jewish daughter of Latvian and Lithuanian parents who had immigrated to South Africa in 1906, First was an active member of the South African Communist Party (SACP) her parents had helped to form. As an investigative journalist and socialist activist, First shifted her allegiance to the ANC when the Nationalist Party banned the SACP in 1950. Alongside 156 other members of the Congress Alliance, First was put on trial for treason from 1956–1961 for her involvement in producing its Freedom Charter. She was imprisoned without charge in 1963 and spent nearly four months in solitary confinement, during which time she attempted suicide. After her release, First went into exile, writing her account of apartheid – *117 Days* (2010 [1965]) – from England. She later moved to Mozambique, where she remained active in the struggle until 1982, when the SAP assassinated her by means of a bomb received through the mail. In the following excerpt First provides testimony of apartheid strategies for dealing with White activists. Her testimony illustrates the punishment that awaited White South Africans who challenged the apartheid system. It also suggests that the social privileges accorded to the ruling white class served to obscure their own lack of liberty in a society where the police were empowered to detain and torture anyone who refused to fit within their designated racial boundaries (First, 2010 [1965], p 318):

> My release had to be part of a wider tactic for dealing with political whites, the errant who would not go into the laager[3] of whites against Africans. How to deal with us? Some were permitted to leave the country: this was one way of physically removing opposition. If among those locked up there were men who broke under the strain of detention and interrogation, they would be used for information by the Security Branch. Those who were unbreakable were given long spells of imprisonment – eight years, twelve years, twenty years, life. In my case the first spell of detention had not given them the information they wanted from me, nor the evidence in all its strength that they needed to convict me. They could have been releasing me to watch me again and catch me in the act. Viktor[4] delivered a warning against my trying to evade my bans or make a dash over the border by the escape route. 'If you try that,' he said, 'I'll be there to catch you.'

IV. Radically open

Simon Tseko Nkoli (1957–1998) was born into the Johannesburg township of Soweto to a Sotho-Twana family. He was arrested for his involvement in the resistance in 1984 and publicly came out as gay during his trial. Upon his release from prison in 1988, Nkoli founded the Gay and Lesbian Organization of the Witwatersrand (GLOW), where he collaborated with Beverley Palesa Ditsi, a Black lesbian activist and filmmaker, to organize South Africa's first Pride march in 1990. In his speech to Pride participants, Nkoli identified the intersectionality of oppression and called for gays and lesbians to fight for radically inclusive democracy (Cameron, 2006, p 37):

> This is what I say to my comrades in the struggle when they ask me why I waste time fighting for moffies.[5] This is what I say to gay men and lesbians who ask me why I spend so much time struggling against apartheid when I should be fighting for gay rights. I am black and I am gay. I cannot separate the two parts of me into secondary or primary struggles. In South Africa I am oppressed because I am a black man, and I am oppressed because I am gay. So, when I fight for my freedom I must fight against both oppressors. All those who believe in a democratic South Africa must fight against all oppression, all intolerance, all injustice. With this march gays and lesbians are entering the struggle for a democratic South Africa where everybody

has equal rights and everyone is protected by the law: black and white, men and women, gay and straight.

V. Repair

As the author of this book, my positionality straddles uncomfortable borders. My embodied heritage is that of a working-class White woman who grew up in the settler colonial American West, but my consciousness is Black. In South Africa, I lived almost entirely within coloured community, but I also was in contact with Afrikaner society, and a way of being that mirrored that of the American West. While I had a couple of Afrikaner friends who felt like family to me, my broader relationships were tense. After moving to Pniel, my interaction with Whites largely became reduced to the public sphere, and it seemed that I angered people whenever I passed through the elite Afrikaner world of Stellenbosch. Shop owners chastised me for using the coloured pronunciation of Pniel rather than the Afrikaner way, or for ordering a birthday cake with the coloured spelling of a friend's name rather than the White.[6] It felt as if, through my association with coloured South Africa, I too became defined as the Other, as had happened in my youth when I was violently attacked by skinheads.

In South Africa, I found myself avoiding White spaces as much as possible. In coloured community, my emotional experience was one of belonging, despite the colour of my skin. Perhaps this feeling was possible due to a similar class consciousness and a shared value system, or it might have been that we simply chose to be radically open with one another, in the spirit of antiracist work. Whatever the cause, I felt most at home in coloured community, its warm and supportive relationships like those of my own extended family. My occasional forays into Stellenbosch or Clanwilliam often felt to me like plunging into a low-simmering cauldron, swirling with hot microaggression. Whether directed toward me, others with my social or physical attributes, or racial minorities to whom strangers presumed I had no affiliation or care, these microaggressions were hard to endure. In those icy moments, I felt as if apartheid had somehow climbed inside of me, sapping my desire to live and making me want to fight. This sensation was far from foreign: the frontier aggression that I experienced growing up in the American West had sparked the same feelings of nihilism and rebellion.

My few White friends modelled another way of being, one that was culturally and linguistically Afrikaner, yet open to racial and ethnic difference. In one another, we recognized our common history and shared struggle. As the descendants of European peasants who had fled persecution to seek a better life in rugged geographies, we valued land, family, and freedom. As the descendants of colonial migrants who propagated European imperialist ambitions on foreign soil, we struggled to reconcile these aspects of our heritage with the brutal legacy of settler colonialism and White supremacy. As politically progressive Whites working in a world where so many of our White brothers and sisters continued to re-enact racial inequity, we seemed to move between hope and suffering, mutually dazed and critically conscious. During times spent camping under the stars, we experienced moments of transcendence: our deep conversations and deeper quietude giving us the courage to grow beyond limitations.

Whether the lessons were caring or callous, Afrikaner South Africa taught me that truth and reconciliation is not simply an outward praxis. If we are to break the chains of oppression, we must first look to the abuser within. Several years after returning home from South Africa, I discovered that one of my father's ancestors was a slave owner and, in learning about our ancestry, my father and I have come to understand the afterlife of slavery in a more embodied way. My father's father was a cold and distant man who had emotionally abandoned his children. Although my grandfather had chosen to reject the virulent racism of his father by never speaking a racist word in his own home, he could not surmount the dehumanizing experience of having been raised in a family that did not know how to show love. I was frightened of my grandfather as a child, but now that I know our history, I feel great sadness for the fractured child he must have been.

Just love

I. Justice

According to Desmond Mpilo Tutu, socially just societies are forgiving societies. In the *Book of Forgiving*, Tutu and Tutu (2014, p 49) describe the Ubuntu praxis of justice as a fourfold path, or forgiveness cycle. This affective and relational spiral of engagement involves: (1) telling the story; (2) naming the hurt; (3) granting forgiveness or recognizing shared humanity; and (4) renewing or releasing the relationship. The following excerpt shares Stefaans Coetzee's experience with this praxis, as described by Tutu and Tutu (2014, pp 168–169):

> On Christmas Eve in 1996, when he was seventeen, Stefaans and a trio of members of the white supremacist Afrikaner Weerstandsbeweging (AWB) planted a series of bombs in a shopping center in Worcester, South Africa. Their target was a venue frequented by the black population of the city. Their goal was to exact the maximum death toll. Only one of the bombs exploded, but it injured sixty-seven people and left four dead. Three of those who died were children. Shortly after the incident, Coetzee expressed his disappointment at the low death toll.

It was a fellow prisoner who set Coetzee on the healing journey. Eugene de Kock, nicknamed 'Prime Evil' by the media for his role in numerous apartheid era murders, became Coetzee's mentor. 'Unless you seek forgiveness from those you have harmed, you will find that you are bound inside two prisons – the one you are in physically and the one you have around your heart. It is never too late to repair the harm you have caused. Then, even though you are behind bars you will still be free. No one can lock away your ability to change. No one can lock away your goodness or your humanity.' On Reconciliation Day in December 2011 a letter from Stefaans was read to a gathering of the surviving victims of the Worcester bombing. In the letter, Stefaans expressed his remorse and asked for forgiveness. Many have forgiven him for his horrific act. Indeed some of the surviving victims of the bombing have visited him in jail. Some have not yet been able to forgive. Stefaans understands that he cannot demand forgiveness, but he describes being forgiven as a 'grace … that resulted in freedom beyond understanding.'

II. Unity in diversity

Malika Ndlovu (1971–) was born in Durban, where she grew up writing poetry. She secured a degree in Performing Arts during the transition to democracy in the early 1990s then moved to Cape Town. In addition to writing and directing several theatre productions, including the critically acclaimed play, *A Coloured Place*, Ndlovu co-founded the women's collective, WEAVE. Given the racial and ethnic diversity of its members, WEAVE is a living example of unity in diversity. Published in its 2002 volume, *ink@ boiling point*, Ndlovu's poem 'Instruments' expresses the liberating source and feeling of this Ubuntu concept (p 192):

We are light beings
Some slumbering
Some awakening
To the truth of who we are
Indestructible stars
Housed only for a while
In these temples of flesh
Once our memories are refreshed
We can see
That this life
This body
Is simply a veil
A vision
A temporary reality

That we are more
That we hold perfection within
Just beyond our imagining

We are light beings
Portals of love
Makers of peace
Creators of beauty
We are healers
We are believers inherently
Rediscovering our way
Homeward
Inward
Out of Earth-time
Where free is our natural state
Where love is the only way
We are born to bring light
To honour the blessing of each life

III. Freedom

Nelson Rolihlahla Mandela (1918–2013) had a lot to say about freedom. Prior to his presidency, he spent 27 years in prison, first at Robben Island where he and other prisoners were subjected to meaningless hard labour, then at Pollsmore Prison, where he contracted tuberculosis, and finally at Victor Verster Prison, where he completed his law degree. When Mandela was released from prison in 1990, he could have walked out of its doors with vengeance in his heart. Instead, he chose to leave his anger behind, for he desired, above all else, to be free. In the conclusion of his autobiography, *Long Walk to Freedom* (2008), Mandela shared his experience with the Ubuntu ethic of freedom (pp 624–625):

> It was during those long and lonely years that my hunger for the freedom of my own people became a hunger for the freedom of all people, white and black. I knew as well as I knew anything that the oppressor must be liberated just as surely as the oppressed. A man who takes another man's freedom is a prisoner of hatred, he is locked behind the bars of prejudice and narrow-mindedness. I am not truly free if I am taking away someone else's freedom, just as surely as I am not free when my freedom is taken from me. The oppressed and the oppressor alike are robbed of their humanity.
>
> When I walked out of prison, that was my mission, to liberate the oppressed and the oppressor both. Some say that has now been

achieved. But I know that is not the case. The truth is that we are not yet free; we have merely achieved the freedom to be free, the right not to be oppressed. We have not taken the final step on our journey, but the first step on a longer and even more difficult road. For to be free is not merely to cast off one's chains, but to live in a way that respects and enhances the freedom of others. The true test of our devotion to freedom is just beginning.

IV. Ecological community

Patricia McFadden (1952–) is a Southern African activist from the small kingdom of eSwatini (formerly Swaziland), located to the east of Johannesburg. As a radical African feminist who participated in Southern African independence movements, her scholarship has given voice to the experiences of women activists. In more recent work, McFadden (2018) is contributing to the African discourse on ecological community by sharing her praxis of self-nature interaction, balance, and sufficiency. This feminist framing goes further than other studies that describe the Ubuntu teaching on human–nature harmony, in that it centres, rather than ignores, issues pertaining to status and power. As a middle-class eSwatini woman who has returned to a rural and agrarian way of life while challenging its patriarchal traditions, McFadden argues that one cannot build ecological community without also unlearning patriarchy. The following passage describes her personal journey. Evoking the Ubuntu relationship between community and ecology, McFadden provides a cognitive bridge for joining the Ubuntu teaching on community building with the ecocultural lessons of the Latvian Dainas (2018, pp 427–428):

> Beyond my personal experiences as I live a life that is attentive to the earth and its bounty, its boundless spiritual, nurturing, and aesthetic gifts, I have also been able to initiate new relationships with some of my neighbors on the mountain. Over the past few years, I have supported and encouraged a neighbor who lives very precariously; she and her partner are living with HIV/AIDS, their son with Down Syndrome is in a wheelchair, and the only income they have is a measly, unpredictable social grant twice a year that barely suffices. One day, I suggested to my neighbor that we clean out a little patch of land adjacent to her two-room house and rebuild the land so that she can grow some food. We spent a week removing the broken bottles, tins, and rubber, and slowly we brought in the manure, the compost, the seeds, and the love. It was magical. Today, she looks forward to the rainy season, when she can put the seedlings down, and the joy on her face when she has a successful crop is irreplaceable.

This initiative has changed our relationship in several ways. She, a working-class woman with minimal education, and I have been able to build a bridge of solidarity between us based on a sense of integrity and self-exploration. We share knowledge about seed preservation, and she often teaches me about indigenous greens that have come back on that land – changing my own attitudes toward 'weeds' and their immeasurable value to health and healing. She has planted a little corner with some of the basic herbs needed to control flu, pain, stomach upsets, and more. We have become these new women in ways that neither of us imagined.

In terms of class solidarities, this relationship has enabled me to step away from the prejudices that are inbuilt in relationships of class and social status. Initially we had to work our way through much of the baggage that constructs us as Black women in a feudal, patriarchal monarchy. We had to find a language in which to share this knowledge that has changed our lives ... such initiatives must form the core of the new contemporary African feminism.

V. Care

On a spring evening, I returned home, hardly out of my car before Noleen pushed me into hers: I was going along for a neighbourhood watch. Sitting in the backseat, alongside several friends, Noleen first drove us down by the river, where we witnessed a drug dealer selling to young children. Noleen tore off toward the police station. Along the way, she told me that she wanted me to go into the station with her, because the police never listened to her group when they reported problems. Given my distrust of police in general, I reluctantly tagged along, and stood behind Noleen while she talked. Before she had finished speaking, there was a loud crack as an officer threw open the door and several men went running out of the building. Seconds later, these officers drove off, sirens blaring. Sighing in disgust, Noleen walked back to her car with me, saying, 'all the police officers here are coloured, but they still think like apartheid: they don't care for their own people but when the White lady arrives, they are eager to help!'

Later in the night, Noleen barrelled up the mountainside to investigate a low-burning bushfire that had somehow ignited, likely, I was told, by angry teenagers. I remember feeling overwhelmed by the travesty of poverty and racism; and in that moment, the nihilistic lyrics of the Nine Inch Nails song 'Burn' suddenly played out in my mind. Before I could stop myself, I cursed this unjust world, thinking 'let us burn it down.' It was Noleen who taught me that care was the antidote to the nihilistic feelings I occasionally experienced. When she was upset with the world, she did not retreat into herself and listen to angry music as I did. Rather, she would change the frequency by playing love songs on her kitchen radio and cooking dinner for someone in need. Noleen used to say to me, 'why do you listen to that angry music? It's no good for you! You should listen to love songs. They will make you feel better and remind you to care about life!' In subsequent years, I have come to understand that the freedom to care and the care to be free are what sustain my own resistance to the nihilistic and self-destructive seeds of authoritarian monocultures.

Sustainable development in the South African context

In South Africa, the combined forces of colonialism and apartheid sundered human connection. Yet these forces failed to wholly sever human feeling, for Southern Africans always have been among the most heterogenous people on Earth. Over the longue durée history of hominin habitation, Sān and Khoekhoe societies were ethnically and linguistically diverse yet socially interwoven (Barnard, 2008). If contemporary South Africa bears deep psychosocial wounds wrought by the authoritarian impulse to categorize and homogenize everything it sees, its Indigenous heritage offers the antidote to this mental and social disease.

South Africa has made laudable strides in conservation, but the nation continues to face grave challenges when it comes to addressing inequity, suggesting that its market-based approach to sustainability is falling short on its promises (Keahey and Murray, 2017).

South Africa's 2030 development plan acknowledges social and environmental deficits but centres corporate solutions. On one hand, the plan emphasizes diversity, equity, and inclusion. The vision statement presented in *Our Future – Make it Work* (National Planning Commission, 2015), rings with the Ubuntu spirit of South African democracy. It also is imbued with decolonial logic: not only does it engage the modality of storytelling to describe South Africa's commitment to cultivating an ethnically varied and co-extensive national identity, but it also demonstrates a degree of psychosocial and self-reflexive awareness that is rarely found in Western discourse. Consider the following passage:

> Now in 2030 we live in a country which we have remade. We have created a home where everybody feels free yet bounded to others; where everyone embraces their full potential. We are proud to be a community that cares.
>
> We have received the mixed legacy of inequalities in opportunity and in where we have lived, but we have agreed to change our narrative of conquest, oppression, resistance. We felt our way towards a new sense of ourselves:

- Trying, succeeding and making mistakes
- Proclaiming success and closing our minds to failure
- Feeling orientated and disorientated through our own actions
- Affirming some realities and denying others
- Proclaiming openness to the world, yet courting insularity
- Eager to live together, yet finding it difficult to recognize shared burdens
- Learning to recognize and acknowledge shared successes

On the other hand, the 2030 plan also rings with the nationalist language of economic growth and technological modernization. Its constellation of corporate, technological and state welfare solutions may be an outcome of the moderate political path that Mandela's government carved out during the 1990s, when ANC socialists and White capitalists joined forces to construct the post-apartheid state. Yet this situation essentially has provided impoverished people with some measure of life support while continuing to concentrate wealth among the South Africa's most elite citizens, most of whom are White (Ferguson, 2010). From a critically conscious standpoint, the rhetoric of diversity, equity and inclusion may be the latest ideological cloak of modernizing empire, in its current configuration of global-national-corporate collusion.

This chapter has given voice to an intergenerational body of activists who guided my socialization into a remarkable culture of truth and reconciliation. If my earlier coverage of Daina philosophy contributes to Indigenous science by unpacking the praxis of *padoms* (wise thinking), then Ubuntu philosophy provides further scope into this praxis from the differently situated positionality of South African society. According to the Moravian theologian, Karel Thomas August (2005), the lifeway of Ubuntu is one of choosing understanding rather than vengeance, reparation but not retaliation, empowerment and not victimization. Wherever we may be in the world, such choices are always available to us. Whatever has been done in the past, we can choose to change our words and actions today, not simply for the sake of generations not yet born, but also for ourselves, and our own burning hunger to be free.

Organic Farming and Slow Food in Post-Soviet Latvia

Latvian folk song

Planted I a lovely oak tree	Iedēstiju ozoliņu
In the middle of my clearing.	Tīrumiņa vidiņā.
Hum my bees and sing my sisters,	San bitītes, dzied māsiņas,
All round my field of rye.	Apkārt manu rudzu lauku.

— translated by the Latvian American linguist, Ieva Auziņa Szentivanyi

Land and freedom

It is an early morning on Ataugas Farm. I awake under the wooden rafters of Aivars and Lilija Ansoni's home and groggily make my way down the stairs, unsure what the day will bring. I arrived on the farm the evening before, having arranged to work in exchange for an account of Latvia's organic farming movement from a couple who has been involved since its inception. Aivars is in the kitchen, frying eggs in a skillet. He adds a generous dollop of sour cream to the sizzling eggs then slides them onto a plate and hands the food to me, blue eyes twinkling. I inhale the rich aroma with surprised pleasure. Aivars laughs and tells me that this is one of the many benefits of being a farmer: 'I have always loved sour cream on fried eggs,' he says, 'but it was too fattening to eat when I worked in the city. This will give you the energy to work hard today!'

The agrarian ideal runs deep in the Latvian national consciousness for, in this formerly colonized society, land is a potent symbol of cultural freedom. When Latvia first secured its independence from foreign rule in 1920, the young Republic immediately passed the Agrarian Reform Law. Transferring land ownership from the Baltic German nobility – who at the time were less than 4 per cent of the population – to Latvian peasants, the Republic abruptly dismantled a colonial production regime that had been in existence since the fourteenth century (Plakans, 1995). This act radically transformed the agrarian landscape, as large estates were carved into small-scale family farms. When Latvians again declared their independence in 1990, the transitional government re-enacted the agrarian reforms of the First Republic, encouraging a new generation of Latvians to return to the land and take up the national tradition of homesteading (Žakevičiūtė, 2016).

During both periods of political transition, small-scale farmers struggled to surmount vast economic challenges. In the case of the First Republic, Latvian industry had been devastated by the First World War. Agricultural holdings had been decimated, and the nation had broken away from Russian markets, meaning that producers had to establish new trade networks during an interwar period marked by global instability and economic recession (Norkus, 2018). A similar scenario occurred around the turn of the twenty-first century, when Latvia again faced the problem of rebuilding the agro-food system without capital (Zobena, 1998).

Communicated through the Dainas, the **social imaginary** of Latvian ecoculture not only has motivated Latvians to demand their right to nationhood, but this symbolic dimension of existence also has provided Latvians with a blueprint for enacting agrarian reform. During the resistance movements of the nineteenth and twentieth centuries, the Latvian imaginary gave rise to a cojoined politics of nationalism and environmentalism. Indeed, the Singing Revolution of the late 1980s initially began as an environmental protest. In 1986, the Soviet state announced its plans to build a hydroelectric dam on the Daugava River, a sacred waterway and potent ecocultural symbol of Latvian lifeblood (King, 2012). Latvia erupted in protest, for under the banks of this river of fate lie the bones of mythological heroes and ancient freedom fighters who had given their lives in an effort to repel iron-clad crusaders. In planning to yoke the Daugava's waters to Soviet development, the Latvian SSR had invoked the ancestral memory of servitude to foreign masters; and in the telling of deleterious environmental impacts wrought under Soviet rule, Latvians remembered their own suffering at the hands of an authoritarian police state.

By 1988, the environmental protection movement had morphed into a nationalist campaign for independence, commonly known as the Third Awakening. A new generation of Latvian intelligentsia harnessed the populist pressure from below to form the Latvian Popular Front, a political bloc that demanded the restoration of the Republic (Penikis, 1996). By 1990, the Popular Front had stormed the Latvian SSR, where it secured the political support needed to disband the Supreme Soviet and install a transitional parliament. This Supreme Council declared the Soviet invasion of Latvia to be illegal and immediately began to dismantle the despised Kolkhoz (collectivized) farm system by passing several land reform measures (Plakans, 1995).[1]

In 1993, Latvians voted the first post-Soviet Saeima into power, and its governing coalition of parties elected Guntis Ulmanis – the great nephew of Latvia's first prime minister, Kārlis Ulmanis – to serve as Latvia's fifth president. As the leader of the centre-right Latvian Farmers' Union, Ulmanis succoured an alliance with the newly formed Latvian Green Party and in 2002, these two parties established the Latvian Union of Greens and Farmers (Auers, 2012). Unlike in Western Europe, where green activism developed from the political left, environmentalism in Latvia emerged from the nationalist right wing and has retained a distinctly conservative ethos.

The post-Soviet government inherited the decaying remains of an industrialized and unproductive agricultural system. During the 1940s and 1950s, the Soviet Union had enfolded Latvia's network of small-scale farms into large industrial units. These Kolkhoz farms became the basis for the development of industrial agro-towns, where production and manufacture occurred as one unit, with labour producing, processing and shipping goods across the Soviet Union (Donato, 2018). In the 1960s, the state enacted a policy of melioration, draining Latvian wetlands that were situated near Kolkhoz farms to extend fields and achieve the farm size needed to accommodate large machinery (Melluma, 1994). Having invested heavily in petrochemical development, the Soviet Union instituted agricultural policies that encouraged the overuse of chemical inputs. By the 1980s, Baltic waterways had become inundated with chemicals, causing two-thirds of the Baltic Sea to become de-oxygenated dead zones (Darst, 2001).

While the incoming government effectively halted environmental degradation by passing populist land reforms, President Ulmanis also curried favour with Western capital by promoting neoliberal market policies that opened the Latvian economy to foreign investors. Although land reforms had provided would-be farmers with agricultural holdings, the first generation of post-Soviet producers lacked access to subsidies for commercial development; and likewise lacking the funds to rebuild, Latvia's processing sector had all but collapsed, meaning that farmers had to establish alternative markets.

After my first full day of work at Ataugas Farm, during which I had harvested plums in the orchard, I sat with Aivars and Lilija around the dinner table listening to their thoughts about the future. Despite the lack of subsidies, they had managed to establish an economically viable farm, but they were worried about the future of the organic farming movement. In the wake of Latvia's 2004 accession into the European Union (EU), Latvian supermarkets had become glutted with imported food items, and Latvia's rural youth were emigrating en masse to Western Europe, where there was work to be found on industrial farms. At the same time, EU accession had enabled Latvian farmers to secure subsidies for organic conversion, and movement activists had begun to invest in local and slow food initiatives in a bid to distinguish the Latvian organic label from organic imports. When I departed from Ataugas Farm, I used the information that Aivars and Lilija had provided me to design a multi-commodity study set at a national scale. My goal was to answer two broad questions: (1) what had the organic farming movement achieved during Latvia's first 15 years of independence; and (2) how was EU market integration impacting the producers involved in the movement?

Framing and methodology

This chapter draws from three sociological concepts to develop an in-depth analysis of Latvia's organic revolution during a fast-paced era of social transformation. First, I draw from Laura Raynolds' (2004) scholarship on organic agro-food networks to examine the actor networks and quality conventions shaping organic development in Latvia. By mapping the organic food sector and unpacking its conventions, I show how Latvians have constructed an alternative political economy at the margins of post-Soviet markets. Second, I introduce the Foucauldian concept of heterotopia to situate Latvia's organic food sector as an alternative world situated both within and against the dominant world of neoliberal market economy. This framing enables me to examine the tense, contradictory and transformative conditions shaping the organic movement at a time when Latvia was integrating into the European single market (Foucault and Miskowiec, 1986). Third, I apply a more-than-representational lens to investigate multi-sensual and embodied dynamics of organic development, showing how the Latvian ecocultural imaginary has informed its values and practices (Sarmiento, 2017).

My research findings largely derive from 10 months of fieldwork that I conducted in 2005. Funded by the US Fulbright Program, this study employed a mixed methods modality to examine organic development across multiple commodity sectors and at a national level of analysis. Latvia's diminutive size, my language proficiency and my contacts at the Latvian University of Agriculture (LLU) made this scale of inquiry possible. I began fieldwork by using a combination of unobtrusive measures, unstructured interviews, and participant observation to gather initial information and establish contacts. During this initial phase, I visited supermarkets and farmer markets around the country and attended whatever conferences, seminars and meetings I could access.

I secured most of my data through a combination of farm case studies, semi-structured interviews, and telephone surveys. After completing my initial case study at Ataugas Farm, I conducted case studies of three other family produce farms, purposely selected to match the identified categories of farms prevalent in Latvia in 2005. Mapped in Figure 5.1, my four farm case

Figure 5.1: Case study farm sites

Key
1. Ataugas Farm
2. Jaunpātes Farm
3. Priedinas Farm
4. Salenieki Farm and Health Retreat

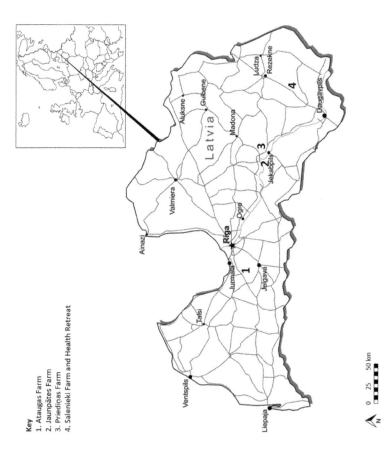

Source: Adapted from Keahey (2009)

studies thus comprised: (1) the organic Ataugas Farm; (2) Jaunpātes Farm, which was in the process of converting to organic production; (3) Priediņas Farm, a conventional holding situated in and around a wildlife refuge; and (4) and Salenieki Farm and Health Retreat, a combined organic farm and ecotourism venture. Next, I conducted semi-structured interviews with four agricultural experts, four retailers and restaurateurs and five organic food processing firms, the latter of which involved artisanal bread, juice, honey, dairy and meat processors. Finally, I conducted structured telephone interviews with an array of conventional food processors to survey national interest in organic conversion, ultimately completing 22 surveys across Latvia's meat, egg, dairy, grain and produce sectors. To assist with the surveys and provide cultural insight during first-stage data analysis, I hired a Latvian student to serve as my research assistant during the final stage of fieldwork; and after completing the study, I hired a translator to convert my work into Latvian and then disseminated copies to research participants.

Organic transitions

Aivars and Lilija Ansoni were members of Latvia's first generation of post-Soviet farmers. They bought their country house in 1987 and 15 hectares of surrounding land in 1992. During the 1990s, they converted the land into an organic farm. The Ansoni assumed the full cost of conversion, for at the time there were no subsidies available for conversion; however, they were able to access an organic farming course in a nearby town. By the early 2000s, the Ansoni were producing a diverse array of organic and biodynamic certified fruits, vegetables, and flowers, counting among their buyers two Rīga restaurants and a Rīga kindergarten. Each week, Aivars loaded the farm truck with fresh produce to deliver to this network of private buyers, and he also rented stalls at outdoor farmer markets, where he had established a loyal consumer base.

For the Ansoni, organic farming was a project of love, made as a devotion to the restoration of land, the reclamation of freedom, and the revitalization of Latvian ecoculture. Finding the beyond-organic principles of biodynamic agriculture to be congruent with their own moral ontology, they had ended the soil's reliance upon any inputs that did not originate on farm. In practice, this meant generating their own fertility through such techniques as animal integration, composting, cover cropping, and crop rotation. From a small plot of land whose soil had been devastated by decades of chemical inputs, the Ansoni had established a thriving and genetically diverse orchard with 60 plum, 40 apple, 17 pear, and 19 cherry varieties. Buzzing with wasps and humming with bees, this fragrant space was fertilized by a small and contented flock of sheep, whom the Ansoni raised for this purpose and did not sell for meat. The wetlands bordering the farm had slowly recovered

Figure 5.2: National organic movement network

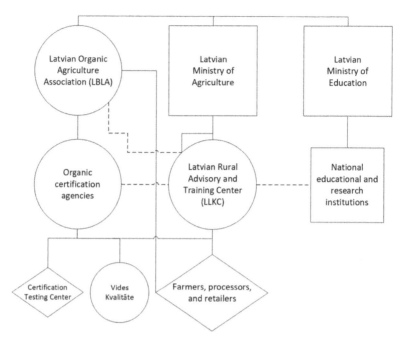

Notes: Squares depict state institutions, circles are non-governmental organizations, and diamonds symbolize private enterprise. Solid lines denote well-developed inter-institutional relationships while dashed lines indicate less developed ties.

Source: Adapted from Keahey (2009)

from the environmental degradation that had occurred under Soviet rule, and the Ansoni took pleasure in witnessing the return of once-scarce wildlife to the lushly forested watershed in which Ataugas was situated.

By 2005, several organizations were involved in organic development; Figure 5.2 maps these institutional relationships. To begin, LLKC – the Latvian Rural Advisory and Training Centre – played a key role in promoting organic conversion. During the first decade of post-Soviet transition, the Latvian state had privatized several government agencies, causing LLKC to reform as a non-governmental consultancy. Although privatized, LLKC worked in partnership with the Latvian Ministry of Agriculture and had connections to various agricultural education institutions that operated under the auspices of the Ministry of Education. LLKC also communicated with certification agencies, and it had close ties to the Latvian Association of Organic Agriculture (LBLA), which controlled the rights to Latvia's nationally accredited organic label. As a democratically organized association of organic farmers, processors and organizations, LBLA used its membership fees and annual dues to maintain the organic label and engage in political advocacy campaigns that called for investments in organic production. In 2005, LBLA's president was an associate professor and former Dean of the Agricultural Faculty at the Latvian University of Agriculture. Her ties to the International Federation of Organic Agriculture Movements (IFOAM) had enabled LLKC to engage with the global movement of organic farmers, bringing its members into conversation with producers in other European countries.

To the east of Ataugas Farm, not far from the Daugava River town of Aizkraukle, Jaunpātes Farm was undergoing organic conversion. Although the farm boasted 32 hectares, it was located near the southern banks of the river and subject to seasonal flooding that washed away topsoil. This reality forced its proprietor, Vēsma Toča, to think creatively about the farm's development. Fortunately, regional market integration had provided Vēsma with access to EU subsidies for organic conversion. Following a half-generation behind the Ansoni, Vēsma had moved to Jaunpātes in 2003. She had inherited the farm in 2000, when her husband's parents had passed away, and the farmhouse had stood empty for three years, visited only during brief country retreats from Rīga, where Vēsma had worked as a potter for a ceramic factory. In 2004, she began converting the land to an organic strawberry farm while taking an organic farming course offered by her district LLKC. In 2005, she invested in a modern greenhouse, and when I met Vēsma, she was busy experimenting with different strawberry varieties to determine those most suitable for off-season cultivation. When I asked Vēsma to explain her interest in organic farming, she told me that this agrarian technology aligned with her Latvian worldsense, which she expressed as the moral value of "living harmoniously with nature".

Vēsma's story provides a glimpse into the organic revolution occurring on Latvian family farms during the second decade of post-Soviet reconstruction. As EU subsidies became available for organic conversion, a new wave of back-to-the-land activists retreated from jobs in Rīga to invest in family farms. Only 39 Latvian farms had secured organic certification in 1998, but by 2007, more than 4,000 farms were certified, and Figure 5.3 charts this rapid growth in organic certified hectares.

When considering this information in relation to the broader data on Latvian farms, a clear demographic pattern emerges. According to data compiled by Eurostat (2008) there were a total of 107,750 registered agricultural holdings in 2007. Among these, only 44,400 holdings were around the average size of one Western European industrial unit. More than 49 per cent of the holdings were comprised of subsistence producers and 68 per cent were less than 20 hectares. Nearly half of the holdings' sole owners were women, and nearly half again were over the age of 55. If this data suggests that most Latvian farms were owned by people who had retired

Figure 5.3: Organic expansion in Latvia

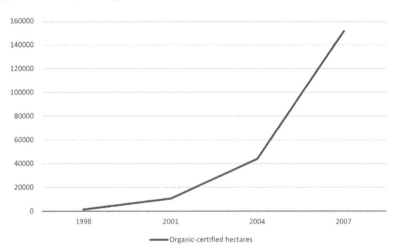

to the countryside to take up the family farm, Vēsma's story and the broader trend in organic conversions indicates the desire of subsistence farmers to engage the organic modality to restore the land in accordance with Latvian ecocultural values.

Along the northern banks of the Daugava River – not far from the river town of Jēkabpils – Priediņas farm was situated in and around a local nature reserve.[2] Its proprietor, Jānis Bogdanovs, was one in a scant minority of young farmers. After a stint of working at a fertilizer factory in England, Jānis had returned home to run the family farm. In 1991, his parents had bought the house and land. Having previously worked for a Kolkhoz unit, they decided to establish an independent produce and dairy farm. While Jānis had decided to forgo organic conversion, he had taken advantage of newly available EU subsidies for environmental conservation. In exchange for payment, Priediņas Farm had put 17 hectares aside for ecological protection, maintaining these as natural grasslands and retaining the right to mow for hay. Further to the east, Salenieki Farm was busy producing healthy food for farm guests. In 1996, Ruta Nokārkle bought 60 hectares of land to accompany the 40 hectares she inherited through family.[3] Leaving Rīga for remote Latgale, Ruta had established a joint organic farm and health retreat, providing her guests with meals prepared from farm produce and equipment for outdoor sports.

Given the collapse of the industrial processing sector in the wake of Soviet dissolution, organic farmers either sold fresh food or entered processing. By 2005, a small network of organic processing firms had surfaced around the country, including: (1) Zaube Cooperative, Latvia's sole organic slaughterhouse; (2) Ķeipene Dairy, which packaged its organic milk in distinctive brown bottles; (3) Zelta Kliņģeris, with its celebrated black rye bread produced through a traditional process of grain fermentation rather than through the modern application of yeast; (4) Parsla Enterprise, a Latgalian-based juice processor of which 50 per cent of its product line was certified organic and the remainder was largely organic by default; and (5) Kalna Sondori, one of many organic honey enterprises in a land where bee-keeping is a key cultural tradition.

Organic processing firms typically distributed their goods to specialty organic shops in Rīga and supplied regional schools with healthy food. However, these firms struggled to enter supermarkets due to a perceived lack of demand and low consumer purchasing power. Zelta Kliņģeris and Parsla had tackled this barrier by using EU membership as an opportunity to enter into organic trading agreements with European buyers, and Parsla additionally sold natural forest products to Russia and Canada. As a small start-up, Ķeipene Dairy had secured governmental subsidies to begin operations in 2002. Producing unpasteurized dairy products under a standardized testing system, Ķeipene had given Latvia the distinction of being the only European country besides France to have achieved this feat.[4] While organic farmers around the nation were clamouring to sell their milk to Ķeipene, the firm was unable to grow beyond its half-ton daily production, because it lacked the land needed to secure a bank loan for expansion. Finally, other smaller-scale processors, like the Kalna Sondori honey enterprise, had invested in processing by repurposing village apartments into modern facilities, typically selling their produce directly to neighbours and through rented stalls in open-air markets.

Whether produced on farm or at a processing facility, most of Latvia's organic food sales were made in Rīga, where professional inhabitants had greater purchasing power. Key movement activists also were stationed in the city, where they operated specialty organic shops and restaurants. However, Latvian organic goods were almost entirely absent from supermarkets. During interviews with this group of retailers, I typically was told that stores did not stock organic Latvian products due to the low purchasing power of the general populace. Yet, when comparing top-brand supermarket items with the organic counterpart sold in specialty shops, the organic products often were less expensive, suggesting that the primary challenge facing organic producers was one of scale rather than cost.

Regional market integration

Within the broader scope of the post-Soviet political economy, neoliberal reforms had created a market that privileged industrial producers. As there were no regulations or subsidies in place to promote sustainably produced goods, markets largely reduced product quality to the industrial and market conventions of standardized quantity and price. Although a handful of industrial food processors had survived Latvia's transition to a market economy, even these conventional brands struggled to remain competitive within the single European market. The nascent organic markets that a generation of producers had managed to carve out during Latvia's first decade of independence became in its second decade a critical heterotopia for the nation's predominantly small-scale farming population. At the forefront of this heterotopia, LBLA's organic label challenged industrial and market conventions by redefining quality in terms of domestic and civic norms that added value to socially responsible and environmentally sustainable practices. Because organic producers tended to cultivate food in accordance with terroir-based traditions, Latvia's organic label also had become a symbol of artisanal production, appealing to reputation conventions that drove luxury brands.

In 2005, the organic market heterotopia was struggling to remain visible amid the influx of cheaper organic goods. Produced and traded by large European firms these goods were desirable to supermarkets because they met industrial conventions pertaining to scale and standardized quality. This influx of imported goods not only reinforced the structurally unequal playing field upon which Latvian organic producers were marginalized, but large firms sought to capitalize from growing consumer interest in artisanal and sustainable goods, not by restructuring their own production processes in accordance with domestic or civic conventions, but rather by investing in slick marketing campaigns that echoed the claims of the movement, in a simulacrum of care. The growing diversity of industrial food items on supermarket shelves was accompanied by a dizzying array of market labels. While some of these denoted a sustainable product monitored by a third-party certification system located in the original country of production, other labels were fanciful private inventions that simply implied an ecological orientation.

The post-Soviet state exacerbated this situation by launching the Zaļa Karote (Green Spoon) label. Despite its ecological imagery, Green Spoon was not an organic label but a local one. To use it, a processor simply had to source 75 per cent of the ingredients in its product from Latvian farms. The farms supplying these ingredients were among Latvia's largest agricultural holdings, suggesting that the state-funded and aggressively marketed Green Spoon label was little more than a greenwashing campaign designed to promote the interests of Latvia's large industrial producers.

As a heterotopian market system, Latvia's organic food sector had worked hard to establish consumer demand for goods produced in accordance with domestic norms that cared for nature and locality and civic norms that supported health and fair labour. However – like any heterotopia that emerges in resistance to the broader world in which it is situated – this sector's labelling practices were confusing as well. In 2005, there were three Latvian organic certifiers, but only one nationally accredited label, *Ekoprodukts*, which was controlled by the LBLA. Certified farmers who were not members of this umbrella organic farmers association were barred from using the label and informally marketed their product as organic. LBLA members who had the rights to the label reproduced it on their packaging in various ways, their financial capacity and technical know-how determining whether it was a hazy stamp or a prominent and colourful symbol. Buffeted by a diverse array of labels, consumers often thought they were buying organic or otherwise sustainably produced goods, when in fact they were purchasing conventional products.

Given the challenges of market access, most of Latvia's farmers had remained locked into subsistence production in a countryside increasingly emptied of people. Within the world of European rural development, such holdings were classified as 'hobby farms' and considered to be a lifestyle choice, not subject to policy response (Lougheed, 2009). While subsistence farming may have been a chosen lifestyle for some households in affluent European countries, this subsistence demographic was far from the norm, and the situation in Eastern Europe was quite different. In Latvia, subsistence and semi-subsistence farmers were far more likely to be living in extreme poverty than small-scale farmers who had the means to invest in commercial operations. When I was in the field, several informants told me that there was an urgent need to institute rural development policies that would support farmers who supplied their families with food.

Latvia's network of subsistence farmers traditionally has played a key role in ensuring food security during periods of political upheaval and economic disruption. As one case in point, the Latvian custom of food gifts helped people survive market shocks in the early twentieth century, during Soviet-era food shortages, and again during the collapse of Latvian industry in the early 1990s. Even when Latvians were barred from owning land during the colonial and Soviet eras, country folk maintained ancient Latvian foodways by cultivating horticultural gardens, gathering forest foods, fishing and hunting and trading food and favours with kin. When Latvia regained its independence, land reforms gave new life to Latvian food customs. Family members who had returned to the land sent produce to urban relatives, who in turn provided their country kin with assistance during harvests and for farm repairs. By 2005, urban Latvians had adapted to the higher cost of living, but even during this time of rapid economic growth, the food gift custom remained so central to Latvian society, that the organic farming sector struggled to establish consumer demand. In a country where most urban Latvians had country family who kept them in fresh food produced without chemical inputs, there was little demand for organic food labels and farmers' markets.

Slow food

After a decade of movement formation and organizing, organic activists spent the second decade of post-Soviet reconstruction building a slow food campaign that explicitly joined ecology and culture. Extolling the virtues of local culinary traditions, organic retailers and restaurateurs marketed dishes prepared with artisanal, organic and locally sourced ingredients. The Latvian Slow Food campaign occurred within the broader context of international agrarian activism, as cultural producers sought to preserve traditional foodways amidst the onslaught of fast food. In a study of the history of the international Slow Food movement, Fontefrancesco and Corvo (2020) state that the post-Second World War Green Revolution – otherwise known as agricultural industrialization – 'led to a widespread abandonment of traditional practices and varieties, leading to a worldwide depletion of bio-cultural diversity' (p 767). As the international organic farming movement opened market heterotopias at the fringes of global North economies, these spaces became key sites of resistance not only to the expansion of the global agro-food regime, but also to neoliberal ideology of fast and reckless development.

In geographical terms, the Slow Food Movement originated in the food-centric country of Italy, where its founder, Carlo Petrini, raised awareness of the concept by participating in a 1980s campaign against the fast food giant, McDonald's, which had opened a franchise by the Spanish Steps in Rome (Leitch, 2018). The campaign to protect endangered cultural foodways from the onslaught of agricultural modernization soon moved to France, where the farmer, activist, and Green Party politician, José Bové famously disrupted the complacency surrounding neoliberal globalization by driving a tractor into a McDonald's restaurant. In Latvia, the slow food paradigm paired well with the ecocultural imaginary, as it extended the domestic convention of nature and locality to include the value of traditional food cultures. Consider the following excerpt from the Slow Food Manifesto[5] in defence of the right to pleasure:

> Born and nurtured under the sign of industrialization, this century first invented the machine and then modelled its lifestyle after it. Speed became our shackles. We fell prey to the same virus: 'the fast life' that fractures our customs and assails us even in our own homes, forcing us to ingest 'fast food'.
>
> Homo sapiens must regain the wisdom and liberate itself from the 'velocity' that is propelling it on the road to extinction. Let us defend ourselves against the universal madness of 'the fast life' with tranquil material pleasure.
>
> Against those – or rather, the vast majority – who confuse efficiency with frenzy, we propose the vaccine of an adequate

portion of sensual gourmandize pleasures, to be taken with slow and prolonged enjoyment …

Real culture is here to be found. First of all, we can begin by cultivating taste, rather than impoverishing it, by stimulating progress, by encouraging international exchange programs, by endorsing worthwhile projects, by advocating historical food culture and by defending old-fashioned food traditions …

In 2005, Mārtiņš Rītiņš was the president of the Latvian Slow Food Association. This celebrity chef founded Vincents Restorāns in 1994, when he opened a small art-gallery café in Rīga and subsequently grew it into Latvia's foremost fine dining experience. An ardent environmentalist, Rītiņš was involved in the organic movement from the start, and he co-founded Rīga's Green Market in the early 2000s. This open-air market operated in a central Rīga square on Friday and Saturday evenings during the summer and autumn months, providing farmers with space to sell their produce while also operating as an organic advocacy campaign. The market made savvy use of cultural symbology; for example, one of its slogans encouraged people to put their money directly into a 'farmer's black hand', invoking the ecocultural imagery of a hardworking homesteader, devoted to the soil. The Latvian Slow Food Association also hosted Slow Food Festivals in towns around the nation, where Rītiņš drew in crowds by performing cooking demonstrations, organic producers offered tastes of local delicacies and artisans sold cultural handicrafts, including fine silver jewellery, beeswax candles, leather books, pottery and hemp clothing. However, Latvian activists were by no means fundamentalist when it came to cultural tradition, for the movement not only supported intercultural engagement, but it also brought in new tastes through the creation of Latvian fusion cuisine, feeding the post-Soviet desire for travel and cultural exchange.

Organic and slow food had spoken to the ecocultural desires of a decolonizing nation. Yet the promise of rural revitalization had yet to materialize. Apart from a few compelling stories – such as Ķeipene's success in launching an unpasteurized dairy operation – the organic heterotopia was a small bubble of refuge, more broadly situated within the maw of neoliberal globalization, with its turn-of-the-century market casino policies and cutthroat European competition. Although EU membership had made European Fund monies available to Latvian producers, individual member states determined how to spend these allocations; in the Baltics, Lithuanian farmers were receiving approximately four times the assistance as their Latvian counterparts. In 2005, Lithuanian organic food items had begun to appear on Latvian supermarket shelves, while Latvian organic goods remained relegated to specialty shops and outdoor markets. Adding salt to these wounds, the Rīga City Council suddenly refused to approve the

Green Market's return in the summer of 2005, causing farmers to scramble for new space to sell. Rumours raced through the organic community, as activists struggled to discover the reason for this refusal. Some believed that wealthy business executives did not like the disruption of the evening market, and others thought that the Council may have demanded fees beyond what LBLA could afford. Mārtiņš Rītiņš told me that no one knew the details, but he believed political corruption was involved.

Although I met several people within the Ministry of Agriculture who tirelessly supported the organic farming movement, my research uncovered systemic underdevelopment and a lack of meaningful state support. By 2005, the Latvian state had recognized the need to invest in the food processing sector, and it had allocated funds for this purpose. However, it pegged these funds to bank loans and a complex value-added tax system that discouraged subsistence farmers from participating in commercial markets. Under the enterprise programme, a producer assumed a standard five-year loan to fund an enterprise development project, assuming half of the debt on their own. The government dispersed funds for the other half at the end of the first year, enabling the beneficiary to pay off a portion of the loan. While this scheme appealed to nationalist politicians who emphasized the Latvian value of self-sufficiency, in practice all but the largest commercial firms found the assistance to be negligible, for a full 40 per cent of the funding allocated by the government went to bank coffers in the form of interest payments.

In another study of Latvia's organic farming movement, also conducted during the 2000s, Guntra Aistara identified a similar pattern of incongruence. In *Organic Sovereignties* (2018), Aistara concluded that the side-by-side paradox of agrarian demise and organic resurgence was an effect of Latvia's peripheral position within both the global and regional European economies. She introduced the term 'interstitial organic solidarities' to illustrate the multi-scalar and multi-temporal nature of agrarian struggles, which in practice 'occur not on given scales or time frames, but always across them' (p 212). If Latvian ecoculture is a timeless and immaterial space, then past, present and future also are intermingled within the materialized realm of this nation's agrarian struggles. When considering agrarian resistance in the global context, sites of resistance serve as social bridges across temporal and spatial distances.

The Foucauldian concept of heterotopia augments this analysis by showing how the coloniality of power is reproduced within fragmented nodes of resistance. On one hand, alternative food heterotopias have arisen across the world as a challenge to the authoritarian monocultures of agricultural industrialization and the rationalization of food. On the other hand, these heterotopias are permeable to outside influences, and subject to reproducing the power structures they are attempting to change. Indeed, a growing body of critical scholarship has investigated the commercialized co-optation of a range of sustainability standards and certifications, from organics to fair trade (Jaffee and Howard, 2010; Daviron, 2011; Besky 2014; Mook and Overdevest 2020).

In a recent doctoral study on the ethics and practice of care in the Latvian organic movement, Agnese Bankovska (2020) conducted a multi-sited and multi-scaled ethnographic study in 2015, one decade after I departed from the field. This scholar found a similar pattern of interstitial 'connection, disconnection, and reconnection' when examining Latvian familial relationships with food. In one moment, the 'parents in both consumer and producer families in my study were motivated by genuine care for their children when choosing to become part of the food movement' (p 187). Yet at other moments these same families ceded to the demands of a rapid-paced and increasingly urban life by choosing to be careless of food. The gendered politics of care was at once a source of inspiration and a point of struggle. While Latvians desired the ecocultural imaginary of traditional foodways, for many families, the question was one of division of labour, and while Bankovska found that men increasingly were involved in cooking and childcare, few families had the time to take pleasure in the performance of cultural foodwork on more than an occasional basis. Whether these constantly shifting sands of care and lack of care are located at the family dinner table or in the interstitial fields of agrarian resistance, perhaps it through such patchworks of care that decolonization occurs.

Currents, intersections, and contestations

Culture and values are the inner dimension of sustainability, for 'culture is the medium through which people give meaning and assign value to their place and environment' (Horlings, 2015, p 164). Yet culture and morality are by no means isolated from political and economic forces, particularly in agrarian movements that seek to construct sustainable food systems. In this section, I examine the current parameters of Latvian ecocultural politics, employing gender analysis to unpack the interplay between Latvia's traditional cultural values and modern political economies. By combining seemingly disparate threads into one dialectical frame, I move beyond an either/or assessment of tradition and modernity to arrive at a transmodern perspective of decolonization that emphasis relational rather than ideological change.

Although women are present in this chapter, the topic of gender has only existed at the periphery of my coverage. In part, this was due to the nature of the original study that I designed in 2005, when my primary focus was on the political economy of the organic farming movement. While I may not have set out to study the gender dynamics of the movement, women were central to my research experience. Of my 24 key informants in Latvia, 16 were women. Within the movement, women were visible at all levels of engagement, as producers, activists and retailers, but also as scientists, state officials and other professionals. At the time, this came as no surprise to me, for I previously had spent three years working in Latvia's educational sector, and I was well-versed in this nation's matriarchal mythology. For me, the connection between Latvia's pantheon of powerful and yet caring goddesses and the central role that women played in the movement's protection of ecocultural production was clear.

It was only through witnessing a quite different struggle occur within Latvia's LGBTQ+ movement that I began to question the conventional matriarchal narrative undergirding the Latvian discourse on ecoculture, nationalism and organic foodways. If the symbology of Mother Earth provided Latvians with the inspiration to maintain ancient ecocultural values during centuries of foreign occupation, this endlessly nurturing goddess is far from the only archetype in Latvia's matriarchal pantheon. Published in *Six Latvian Poets* (2011) and shared here, Anna Auziņa's poem *Our Mother* revisits the matriarchal meaning of the Latvian mother. As part of a younger generation of Latvian poets who came of age in the early 1990s, Auziņa makes use of gender fluid imagery and otherwise shakes up the myth of the endlessly nurturing mother to challenge the idealized gender norms of Latvian nationalist tradition:

Our Mothers	*Mūsu Mātes*
both our mothers – they are robber molls	mūsu abu mātes – viņas ir laupītajvecenes
sitting by the side of the road with legs spread wide	ceļa malā sēž plati ieplestām kājām
and smoking pipes	un pīpē pīpi
our mothers are also country women	mūsu mātes ir arī lauku sievas
they eat juicy apples and go to mow grass for the cow	aped sulīgu ābolu un aiziet pļaut govij zāli
our mothers are witches	mūsu mātes ir raganas
stoking fires in dark kitchens just like in hell	tumšās virtuvēs kurina plītes gluži kā ellē
stirring some brew	un kaut ko vara
and they are also quite some hetairas[6]	un viņas ir arī baigās hetēras
black with painted eyes	tādas melnas krāsotām acīm
with wine stained lips	un vīnainām lūpām
and our mothers are madwomen	un vēl mūsu mātes ir vajprātīgās
in long white jackets	garos baltos kreklos
with huge eyes	milzīgām acīm

Our Mothers	Mūsu Mātes
without any teeth	bez zobiem
wagging their bony fingers	un krata kaulainos pirkstus
and our mothers are children	un vēl mūsu mātes ir bērni
with damp curls over round cheeks	slapjām cirtām pār apaļiem vaigiem
when after a good cry they finally doze off	kad viņas izraudājušās beidzot aizmieg

As I have discussed in the earlier chapter on Daina philosophy, Māra is a powerful goddess who rules over Earth and underworld (Vīķe-Freiberga, 1997). Her dual aspects are represented in the form of two lesser goddesses Zemes Māte (Mother Earth) and Nāves Māte (Mother Death), who denote the relationship between life and death. Zemes Māte is comprised of lesser mother goddesses who are the spirit guardians of Earth's diverse ecosystems and all the beings therein. From forest and river mothers to mothers of the wind, and sea, these goddesses teach Latvians to care for other species. In the Indigenous written language of Latvian symbols, Māra's name is inscribed as a downward triangle that depicts the grounded and receptive nature of yin energy.[7] This symbol inverts the upward triangle of Dievs, the father god of the sky, and a symbolic expression of the active and elevating nature of yang energy. As two aspects of one whole, great mother and father gods illustrate the energy of procreation, and the regenerative force of give-and-take relationships. Thus, at a more abstract level, Latvia's ecosystem guardians denote differing strands of universal lifeforce, or the spark of relational connectivity that moves through all matter across spacetime.[8]

Also introduced in Chapter 3, the Latvian concept of līgo teaches Latvians to sway in tune with nature. This concept is ritually enacted during song and dance festivals where people harmonize song and movement to enter into a state of līgo, or in other words, sway in relation to the experience of connectivity. Līgo also comes into being in the far less solemn setting of the mid-summer solstice, when women of all ages wear the floral crown of the maiden. In Latvian folklore, lovers are said to retreat into the forest in search of a mythical fern blossom that only blooms on this fertile night of spiritual love and sexual regeneration.

Latvian environmental nationalism interprets this gendered cosmovision in literal terms. Figuratively speaking, the cultural symbology of Earth Mother and Father Sky are storytelling devices that teach one to receptively nurture and actively protect life. However, environmental nationalism favours a fundamentalist interpretation that reproduces soft patriarchy. Whereas women enjoy power and prestige as the matriarchal guardians of Latvian ecoculture, the post-Soviet rhetoric on family values has reduced Latvia's diverse pantheon of goddesses to singular role of receptive nurturer, therein

103

reproducing the patriarchal power relations that have shaped Latvia's colonial existence (Mole, 2011).

During the four years that I lived in Latvia, I moved at the fringes of gay and lesbian society, where I witnessed the underground struggle for sexual liberation. However, the spheres of sexual and environmental activism were so far removed, and I had been so deeply socialized into a matriarchal understanding of Latvian ecoculture that it never occurred to me to consider the implications of its gendered cosmovision from the queer vantage point of my own gender identity. When I began writing this book, I had no intention of incorporating sexual politics into a study on organic farming. However, after conducting more recent research into Latvian environmental discourse, I found that sexual and environmental justice activism have come to stand in ideological opposition. Not only has Latvia received the dubious distinction of being the worst country in Europe to be gay, but the European Green Party (EGP) expelled the Latvian Green Party from its membership for failing to adhere to the social values espoused in the EGP Charter. In a story released by the Baltic News Network (2019), Edgars Tavars, the head of the Latvian Green Party, cited the party's stance against same-sex marriage as the reason for expulsion. In his words, 'the green idea has nothing in common with the pre-condition for being sexually, ethnically, economically left-wing, modern or correct. Our flag is green–white–green, not rainbow-coloured or red.' By equating the rainbow symbol of sexual liberation with the monochromatic 'red' flag of the Soviet Union, Tavars delivered a coded message to Latvian nationalists that situated sexual minorities as a foreign and oppressive threat to Latvian family values.

In an earlier study on the Latvian politics of sexuality, Waitt (2005) found that nationalist rhetoric equates the liberal European position on gender equality to the Soviet command for genderless modernity. This rhetoric is historically inaccurate, for if revolutionary Bolshevik ideology extolled the rights of women, strongman Soviet leaders soon reproduced the patriarchal and heteronormative gender relations of imperial Russia. Making homosexuality punishable by law, the Soviet Union shackled even the most intimate dimension of human existence to the spying eye of the Soviet police state (Healey, 2002).

That said, Latvian nationalist claims of neo-colonialism are not without merit. Not only are this nation's organic farmers structurally marginalized within a single European market system that privileges industrial production under the influence of Western European capital, but EU membership has hindered the ability of Latvian farmers and greens to lobby for a more socially and environmentally responsible approach to food production and trade, as distant European bureaucrats have supplanted the Latvian state in policy making (Aistara, 2018). From the vantage point of the average Latvian farm, the structure of the European political economy is not so different from that imposed by the Soviet Union. Hierarchically organized and managed by geographically distant elites who command standardized practices in accordance with modern rational assumptions about the nature of reality and meaning of existence, the European development regime may claim to support the preservation of biodiversity, foodways, and rurality, but its imperial organizational structure reproduces the socially and environmentally destructive modality of authoritarian monocultures.

Both European and Latvian greens recognize the destruction of lands, cultures and ecologies at the hands of a globalized agro-food regime. Yet both groups mistake the root cause of the problem by arguing about ideology rather than revisiting structural relationships. For Latvian nationalists, who have suffered nearly 800 years of colonization and subjection to foreign masters, the idealized heterotopia of the ecocultural imaginary has been a powerful site of refuge, enabling the clan and land to maintain its Indigenous Baltic way of life. In proclaiming tradition to be the source of all good and modernity as a threat, environmental nationalists may seek to recover the precolonial experience of cultural freedom, but in relational action, this group reproduces the either/or logic of imperial gnosis, leaving the root problem of self-other conflict unresolved. In proclaiming secular rationalism and progressive modernity to be the source of all good, liberalism also reproduces oppression, refracting its form of expression in opposition to its perceived nationalist and religious enemies.

In a world ravaged by military conflict and unceasing culture wars, a transformative perspective is sorely needed. I posit that human societies cannot hope to build institutions that are capable of responding to the social and environmental challenges of our time without making a fundamental shift in consciousness, relationships and praxis. To heal from the psychosocial wounds wrought by coloniality, imperialism and modernity, people around the world must commit to enacting more peaceful, productive, and emotionally fulfilling self-other relationships across all spheres of everyday life. By healing our fractured selves, families, communities, professions, knowledges and practices we may begin the collective process of transmuting the modern-colonial psychosis of anomie, conflict and fear of difference into a transmodern mindset of self-other reconnection, peace and love.

For all its decolonized underlayers and recolonizing overlayers, the Latvian ecocultural imaginary is but a cultural cloak to the deeper and more fundamental truth of our inevitable interconnection as humans residing on a tiny blue planet and surrounded by the immense vacuum of outer space. Although I find myself at odds with the Latvian Green Party's statement that there is no room in its green politics for queers like me, I remain deeply inspired by the gift of Latvia's ecocultural wisdom and knowledge, as I have learned it through the teachings of the Dainas, and as I have experienced it during the four years that I lived among Latvians. I have only love and respect for the defenders of a nation that has experienced tremendous suffering at the hands of foreign invaders; and I recognize that the future is all too unclear. As I write, the Russian president, Vladmir Putin, has stoked up the imperial war engine by invading Ukraine. To the south of the Baltics, Hungary has turned away from the false promise of European liberalism to flirt with the false promise of illiberal authoritarianism (Innes, 2015). More broadly, the world has witnessed a resurgence in neo-fascist movements that are actively demonizing ethnic minorities and other marginalized social groups around the world (Heller, 2020).

While societies around the world fight with one another over cultural and political differences, a highly competitive global power elite, unfettered by domestic or civic conventions, and having forgotten how to love, is laying waste to lands and peoples in its rapacious greed to fill a deep void of emptiness within a lifeforce gone cold. The decolonial feminist scholar, Rita Segato, identifies the psychosocial illness of our times as one of apocalyptic psychopathy, or an absence of feeling and care in a world where life still has little meaning (Segato, 2016). If the condition of psychopathy is characterized by a state of detachment, a lack of empathy and an inability to feel emotion, then the solution to this global mental health crisis does not lie in modern rational praxis, which, in the name of objectivity, encourages people to bury emotion, perform detachment and widen the already formidable gulf between knowledge and action, ideology and practice.

There is an urgent need to recover our basic humanity by investing in poetics, arts and literature, by reconnecting with ourselves and others with peace in our hearts, by rediscovering the songs of our ancestors and by reinvigorating myriad cultures and ecologies of knowledge for the sake of generations yet to come. Forged in liberty and maintained during centuries of oppression, the Latvian lifeway is one such antidote to the prison of our collective detachment, providing us with the means to converse with other species, sing with family and friends and take joy in the simple things in life. In the world of the Dainas, to view an unploughed field blooming with bright yellow dandelions or quiet falling snow on a dark winter night are sacred gifts from a participatory universe, and a reminder to love.

To date, Latvia has managed to hold onto its fledgling democracy, despite having lost nearly a fifth of its population to economic emigration in the wake of EU accession. As a diminutive society of horticulturalists, poets and artists, uncomfortably situated between Western and Eastern empires, Latvians have always recognized the precariousness of their ecocultural existence; however, as the cultural victim of centuries of psychosocial abuse, Latvia also runs the risk of reproducing the violence that it has endured, in the same way that an abused child may grow up to abuse children.

In reflecting upon the challenges facing rural Latvia in the twenty-first century, I am reminded of the wisdom provided by a small-scale honey producer in Latgale. During my interview with the proprietor of Kalna Sondori, Antons Korsaks told me that the post-Soviet government had "thrown the baby out with the bathwater". In his estimation, the nation had failed to safeguard the positive aspects of a socialist society by transitioning too rapidly and too extremely to a neoliberal capitalist economy. Citing the devastating effects of mass youth flight, Korsaks believed that Latvia was facing the destruction of agrarian knowledge and Latvian *padoms* (wise knowing) that has enabled countless generations of Latvians to retain and reimagine their unique ecocultural identity.

Situated in the multi-sensual terrain of food and heritage, Latvia's organic farming and slow food movements have carved out alternative markets at the fringes of the post-Soviet economy. While the struggles facing organic farmers are multifaceted and ongoing, the market heterotopia that the Latvia's generation of post-Soviet farmers worked so hard to construct has the *padoms* to construct transmodern foodways that harmonize Latvia's agrarian traditions and urbanized modernities. It is unclear whether the movement will succeed in bringing the next generation of Latvian youth home to the countryside where they may learn the ecocultural knowledge of their elders. However, if history repeats itself a new generation will leave the city, as eager as their predecessors to make hay and sway in the life-affirming way of their ancestors. Will the Latvians wearing rainbows be welcomed home?

6

Fair Trade and Rooibos Terroir in Post-Apartheid South Africa

I have come to take you home

I have come to take you home.
Home. Remember the veld?
The lush green grass beneath the big oak trees?
The air is cool there and the sun does not burn.
I have made your bed at the foot of the hill,
your blankets are covered in buchu and mint,
the proteas stand in yellow and white
and the water in the stream chuckles sing-songs
as it hobbles along over little stones.

— Excerpt of a poem by Dianna Ferrus,
in tribute to Sarah Baartman[1]

Space to breathe

'Sometimes I walk in the mountains and sing my memories into my recorder. People say "Tannie aren't you afraid of the baboons and leopards? What will you do if you fall and break your leg?" But I tell them that I am afraid of nothing.'

— Marie Ockhuis of Heuningvlei, Wupperthal

It is a blustery winter evening, and I am sitting by the fire, fingers wrapped around a mug of Rooibos tea. I am listening to Marie's stories. Raised in a coloured household on the remote Moravian mission of Wupperthal, Marie left the Cederberg Mountains of the Western Cape to work for White men during the apartheid era. As a single mother and democracy activist, she fought to give her son access to the education she had been denied. In the post-apartheid era, she has taken great pleasure in witnessing her son's contribution to educational reform in Cape Town, and when she retired, he invited her to move in with family. Through all the years of her life, Marie had never stopped longing for the wide-open lands of her childhood, so she returned to the Cederberg instead. Now Marie lives in a spartan cottage in the centre of the mission hamlet of Heuningvlei, located at the base of *Pakhuis* Pass where arid mountain meets agrarian marsh. Known to all in Wupperthal as *Tannie Nuus* (Auntie News), Marie is famous for her fierce intelligence and neighbourly spirit. Scrambling to survive on her meagre pension, a small hillside crop of Rooibos, and a micro used-clothing enterprise that is more charitable than profitable, she says that life is bitter, but the Cederberg gives her space to breathe.

The land that Marie roams is breathtakingly diverse. Located in mountain *fynbos* territory at the geographical origin for *aspalathus linearis* – the Cederberg shrub that gifts us Rooibos tea – Wupperthal is enfolded in a biodiverse ecology and a rich cultural heritage that formed through the merger of Afro-Asian, Khoe-Sān and European peoples under the fraught conditions of colonialism and apartheid (Keahey, 2019). The global supply of Rooibos derives entirely from the greater Cederberg region, and this culturally distinctive red tea is the lifeblood of mission communities, where approximately 60 per cent of the industry's small-scale producers reside. Rooibos tea farmers have been augmenting traditional subsistence activities with a heritage development strategy that combines Fairtrade and organic certified tea production with ecotourism, the production of Rooibos-based body products and micro-cultural enterprise.

This chapter engages a critical heritage and alternative trade lens to examine Wupperthal's involvement in sustainability initiatives during a pivotal moment of economic crisis and political uncertainty. Sharing findings from a 2010 participatory action research (PAR) study, I unpack alternative economies from the perspective of small-scale producers, challenging a national discourse that treats coloured people as rootless and lacking in heritage. I also challenge Western discourse that treats terroir as pure, timeless and unchanging. Wupperthal's multi-rooted expression of Rooibos terroir may not be purely Indigenous, given that purity is an ideal concept, but its mixed nature may more accurately reflect the evolution of South African Indigeneity in its material life.

As I will argue in Chapter 7, the categorical logic underpinning modern rational discourse is only capable of cataloguing life in its death, for it converts different aspects of existence into essentialized fragments, or the morally dead ghosts of a once living and interconnected whole. My analysis provides an empirical foundation for decolonizing knowledge by centring rather than obscuring the uncertainties and contradictions of Wupperthal's identity and experience. The presence of coloured terroir in a biodiverse land where ethnic tribes have always mixed lays bare the apartheid myth of discretely categorizable existence.

People and land

The first families of Wupperthal trace their descent through slaves who travelled into the interior with Afrikaners during the Great Trek of the early nineteenth century. When *trekboers* entered the Cederberg, White families settled along the wide valleys of the western slope but found the arid eastern range to be unsuitable for extensive use. Seeking their own destiny, many enslaved people left their masters to establish independent homesteads in the hidden hollows of the craggy eastern slope. According to oral accounts, these ex-slave settlers intermingled with Khoe-Sān families who also had been displaced by colonial expansion.

In 1830, two German missionaries established a Rhenish mission station in the hollow of what is now Wupperthal Sentrale, the centrally located mission village. The church soon annexed ownership of coloured farms in the area, but due to the remoteness of the region, inhabitants managed to retain considerable autonomy in their everyday lives (Bilbe, 2009). By the early twentieth century, Wupperthal had become a fairly prosperous mission station comprised of gardeners, pastoralists, artisans and teachers. Having combined an Indigenous gathering and sheep herding economy with small-scale vegetable production and mission-based enterprise, the people of the time drew from various sources of cultural knowledge to tame the first Rooibos seedlings for agriculture (Patrickson et al, 2008).

Wupperthal's fragile prosperity collapsed in the mid-twentieth century when South African mission stations became designated as rural coloured areas and inhabitants were barred from participating in commercial markets. Exacerbating the situation, the Rhenish church arranged to sell Wupperthal to the Dutch Reformed cleric (Ives, 2017). As a Dutch Reformed cleric, DF Malan, had been the first prime minister of the apartheid state; thus, the mission's residents mobilized resistance to this plan. Securing support from the Moravian Church, Wupperthalers asked the Rhenish to sell the mission to the Moravians instead. Having originated in the eastern German state of Saxony, Moravians believed strongly in the human right to freedom (Raphael-Hernandez, 2017). Moravian missionaries to Dutch Suriname and the Danish West Indies previously had helped local people rebel against slavey, and in South Africa, the Moravian Church continued this tradition by standing in political opposition to apartheid.

The Moravian Church assumed ownership of the Wupperthal mission in 1965 (Bilbe, 2009). Amid the turbulence surrounding the legal transfer in ownership, however, Wupperthal lost large tracts of its arable land to White settlers who had entered the eastern slope. Struggling to absorb coloured relatives who were displaced from urban homes through forced removals, and possessing less land for families to farm, Wupperthal became increasingly impoverished.

Today, the Moravian mission of Wupperthal resides at the heart of the Greater Cederberg Biodiversity Corridor (GCBC) displayed in Figure 6.1. The Cape Floristic Region is one of the world's six floral kingdoms, and within it, the Cederberg is a part of a fragile mountain *fynbos* biome (Patrickson et al, 2008). During the 2000s, Cape Nature, the conservation authority of the Western Cape, began an initiative to establish nature corridors that would allow for species migration between the Cederberg's designated wilderness areas. Cape Nature has secured industry and farmer support for the proposed corridors designated in the map as striped sections;

Figure 6.1: The Greater Cederberg Biodiversity Corridor

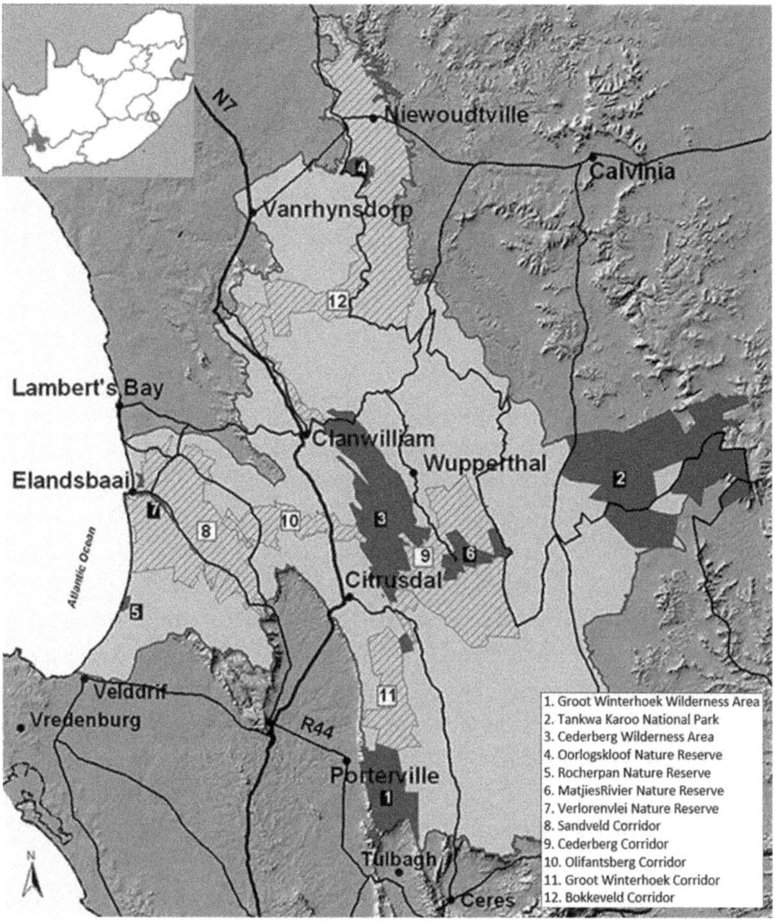

Source: Reprinted from Keahey (2019), with the permission of *Geoforum* (Elsevier) and Cape Nature

however, climate change – in the form of declining rainfall patterns and rising temperatures – is threatening farmer livelihoods and interspecies resilience (Lötter and le Maitre, 2014).

The GCBC has remained de-facto racially segregated, with White-owned estates largely located in the coastal west, and the regional town of Clanwilliam operating as the hub of the Rooibos industry. Wupperthal is located across the mountain from Clanwilliam to the east of the Cederberg Wilderness Area and at the base of a Rooibos heritage route that runs southward from Nieuwoudtville. Having applied for Geographic Indication (GI) in 2008, the South African government secured the designation of Rooibos terroir in 2014 (Biénabe and Marie-Vivien, 2017). The GI system derives from Europe and is designed to support the preservation of ecocultural relationships that inform the production of distinctive goods, such as Champagne, by legally prohibiting the use of product name in cases when the commodity is grown outside of its designated terroir.

Framing and methodology

Critical heritage studies offer dialectic insight into the structural inequities and collective agency informing heritage in development (Winter, 2013). Within this body of scholarship, studies interrogate the impact of colonization, genocide and slavery on cultural heritage, with particular focus on issues pertaining to racial and ethnic identity, and heritage pathways for peacebuilding (Giblin, 2015). Within this discourse, cultural geographers move beyond abstract and categorical understandings of identity by engaging 'more-than-representational theories of heritage' (Waterton, 2014, p 824). Focusing on affective dynamics, these theories posit the vulnerable and contested nature of heritage as expressed through embodied, multi-sensual and relational experiences that ground culture and politics in spacetime.

While scholars who examine the political economy of agro-food systems largely neglect the topic of heritage, a broader body of alternative scholarship has begun to examine the embodied politics of food. According to Michael Carolan (2011), alternative agro-food systems are reviving cultural memories and feelings to challenge industrial practices and transition to sustainability. If food politics are multi-sensual by nature, sociocultural relationships with the countryside are relationally embodied as well for, as Carolan (2008) notes, agrarian perceptions of nature rise from a 'corporeal poetics of everyday life' (p 409). Yet very little is known about the more-than-representational engagement of marginalized farmers in alternative food networks.

As the lead researcher for a 2010 collaborative research and support project, I collaborated with local agencies and small-scale producers to develop a participatory training, researching and networking initiative.[2]

Figure 6.2: Wupperthal communities

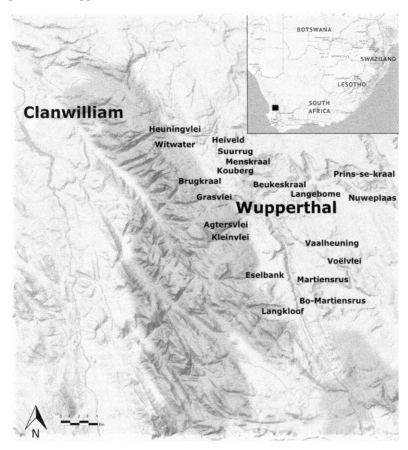

Source: Reprinted from Keahey (2018), with permission from *Gender, Place and Culture*.
Copyright (2017), with permission of Taylor & Francis www.tandfonline.com/

My partners and I worked with the Wupperthal communities depicted in Figure 6.2 to form a grassroots network of ten farmer leaders across five geographic groupings who co-developed the project with us.[3] Including an equal number of democratically elected men and women, the leaders became my co-investigators on a field study that we collaboratively designed.[4] In addition to engaging as participant observers in industry venues, we conducted 48 interviews with a representative sample of mission farmers and solicited oral histories from elders.[5] I further facilitated discussions on power and identity with the farmer leaders, lived with hosts in mission hamlets during fieldwork and interviewed dozens of industry and development actors further afield. This approach enabled us to: (1) examine local livelihood initiatives; (2) unpack social inequities; and (3) identify sources of resilience.

Fairtrade entrepreneurs

'Rooibos is the only possibility for economic survival in this community. The rain falls on the western slope of the Cederberg … we have lower rainfall here, but this is why our Rooibos is so good. The plants grow slower and last longer than in the plantations on the western slope.'

— *Barend Salomo, Managing Director,*
Wupperthal Original Rooibos Cooperative

In 1991, the transitional South African government dismantled the apartheid Rooibos control board and removed racial barriers to commerce. Although large White-owned estates were positioned to dominate neoliberal markets, farmers in Wupperthal were eager to enter an industry that their forebears had helped develop. Various agricultural and environmental agencies assisted Wupperthal in forming a Rooibos tea association, and in 1998 farmers secured funding from the Department of Agriculture to buy a tractor and upgrade the old tea court where the traditional fermentation and drying process takes place. Farmers experienced no difficulty in accessing Eco-Cert organic certification in 1999, for the paperwork was not yet complex, and Wupperthalers had never used chemical inputs to farm mission plots. The young association rapidly grew from 25 members in 1998 to 180 members by 2005.

Having sold organic tea to international Fairtrade buyers since the early 2000s, Wupperthal's farmers mobilized to secure dual Fairtrade–organic certification in 2005. As part of this process, the association was restructured into a cooperative that met Fairtrade International (FTI) standards for small-scale farmer membership. Fairtrade Rooibos standards were not yet defined, but cooperative management believed the eventual introduction of product standards would limit certified tea production to small-scale farmers, as previously had been done in Fairtrade coffee. Encouraged by a web of external actors, the Wupperthal cooperative collaborated with another small-scale farmer organization in the northern Cederberg to meet the projected demand of the certified Rooibos market by adding value to their tea through a Fairtrade packaging scheme. This collectively owned enterprise involved nearly all the coloured Rooibos producers in South Africa as well as a young White entrepreneur who established the packaging firm in Cape Town. Employing many of the farmers' urban relatives, Fairpackers arranged to directly export certified packaged Rooibos tea to buyers around the world.[6]

The groups involved in this joint enterprise lacked the business training needed to navigate export markets at a time of global economic recession. Moreover, when FTI formalized Rooibos standards in 2008, it made the decision to allow Rooibos tea estates into the Fairtrade system under separately designated hired-labour standards. Glutted with cheaply produced plantation tea, the bottom dropped out of the Fairtrade Rooibos market, and Fairpackers lost most of its buyers, causing the small farmer partnership to collapse in 2009. Around the same time, the Wupperthal cooperative lost dual certification after an audit uncovered poorly managed documentation.

The rapid shift to a large cooperative with dual certification and indebted involvement in an export partnership had created a host of managerial challenges. Farmers responded to decertification by voting the cooperative board out of power and installing new leadership largely comprised of farmers with basic market knowledge but no understanding of certifications. Wupperthal splintered into disputing factions and fell prey to unsavoury outsiders, including a lawyer who charged the dying cooperative an obscene sum of money to conduct the legal paperwork for recertification, but who later disappeared without completing the task.

The Wupperthal Original Rooibos Cooperative was instated in 2010 under the guidance of original board members who worked tirelessly to re-certify and rebuild international trade networks. Yet many Wupperthalers realized that Fairtrade membership was no financial panacea, for there simply was not enough land for mission inhabitants to depend upon on tea sales alone. Given the debts accrued from the packaging scheme, the loss of certification, and the interim loss of buyers, farmers had not received payment for their tea between the years of 2007 and 2010. During this time of hunger, many families survived on a combination of subsistence activities and income from state welfare or remittances from urban-dwelling relatives. Those without sources of income fell into a pattern of growing debt. One farmer leader, Rodger Witbooi, succinctly described this downward spiral:

'Many people in the community depend upon Rooibos. If they could use their gardens for subsistence and only sell Rooibos, it would be good, but now they must sell their vegetables for money and later spend money to buy back vegetables.'

As the first small-scale farmers in South Africa to join Fairtrade certified markets, the coloured Rooibos producers of the Cederberg were Fairtrade trailblazers. However, their entrepreneurial energy far outpaced the development of external support systems in a nation transitioning from apartheid. If Wupperthalers lacked the managerial skills and material resources to enter export markets, they also were caught in the snare of a South African neoliberal development regime that had encouraged marginalized producers to lift themselves out of poverty by engaging in risky commercial ventures.

Given the failure of the state to return mission lands that had been annexed for White development during apartheid, enterprise was essential to Wupperthal's future, and people with Rooibos plots were desperate for re-entry into the Fairtrade system. In contrast to conventional markets where Rooibos pricing routinely fell below the cost of production, Fairtrade markets provided small-scale farmers with minimum pricing guarantees as well as an additional 15 per cent above the negotiated price, for the purpose of supporting community development. With dual certification reinstated, Wupperthal Original's cooperative board hoped to improve managerial capacity by securing access to training for both farmers and staff through Fairtrade Africa's newly instituted producer support programme. Discussing the community rift that had occurred over the course of this struggle, the Secretary-Treasurer of Wupperthal Original encouraged the farmer leaders involved in this study to pursue a path of truth and reconciliation:

'I. Me. Myself must admit I was wrong. ... We must all admit there was a time in our life when we were wrong and didn't respect one another. ... We must respect one another and it must not be only one person's way. ... Then we can forgive each other and start the opportunity of a new beginning.'

Enterprise diversification

Wupperthal's efforts to develop sustainable enterprise have moved beyond Rooibos to encompass the mission's broader heritage as a distinctive society located at the heart of the Cederberg. According to Pieter Zimri, an elder residing in the Wupperthal village of Kleinvlei, the mission economy was never limited to the production of a single good, for during the colonial era, households engaged in artisanal occupations that ranged from welding and construction to leatherwork and mixed farming. Not only had Pieter's father, the master builder Johannes Zimri, built the historic Wupperthal church, but homes were hewed by generations of craftsmen who developed a mission aesthetic based on functional yet visually appealing whitewashed architecture.

Pieter also told us that Wupperthal's *trekboer* shoe factory first opened in 1836. As a boy, Pieter had assisted the cobblers, who used the skins of local livestock and dyes from plants, by collecting plant material for their use. Although the factory experienced decline under apartheid – when the last White Rhenish Reverend left the mission and copied Wupperthal's designs to open a commercial shoe factory in Clanwilliam – the Wupperthal factory nevertheless survived and has become recognized as the oldest working shoe factory in South Africa. Catering to locals and tourists wishing to buy handcrafted leather hiking boots, Wupperthal's elderly cobblers have maintained the same artisanal shoe-making process as their forebears.

Nearly 60 per cent of our interview respondents stated that they continued to participate in heritage-based vegetable and livestock production in addition to Rooibos; and 40 per cent said they had expanded into other forms of cultural enterprise, with somewhat more women than men involved in these investments. If vegetable gardening and animal husbandry was largely undertaken by men for household consumption as well as for barter and small-scale sale, women made jewellery and operated shops and bakeries out of their homes. People of all genders participated in ecotourism development, and women bakers marketed mission bread to tourists seeking a taste of the Cederberg. Baked in small batches according to artisanal method, the production of Wupperthal ash-bread involved superheating outdoor clay ovens with fragrant and slow-burning hardwood then sweeping out the ashes and inserting loaves to bake.

Up on the escarpment in Langkloof, Kosie and Ann Salomo had opened their home to tourists who came to view the spring floral bloom and as a base for backpacking trips into the Cederberg Wilderness Area. A regional environmental agency had provided the Salomos with a solar powered water heater, enabling them to offer warm baths to hikers fresh off Gabriel's Pass. To the northwest, a regional development agency was paying farmers to build a campground in Kleinvlei and improve the road to Heuningvlei so that tourists could access its collectively owned guesthouse with greater ease. Private households with requisite resources also ran guesthouses around the mission while welders crafted traditional metal harnesses for donkey carts whose owners marketed day trips to tourists. Finally, a USAID-funded empowerment project had helped a group of women establish Red Cedar in 2003. Using Rooibos and other natural ingredients to produce an array of natural body soaps, creams, and ointments, the women running this business sold their product line in a Wupperthal shop, made national sales online, and traded internationally through the Moravian Church network. While numerous interview respondents possessed artisanal skills and shared several ideas for heritage-based development, most said that they lacked the funds needed to establish micro- or small-scale enterprise, particularly given the loss of income resulting from the Rooibos tea crisis.

Systemic scarcity

'I can't afford my basic needs very often. I get by crying and I think of leaving and looking for a job, but I can't leave my family behind with nothing.'

– Patricia[7]

Despite their efforts to establish a local mixed economy, most Wupperthalers experienced material deprivation. Discussing the importance of income to everyday life, farmer respondents told us that one could survive with very little money during apartheid, but the rising cost of living in the post-apartheid era had made it impossible to survive on subsistence livelihoods alone. While livelihood training was needed and intermittently available to mission communities, the income and skills derived from these development projects were not enough to ameliorate multi-generational poverty wrought by centuries of dispossession and decades of underdevelopment at the hands of a White supremacist state. At the root of the problem was the severe shortage of land that prevented producers from expanding sheep and Rooibos production, as White farmers in the region had done. Much of the terrain surrounding Wupperthal was comprised of rocky escarpments designated for wilderness conservation, and access was strictly controlled. All the respondents we interviewed expressed strong support for Cederberg conservation, but these shifts nevertheless prevented people from accessing terrain that their ancestors had relied upon for food, medicinal herbs, and firewood.

Wupperthalers who were involved in organic gardening and Rooibos production secured access to small plots of land. These were owned by the Moravian Church which managed access through nominal rents; however, in practice, individual access largely passed down through families, typically with sons – and in some cases daughters – inheriting plots from fathers, and wives inheriting from deceased husbands. More broadly, however, the amount of available land was insufficient for agrarian development. Younger and poorer people had to wait years, if not decades, for those with plots to retire, and there was not enough arable land to provide all households with plots. On average, household production was exceedingly small-scale: about 60 per cent of the mission's farmers produced less than three tons of Rooibos per year, and only 8 per cent produced more than seven tons.[8] Offering further perspective, an industry extension officer who had mapped Wupperthal's tea fields told me that more than 200 Rooibos farmers and their extended families were trying to survive on income generated from rented parcels that combined would be two White estates of typical size.

Eighty-three per cent of the mission population had no savings to rely upon in cases of emergency. During lean times, people survived on little more than flour and sugary tea, and residents ironically referred to flour dumplings boiled in water as a 'local delicacy'. Further research is necessary to generate reliable health data, but the farmer leaders believed that the local starvation diet of bread and sugar was a primary health issue, for they told me that numerous people were taking medication for diabetes after one interview with a lean and elderly farmer who told us that he had lost both of his feet due to problems with his blood sugar. Although fresh vegetables were available during the growing season, there was precious little to conserve, and few households had access to fresh foods during the winter months. Given the costs involved in travelling to Clanwilliam where supermarkets were located, Wupperthalers generally purchased canned goods that would not spoil when pooling their resources together to make the trip to town.

The lack of reliable income fuelled youth flight, with many leaving the mission for secondary education or in search of work as soon as primary schooling was completed. Among those who remained, most expressed a desire for further education but said that their families lacked the resources to send them to secondary school or to enrol them in vocational training. Berna-Leigh Veloen, a young farmer leader who had wanted to become an emergency medical provider, informed me that she was unable to pursue her goal "because there is not enough money to pay for training". During an interview, a young male farmer who had trained in welding told us that there were no local opportunities to make a living from this occupation, saying "my problem is that I must go to Cape Town to work as a welder, but I don't have a place to stay there". Young mothers typically resided in parental homes and expressed feelings of guilt for their inability to contribute to household income due to childcare responsibilities that made it impossible to leave the mission for work. Young people typically resided in parental households well into their middle years when they finally began inheriting farm plots.

These accounts of systemic scarcity illustrate the ongoing segregation and underdevelopment of rural coloured areas, suggesting a de-facto reality of neoliberal apartheid. Like other former homelands in rural South Africa, Wupperthal has continued to depend upon subsistence farming and the cultivation of traditional foods for survival; yet the rising cost of living in a neoliberal economy has meant that food security can no longer be achieved by subsistence practices alone. As the lifeblood of the mission, Rooibos has provided farmers with a critical opportunity to cultivate a cash crop on dry lands unsuitable for vegetable production, but fields are small and export markets are volatile. The mountains surrounding most of Wupperthal have been designated for environmental conservation, and the arable lands surrounding parts of the mission remain under White ownership. National failures to establish a viable strategy for land reform have prevented coloured farmers from expanding production, making Fairtrade and organic certifications a prerequisite for market entry. Although Wupperthalers readily acknowledged these systemic barriers, they also saw themselves as hardy and independent people. They identified a range of social and ecological benefits that helped them to live culturally rich and emotionally nourishing lives.

Ecocultural resilience

'I moved back here because my uncle was shot in the taxi violence. There were two attacks and he was killed. I also was almost killed in a bad neighbourhood. I wanted to come home where there are no streets and it is safe – to see everyone and talk to everyone, and live closer to the bible.'

– *Willem*[9]

Wupperthalers either rented or owned cottages that maintained the aesthetic appeal of the mission, but in almost all cases these were equipped with the modern convenience of electricity. While many homes lacked indoor toilets, most were plumbed with running water piped in from spring-fed rivers. The materials used in home construction and comfortable porch *stoeps* allowed for the movement of air during the arid summer. When winter rains shrouded the mountaintops in chilly fog, families gathered by the fireplace, with elders passing oral histories down to the next generation and friends coming together to watch television. Most households did not have telephones due to outdated mission infrastructure, and there was no wireless coverage, so communication generally travelled by foot.[10] If the lack of modern telecommunications hindered enterprise development, it also provided people with a sense of distance from the problems of the modern world. Despite the hardship and poverty, Wupperthalers agreed that life off the paved road was better than the daily grind of urban South Africa, where their working-class relatives contended with racism, violent crime and exhausting work schedules.

When asking farmers to describe what they most enjoyed about living in Wupperthal, respondents emphasized feelings of safety and serenity. Women who lived alone felt safe in their homes; mothers said they liked living on the mission because they could allow their children to explore the world without fear for their safety; and elders like Marie Ockhuis sensed no danger in taking long walks alone in the mountains. The feeling of safety was so profound that few people felt the need to lock their doors and often slept on the porch *stoep* on hot summer nights. Fights were common among younger men, and some instances of domestic abuse did occur; yet such acts of violence were culturally discouraged, particularly in communities where women were active leaders and had made it known that domestic abusers would be taken to court.[11] The strong sense of physical safety expressed by most women in Wupperthal was remarkable in a post-apartheid nation that more broadly has continued to grapple with high rates of rape, domestic abuse and femicide.

Wupperthalers historically have held education in high regard, but education was stifled under apartheid, when children had to work to help their families survive. This situation was redressed in 1994 when the incoming government legislated compulsory free education for all children through the ninth grade. Mandela's non-conditional Child Support Grant has been instrumental in terms of helping children in Wupperthal complete primary school, particularly among the children of outstations who lodge at the mission school during the week. Wanting their children to grow up safe and happy, urban-dwelling parents often sent their children to live with grandparents in Wupperthal, enabling elders to secure child support funds and children to know their heritage. If Wupperthal's youngsters learned about the broader world as part of their formal education during the school week, they gained an informal education from their grandparents over the weekend and on school breaks, when they learned how to cultivate crops and care for livestock as well as to respect and relate to the Cederberg ecology.

Intergenerational knowledge sharing was not formally developed through apprenticeships as some youth desired. However, it informally occurred in multi-generational households. Having secured at least nine years of formal education, the post-apartheid generation possessed skills that many elders lacked such as the ability to speak in English. Apart from helping semi-literate elders with paperwork, Wupperthal's young adults were interested in digital information technology as a tool for development. In contrast, elders had greater knowledge in relation to agrarian production practices and possessed an intimate understanding of the local ecology, including an awareness of environmental changes over time. Given the prevalence of youth flight, the youth who remained believed that the blending of these knowledges was essential for ensuring Wupperthal's ecocultural resilience. Generational disagreements did occur, but elder–youth relationships generally were positive. According to Paul Zimri, a 26-year-old farmer leader who had lived in Kleinvlei all his life, "we can't be angry for long because we are too close. We walk into each other so anger only lasts one week."

If social affiliation was a primary source of wellbeing, the cultural value of mutual support also helped people survive periods of economic hardship. People regularly participated in the sociocultural life of the community and customs related to social reciprocity helped to reaffirm family and social ties. While young people played sports and formed musical bands, middle-aged adults and elders were active in mission politics and religious life. And when discussing sources of household income, interview respondents often spontaneously expressed a sense of gratitude for the contributions of other family members. People often shifted from discussing their experiences with poverty and deprivation to sharing their feelings of self-determination and emotional connection in conversational midstream. For example, after talking about her experiences with hunger and fears about providing for her family, Patricia shifted the mood of the discussion, saying "I enjoy living here … everything is very quiet, and I am free." In a similar vein, Yvonne[12] stopped talking about her struggle to put food on the table by taking a deep breath and stating, "God and my children give me strength, and being a single mom is the best thing because of the feeling that my children love me and that we can all depend on each other for help."

This sense of relational affiliation extended to other species. During interviews, respondents told us that they spent several hours a day communing with nature, either during breaks from their work or through recreational pursuits such as hiking and swimming. Having recently come of age, Theo[13] told us that he had decided to remain on the mission and work as an organic farmer because he wanted to live in a neighbourly society and did not want to lose the ability to go "hiking in the mountains alone". As the mission's only White resident, Hennie van der Westhuizen had married into the community of Heuningvlei. Welcoming me into a cosy cottage filled with books, Hennie told me that he had moved down a social class when he married but despite the physical hardship, felt "rich beyond belief". He attributed the source of his wealth to a happy marriage and the ability to spend much of his time "reading, writing, and hiking in the mountains". Over in the main village of Wupperthal, Jessica Mouton, who worked at Red Cedar, had started a hiking club with another avid explorer, providing an opportunity for people to hike together. Given the strong respect for nature that Wupperthalers expressed, it was difficult to determine where mission land ended and conservation zones began, for the land was unburdened by litter and largely allowed to remain in its natural state.

Finally, access to basic healthcare represented a key source of resilience. In Wupperthal, a free health clinic provided consultations and dispensed medicines, and clinic nurses visited the various mission communities monthly. The state also provided Wupperthalers with free ambulance service to state hospitals in cases of emergency, which in more remote areas was conducted by helicopter. Most respondents told us that state hospital services were affordable, but when facing protracted health issues, they struggled to access expensive private facilities that provided superior quality. Although the public healthcare system has remained underfunded and is less equipped to deal with major medical problems than the private medical sector, Wupperthal's free clinic and regional state services have enabled people to maintain a rural way of life without losing access to basic medical care.

More-than-representational heritage

'We are raised to look after one another. If a household is struggling, everyone in the community is expected to help out. So even the poor have basic support ... we have little, less than people in the cities, like supermarkets and liquor stores, but actually we are happier than they are. They say to us, you have nothing and we say, yes, but are you happy and they say no. We accept more than they do. We can live with a problem and keep working on it.'

– *Craig Bantom, Farmer Leader of Wupperthal*

If scholars working in Europe have noted that the concept of heritage can be harnessed to revitalize economically marginalized rural landscapes (Bowen and De Master, 2011), scholars operating in the formerly colonized global South note that concepts related to heritage and terroir are enmeshed with histories of dispossession and bondage, such as Sara Besky (2014) describes in a vivid study on Fairtrade Darjeeling tea in India. While the research that I conducted with Wupperthal's Rooibos tea farmers corroborates Besky's findings, raising questions about Fairtrade and terroir-based development approaches, I also find that experiences with marginalization were only one part of Wupperthal's multidimensional heritage, which also included the story of a people who have drawn from multiple ethnic traditions to cultivate Rooibos terroir from the soil of a hardscrabble land.

Given the racialized terrain of South Africa's Rooibos tea industry, large White-owned estates are commercially positioned to benefit from geographical indication rather than the industry's dispossessed farmworkers and small-scale farmers (Coombe et al, 2014). Yet Wupperthalers claim that it is the coloured producers of the eastern Cederberg who embody the Indigenous spirit of Rooibos terroir. Their experience challenges conventional understanding by showing that: (1) heritage and terroir are not the sole domain of European cultural geographies; (2) disembodied notions of pure heritage and timeless terroir are empirically inaccurate; and (3) racial and ethnic identities are neither pure nor static.

The embodied politics of Rooibos terroir

The artisanal production of Rooibos tea was first developed by the Khoe-Sān peoples of the Cederberg who harvested wild Rooibos shrubs by cutting and fermenting their needle-like leaves. Having intermingled with displaced Indigenous communities, the ex-slave societies of the eastern Cederberg are situated at the geographic point of origin for this product. During oral histories, Wupperthal elders recounted childhood experiences with Rooibos during the early twentieth century. From their elders they had learned that 'bushmen'[14] taught ex-slave settlers about a shrub that could be turned into a restorative tea. According to Piet Salamo of Langkloof, a locally renowned wood carver born in 1925, Rooibos was a central component of Wupperthal's historical diet, with families drinking "bush tea for breakfast, lunch, and dinner". Although coffee was popular, it was deemed a luxury, and all the elders we spoke with had helped gather and process wild Rooibos as children. Following the Indigenous method, households harvested the leaves during the hot summer months. After spreading these out to dry, the green leaves were sprinkled with water and covered to ferment, over time taking on their distinctive 'red bush' hue.

In addition to retaining Khoe-Sān production knowledge, Wupperthalers played a direct role in developing seedlings for agricultural cultivation. Having spent a decade travelling the Cederberg as a peddler at the turn of the century, a Russian immigrant by the name of Benjamin Ginsberg opened a shop in Clanwilliam around 1912 to market and sell wild harvested Rooibos tea (Gorelik, 2017). As consumer demand grew, the local ecology became degraded, with White and coloured producers alike burning land to stimulate the germination of wild Rooibos seeds. In the 1930s, Pieter Le Fras Nortier – the Afrikaner district surgeon of Clanwilliam – proposed agricultural field experiments. An ardent naturalist, Nortier was not interested in profiting from seedlings; rather, his objective was to diminish the negative ecological impact caused by excessive *veld* burning. In collaboration with coloured producers and farmworkers who possessed an intimate knowledge of Rooibos ecology, Nortier developed an agricultural variety that 'became the mainstay of the Rooibos industry' (Gorelik, 2017, p 38). Ginsberg used this variety to establish the first international Rooibos trademark under the Eleven O'Clock brand in the mid-1950s, causing Rooibos to become the primary cash crop of the Cederberg.

Under apartheid, the industry centralized, and in the 1980s, the Clanwilliam Rooibos control board mandated pasteurization after a salmonella outbreak. During the transition to democracy, the board restructured into a large processing firm under the name of Rooibos Limited. According to Dr Frans van der Westhuizen, an Afrikaner farmer who founded the processing firm Kings Products in 1996, pasteurization legislation was needed to ensure public health; however, this also meant that new businesses had to acquire the requisite knowledge and technology to decentralize the industry. Alongside Kings Products, Cape Natural Tea Products broke the Rooibos Limited monopoly by acquiring pasteurization technology for its Cape Town-based processing firm in 1996 (Wilson, 2005).

Given South Africa's history of centralized market control, Afrikaner farmers have been wary of any sustainability initiative that might recentralize industry power (Keahey and Murray, 2017). For this reason, White farmers opposed the development of a Right Rooibos biodiversity label that was designed to shift power from buyers to producers by harmonizing sustainability standards and certifications into one auditing system. In contrast, the small-scale farmers of Wupperthal lacked the finances and expertise to manage two market certifications, let alone access other Rooibos sustainability labels. While coloured producers supported the Right Rooibos campaign, the biodiversity label was never instituted, and White-owned estates have continued to capture more than 90 per cent of all Rooibos sales, reproducing the power dynamics of a de-facto White industry (Ives, 2014).

Despite these racial and class-based inequities, the Rooibos industry has substantiated Wupperthal's claims to the quality of small farmer tea through a series of blind taste tests. Not only did industry informants tell me that the tea grown by coloured farmers possesses a superior flavour due to the slower growth of Rooibos at its more arid point of origin, but the excellent quality may also be due to faster fermentation rates and a production process based upon a *savoir faire* handed down through families across generations (Grant, 2007). Considering the systemic scarcity that coloured producers have suffered, the designation of terroir represents a critical opportunity for small-scale farmers to add market value to their tea. Some Fairtrade buyers, such as the US-based Equal Exchange brand, have advocated for small-scale farmer interests by maintaining direct trading relations with the Wupperthal Original Cooperative and by limiting Rooibos purchases to tea produced by small-scale farmers.

Despite opportunities for interracial dialogue and participatory terroir planning, industry marketing campaigns have reified colonial power relations by portraying Rooibos terroir in power insensitive ways. Erasing Wupperthal's heritage, colourblind Rooibos campaigns have perpetuated South African stereotypes about coloured people as lacking in culture and place (Ives, 2017). This failure of interracial connection is unfortunate given the negative impact of neoliberal markets on all Rooibos farmers. When the farmer leaders involved in this project finally met White farmers at an industry event, they hoped to talk to them in break-out sessions as we had initially planned. However, the White farmers in attendance derailed the schedule. Shouting feelings of anger and bitterness over their experience with inequitable markets, the White farmers threatened to walk out of the meeting. After the session ended, several farmer leaders told me they had realized that White farmers were experiencing "the same problems as we are" and expressed a desire for collaboration.[15] Thus, it is important to recognize that while the coloured farmers of the eastern Cederberg claimed Rooibos terroir, they did not assert exclusive ownership. Far from rejecting White claims to terroir, the farmer leaders wanted to work directly with their Afrikaner neighbours on developing Cederberg heritage campaigns that would foster racial healing and benefit the region as a whole.

On a broader scale, Wupperthal's enterprise diversification efforts reflected the diversity of a global fair trade movement in which FTI's certification system was only one network. Formalizing its approach in the 1990s, FTI instituted a product certification framework to govern sustainability standards for agrarian goods like Rooibos tea (Raynolds and Greenfield, 2015). Traditionally situated in the craft sector, the World Fair Trade Organization (WFTO) pursued another direction by developing a guarantee system designed to monitor both ends of the supply chain (Sahan, 2019). Finally, the South African movement has established a Fair Trade Tourism (FTT) certification system to support investments in sustainable and heritage-based tourism (Strambach and Surmelier, 2013).

At Fairtrade South Africa's annual meeting in 2010, an FTT representative presented a plan for developing 'integrated fair trade experiences' that would support tourism investments in FTI-certified farming communities. However, Wupperthal's farmers struggled to navigate dual Fairtrade–organic certification, suggesting that the movement's segregated governance structures are hindering the potential for enterprise diversification. When the farmer leaders and I began our research, Wupperthalers had never heard of the WFTO or FTT systems, and although the farmer leaders saw the value of investing in a broader fair trade economy, there was no clear path for doing so, and the costs were too high.

According to Mook and Overdevest (2020), the institutionalization of FTI standards reflects a credentialist approach to sustainable development that runs counter to its social justice agenda. Credentialism may satisfy global buyers who want production guarantees, but it also reinforces entrenched inequalities through standardized managerial practices that prevent the emergence of more collaborative and relational forms of engagement, thereby reifying authoritarianism in practice. By treating the concepts of social justice and ecological sustainability as technocratic standards for assessment, credentialist approaches may do little more than maintain the detachment of institutional practice from embodied knowledges, identities and experiences.

Institutional shifts

In the early twentieth century, White farmers had formed into racially exclusive cooperatives to access state subsidies, and in 1922 the state authorized these cooperatives to determine and monitor the farmer members receiving benefits (Ducastel and Anseeuw, 2018). During the global recession of the 1930s, White cooperatives were empowered to set prices as commodity control boards. The establishment of a single marketing system for specific products enhanced the collective power of commercial farmers 'in the value chains and in the boards themselves' (p 558). By the time apartheid was established, White agro-business had become a core constituency of the National Party (NP), which curried political favour by continuing to provide estates with access to subsidized finance (Makhaya and Roberts, 2013).

Within 20 years, nearly three-quarters of South Africa's White farmers had joined large industry cooperatives governed by control boards. These public–private bodies managed a neo-colonial political economy that relied upon state subsidies and dispossessed labour to secure the capital for agricultural modernization. However, White producers did not equally benefit from the apartheid system, for control boards also functioned as industry cartels. To protect incumbent interests, the boards consolidated processing, packaging and distribution channels, preventing the emergence of competitive enterprise (Mncube and Grimbeek, 2016).

The South African government has introduced Broad-Based Black Economic Empowerment (BEE) legislation to address these structural inequities. Within the agricultural sector, the AgriBEE system is supposed to ensure the rights of farmworkers, but as the state has lacked the capacity to monitor estates, Fair Trade South Africa has filled this gap by certifying estates that are willing to bring farmworkers into management and ownership. These moves have met with mixed outcomes. In the wine industry, for example, some estates have become collectively Black-owned, but the industry more broadly has struggled to reconcile its racialized past. Given the national focus on the plight of farmworkers, the plight of small-scale farmers largely has been ignored. While the state has pursued small-scale land restitution projects with specific Indigenous groups, such as the Khoe-Sān of the Kgalagadi desert, these piecemeal efforts have yet to make an impact upon the broader region (Dikgang and Muchapondwa, 2016). Some rural coloured communities have begun to reclaim Indigenous identities in a bid to secure recognition of their ancestral ties to the land; yet for multi-rooted communities like Wupperthal, such a reframing of identity would obscure other meaningful aspects of their cultural heritage. By refusing to agree upon a term to signify their race, the farmer leaders challenged me to learn how to discuss structural power imbalances without reimposing categorical frames that limit the scope of who people are.

Identity and belonging

If terroir marketing campaigns tend to whitewash the historical reality of colonial violence, conventional heritage campaigns commodify and fetishize Indigenous identity (Carrigan, 2011). The critical heritage discourse offers an important corrective by emphasizing the need for power-sensitive and culturally situated engagement (Waterton, 2014). Within this terrain, studies are challenging Euro-Western assumptions about the nature of knowledge and reality, illustrating the importance of Indigenous knowledge to sustainable heritage development (Battiste and Youngblood Henderson, 2000). Yet the tendency of the heritage discourse to distil the complex nexus of heritage and identity into the binary categories of European or Indigenous has obscured the fluidity of cultures and identities, creating the false impression that people do not mix, and that cultures do not evolve over time.

South Africa's multiracial history raises questions about the meaning and limits of Indigeneity. For example, the National Heritage Council has announced plans 'to promote and protect Indigenous knowledge systems' through a heritage-based model of enterprise development (DAC, 2018). Yet the Council does not specify whether the term Indigenous solely signifies people who explicitly identify as Khoe-Sān (approximately 1 per cent of the population) or if its interpretation also encompasses the knowledges of coloured people with some Khoe-Sān heritage, such as Wupperthal. As Blacks often were labelled 'Native' during the apartheid era, one can only assume that the definition of Indigeneity extends to Bantu groups who entered the region approximately 1,500 years ago. Yet more problematic is the Afrikaner claim to Indigeneity as a White African tribe that suffered under British colonial rule. To forge an accommodation with diversity, Mandela's government drew from Ubuntu philosophy to posit 'a South African identity that was at one and the same time plural and various' or in other words 'co-extensive, not oppositional' (Boehmer, 2011, p 270). While his approach has provided a more relational, embodied and fluid understanding of identity and belonging, it also has opened the door to colourblind and racially insensitive heritage investments.

During the initial transition to democracy, the Truth and Reconciliation Commission (TRC) articulated a restorative justice vision of heritage development. By combining material reparation with multicultural learning, it was argued that heritage investments could become a space for interracial healing (Meskell and Scheermeyer, 2008). However, in the neoliberal landscape of enterprise development, scholars have found that South African heritage investments are benefitting White operatives without providing reparation to racially marginalized communities. In an in-depth study with Black communities bordering Kruger National Park, South Africa's largest game reserve, Meskell (2011) found that White commercial actors were fetishizing generic African culture to attract tourists to the park. As tourists were shuttled from White-owned lodges to fortressed conservation lands, they only superficially interacted with Black people who were paid to perform an exotic form of African-ness that had no connection to their own culture.

The creole peoples of the Caribbean offer further insight into the question of coloured identity. According to Knörr (2010), the Caribbean experienced a similar process of colonialism as South Africa, as African slaves intermingled with displaced Indigenous people and European Whites. Yet people in this region underwent a process of Indigenization that has helped them become recognized as belonging to the land, whereas coloured South Africans typically are viewed in non-Native terms. Knörr argues that this difference may be due to the fact that coloured South Africans have failed to creolize, that is to crystallize their multiple identities into a singular whole. The broader discourse on coloured identity likewise finds that mixed-race South Africans are ambivalent about their racial identity. It is important to remember that the coloured label was externally imposed on diverse groups of people who did not fit into the binary world of Black or White, and that this imposition occurred through a stigmatizing process of racial classification and segregation (Adhikari, 2006). In other words, the term 'coloured' does not recognize the degree of cultural variation and racial expression found within South Africa's coloured communities.

Challenging the common belief that coloured people are lacking in place and culture, some coloured communities in the northern reaches of the South African Cape have begun to reclaim their Khoe-Sān identities to showcase their heritage as the original inhabitants of an ancient ancestral land (Besten, 2009). In the southern Cape, a vibrant Cape Malay culture has evolved, with a distinctly Muslim identity and a musical and food heritage informed by the fusion of Afro-Asian influences (Martin, 2013). However, in the Cederberg Mountains, coloured people espoused strong feelings of ambivalence, and the farmer leaders failed to come to a consensus on an appropriate label to signify their racial heritage. If the leaders recognized the persistence of racial inequity, they also felt confined by a racial categorization system that was socially constructed according to foreign notions about the nature of blood and ancestry.

Expressing a more embodied understanding, Wupperthalers defined themselves as a working-class society. People identified as small-scale producers, as Moravian and as South African. Wupperthalers only became 'coloured' when White development actors or tourists entered the mission and feelings of racial difference arose. The detachment from racial identity that many Wupperthalers expressed may be due to the fact that their collective consciousness has evolved at distance from the hegemonic discourse of modern-colonial power (Bilbe, 1999). Although mission communities experienced systemic underdevelopment and racial marginalization during two centuries of colonialism and apartheid, the rugged and remote landscape historically has provided people with refuge from the racial violence and categorically proscribed existence occurring elsewhere. As Lina Salamo of Langkloof told me when recounting tales of a life spent in the embrace of a tight-knit community, "apartheid affected other places, but here, people stood together and lived well".

Living in marshy hollows and surrounded by red-rock mountains, the people of Wupperthal performed their Cederberg heritage as part of an everyday rhythm of togetherness and solitude. Communities relied upon one another for entertainment and support, with extended families travelling between hamlets to visit one another and invoking interfamilial ties to reconcile divisions wrought by the Rooibos conflict. Through fireside tales and by teaching the fundamentals of animal husbandry and agriculture, elders taught children to appreciate their cultural heritage and to value land and freedom. Church leaders discouraged materialistic perspectives and feelings of superiority by emphasizing the religious values of mutual respect, generosity and humility. Grounded in Moravian language, this local iteration of Ubuntu philosophy reminded people that individual and collective wellbeing are interdependent. Community members encouraged one another to 'go better yourself' through hard work and by taking advantage of development projects that would enable their communities to thrive.

While the Cederberg rhythm of togetherness and solitude provided people with a sense of peace in their everyday lives, systemic material shortages necessitated collaborative enterprise development. When discussing strategies to improve commercial endeavours, farmers routinely stressed the importance of standing together to achieve common goals; thus, collaborative enterprise investments were grounded in Cederberg heritage. However, Cederberg heritage also emphasized an appreciation for solitude. When sharing what they most enjoyed about their lives, several Wupperthalers said they were willing to endure the hardship of agrarian life to retain freedom from bosses and externally imposed work schedules. Affiliation with nature was a key feature of Cederberg identity. People routinely spent time communing with land and other species by resting on porch *stoeps* with breathtaking mountain views. Younger and more mobile elders also gardened, hiked and swam in rivers during hot and dry summers.

Wupperthal's story corroborates the claims of broader heritage and food studies that posit a more fluid and poststructural interpretation of identity. At the time of my research, women had moved into community leadership positions that, under apartheid, were designated for men. When explaining this cultural shift, women leaders invoked an 'historical interpretation of Moravian scripture' that recognized the ability of people to move beyond the proscribed social relations of those experienced in biblical times (Keahey, 2018). Farmer leaders informed me that categorical logic was a foreign way of thinking. Whereas Wupperthalers recognized and, to some degree, engaged in categorically proscribed relations, for example by maintaining traditional gender roles or encouraging youth to respect elders, local identities were fairly fluid and shifted in relation to one another. Far from being relegated to a dead past, Wupperthal's sense of heritage was alive, interactive and dynamically evolving.

Scholars should be careful not to romanticize communities where people are struggling with systemic scarcity. However, it is equally important that scholars begin acknowledging what marginalized people in the global South have to teach us about living sustainably. No matter how kindly intentioned the elite core of the world-system may claim to be, this collective body is unlikely to deliver any meaningful solutions to the planetary harm we humans are inflicting, for these problems are a consequence of elite praxis. As Audre Lorde spoke in her address to the women of the American academy in 1979, 'the master's tools will never dismantle the master's house' (Lorde, 2015 [1981]).

Like Rosalba Icaza (2017), whose decolonial scholarship is situated in the different cultural terrain of Latin America, I have found that people who inhabit the liminal spaces of the world-system have retained otherwise knowledges that offer transformative insight into the nature and meaning of our collective existence. These alternative frames challenge master narratives about development, sustainability, identity and heritage. In Wupperthal, most people suffered from poverty but nevertheless found pleasure in living a life largely off the grid. Most people did not have enough to eat, but everyone had time to participate in the cultural life of the mission, in togetherness and in solitude, and in close connection to the land and other species. Their capacity to affiliate with nature was a critical source of wellbeing, for Cederberg's clean air, burbling brooks, and shady nooks provided people with respite, helping people to heal from the wounds that suffering inflicts. By investing in sustainable enterprise, Wupperthalers sought to conserve the land and culture that gave meaning to their everyday lives while carving out a more prosperous future for their children and the generations to come after.

I too have struggled to navigate my own pathway between tradition and modernity and its correlates of identity and heritage. Raised by progressive parents in the culturally traditional world of northern Utah, I grew up experiencing a similar rhythm of togetherness and solitude in close connection with family, community and nature. Like Wupperthalers in the Cederberg, I possess a deep love of the glorious landscapes and hardy species of the American West. Yet my encounters with the afterlife of apartheid have taught me hard lessons. I have learned how to recognize the authoritarian influences and deep-seated inequities embedded in my settler colonial heritage and everyday social existence.

If my privileged race and class positionality set me apart from small-scale Rooibos tea farmers, my outsider status enabled us to open up to one another. Talking over meals, we found relatable ground in our various struggles to navigate the impulses of tradition and modernity. From the leaders, I learned that sustainability is not simply about safeguarding one's land and heritage, but it also involves shifting my own awareness from one of categorical detachment to one of relational knowing. In so doing, I have come to accept a certain level of ambiguity in my work, for I have come to understand that one cannot understand life in its interconnected flow by drawing hard categorical lines. In the next and final chapter, I bring the more-than-representational histories of South Africa and Latvia into conversation with the divergent knowledges informing development and social change. The decolonizing theory of development that I construct softens identitarian lines to lay bare the authoritarian logic and warring impulses undergirding modern rational science and conventional approaches to development.

7

Decolonizing Development

The corridors of power

The corridors of power are busy places
There are discourses
debates
analyses
assessments
and evaluations
monitoring too.

Then there's policy-formulation
policy review
and strategies
for successful implementation.

The corridors of power are busy places

Next there's the inevitable exchange of ideas
it's a proposal, or other recommendations
or even an inquiry when some or other
misdemeanour has been committed.

The corridors of power are busy places

Too busy to nod in greeting
or acknowledgement of their presence
the invisible women
slipping in and out
bringing tea and refreshments.

The corridors of power are busy places

— Gertrude Fester, South African poet

The existential dimension of development

The early twenty-first century sits at the apex of the Anthropocene, a new geological epoch that has come into being over the last century. The Anthropocene is marked by what Christopher Chase-Dunn (2013) has called a converging set of social and environmental catastrophes, ranging from climate crisis and mass extinction events to sharp increases in social inequality, and the re-entrenchment of authoritarianism in response to global precarity. The Cenozoic Era in which the Anthropocene more broadly is placed is known as the Age of Mammals, and given the demise of large mammals and birds occurring now, the climate scientist Roger Barry (2020) suggests that Cenozoic may be ending.

Unlike previous mass extinction events, however, ours has been induced by human activity, wrought by our dependency upon fossil fuels and more than 4,700 forever chemicals, comprised of per- and polyfluorinated alkyl substances (PFAS) that do not occur in nature (Chambers et al, 2021). Introduced in the 1940s, PFAS now are found in everything, from food packaging and cookware, to cosmetics, electronics, cleaning fluids and fire-fighting foams. PFAS have been found in every ecosystem on Earth, including in the blood, breastmilk, and umbilical cords of humans and other species, and magnifying across recent generations via a process of bioaccumulation (Kempisty and Racz, 2021). Once inside the body, these chemicals mimic hormones, disrupting the endocrine system upon which reproduction depends. Since the 1970s, the industrialized global North has witnessed rising rates of sperm-count depletion and female infertility. Moreover, the widespread practice of toxic waste dumping on or near Indigenous lands has resulted in a decline in the birth of boys in relation to girls, with such trends forecasting 'the death of birth' (Hawken, 1993, p 19).

Our collective inaction in the face of the crisis of the Anthropocene suggests that our minds, bodies and spirits have been deeply colonized by a hyper-rationalized world-system frozen in endless Cold War. Yet we have an opportunity to change the fate of our species if a critical mass of people around the world commit to existential change by engaging in three broad actions: (1) speaking truth to power; (2) cultivating a transformative consciousness; and (3) enacting relationships, practices and systems that support the development of socially just, culturally creative and environmentally sustainable ways of life. In this chapter, I coalesce a wide body of knowledge traditions to unpack the existential dimension of development and to articulate a decolonizing praxis of social change.

Sustainable development and the subversion of a transformative ideal

In 1987, the World Commission on Environment and Development (WCED) published *Our Common Future* to map out a plan for social change. Calling for the protection of future generations, this report gave life to the 1992 Earth Summit in Rio de Janeiro, where the mood must have felt revolutionary given the concurrent collapse of the Soviet and apartheid regimes. The delegates in attendance included the final Soviet president and environmental activist, Mikhail Gorbachev (2006), who took advantage of this global moment of glasnost to call for a democratic and peacebuilding approach to development. After Rio, Gorbachev helped form an international commission comprised of scientists, spiritual leaders, philosophers and activists from around the world, including such global South feminists as Wangari Maathai (2003), the founder of Kenya's environmental Green Belt Movement. After great deliberation, the most diverse commission in modern development history published an intercultural ethic of sustainable development, commonly known as the Earth Charter (2000). Detailed in Figure 7.1, the Charter's 16 principles were grounded in four philosophical pillars that strikingly decentre the influence of capital.

While the Charter secured thousands of endorsements from social and environmental organizations, Brundtland's commercialized offspring, the three-pillar 'People, Planet & Profit' model, came to dominate global development policy and practice in the 2000s (Pichler, 2013). According to Susan Strange (2015), who produced an in-depth analysis of this economy in *Casino Capitalism,* the neoliberal revolution had erased material restrictions to capital, empowering financiers to transform markets into a gaming club for the global power elite. As banks sold bets on our collective futures, alternatives to development either were silenced or subsumed into the neoliberal capitalist logic of the aughts (Okereke, 2008). Succumbing to the free-market siren of limitless horizons, global development failed to take advantage of a potentially consequential moment of geopolitical thaw. Far from negotiating mechanisms that would advance the peacebuilding goals of the Earth Charter, global governance instituted instead partnerships with multinational corporations, enabling the masters of capital to rebrand themselves as the captains of sustainability.

Dominated by the interests of powerful oil producing nations, the 2021 UN Climate Summit, COP26, rejected any meaningful plan to mitigate the perfect storm of climate change facing the world today. This does not mean, however, that these nations were unaware of the severity of the problem. Since the market collapse of 2008, the political economy of the world-system has begun to shift from a neoliberal to a neomercantilist formation, wherein corporate – state collusion is producing an 'arms race' in a scramble for territorial control over the planet's diminishing natural resources (Nadesan and Keahey, 2022). Among the COP26 delegates of 27 powerful nations

Figure 7.1: Earth Charter principles

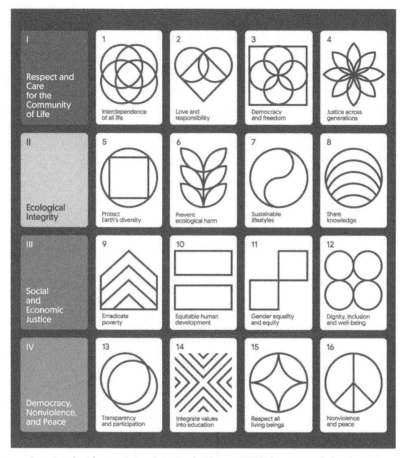

Source: Reprinted with permission from Earth Charter (2020) https://earthcharter.org/

were a consortium of 503 fossil fuel lobbyists who not only outnumbered the delegates of the eight nations most affected by climate change, but who also were more than double the size of the UN's Indigenous constituency (McGrath, 2021). Beyond COP26, the global development discourse has continued to rely upon technocratic sustainability solutions, even when their own scientific reports acknowledge that these approaches are incapable of solving complex challenges (Keahey, 2020).

This inability to change may in part be due to the monocultural influence of ecological modernization theory (EMT) in corporate, national and global governance. Paradoxically assuming that capitalist technologies can be redirected to solve the problems that capitalism has caused, EMT has empowered capital to commander and adulterate alternatives to development (Buttel, 2000).

Scholars who have examined the construction of UN Sustainable Development Goals (SDGs) suggest that EMT's faith in modern rational technologies is misguided. In a study produced by Weber and Weber (2020), the authors show how the UN deployed EMT as an 'inevitable' choice for guiding goal setting, engendering the ideological erasure of other possible approaches during the goal setting process. In a similar vein, Watene and Yap (2015) find that 'the dominant paradigm of goal setting, data collection and measurement – in its universal applicability' drove the erasure of Indigenous contributions from the discussion. As a result, the UN has centred economic goals while ignoring issues pertaining to culture, values and heritage that are the critical inner dimension of sustainability. Given the technocratic scope of the means of implementation, the SDG project is likely to exacerbate, rather than ameliorate social and environmental problems.

The decolonial and Indigenous critique of modernity

Angela Roothaan (2019) unpacks the cognitive forces undergirding these unfortunate developments. Contrasting modern, postcolonial and Indigenous relations to nature, she finds that European Enlightenment scholars who participated in the revival of ancient Greek rationalism reified the imperial logical fallacy of inherent difference, a mindset cultivated through the cognition of categorical separation. René Descartes (1596–1650), a French mathematician working in the Aristotelean tradition, founded the modern European branch of philosophy when he posited the rational mindset of scientific 'man' to be the sole source of living consciousness. Separating mind from matter in his dictum, 'I think therefore I am', Descartes sought to advance scientific method as a systematic and objective examination of natural phenomena. Yet he also redefined living nature in passive terms, with a sweep of the magician's hand converting most life into morally dead matter. The ensuing shift in European consciousness taught 'the scientist who cuts open a live animal to see how the heart works' to no longer feel moral pain for inflicting suffering on a living being (Roothaan, 2019, p 45).

One century later, Immanuel Kant (1724–1804) aligned rational logic with empirical science. This 'father' of the German Enlightenment sought a morality free from the corrupting influences of nature and religion; yet he supplanted the monotheistic devotion of his Pietistic Lutheran childhood with a zeal for monocultural science, therein rebranding the cognition of his forebearers in a secular guise. Rejecting dialectic logic, or conversation with difference, as a mere philosophy of illusion, Kant (1998 [1781]) called for rational reasoning to become grounded in empirical human experience. Although his intention was to strengthen scientific method by combining ideal and material knowledge, Kant's logic freed rational scholars from having to relate to other bodies of knowledge. Viewing humans who did not separate their identities from 'family, clan, the village or the land' as animals lacking in moral reason, Kant reinforced the notion that the rational master alone possessed sentience (Roothaan, 2019, p 46).

Around the turn of the twentieth century, the German sociologist, Max Weber (2012 [1920]), advanced critical theory by deconstructing the concept of rationalism. His work posited the emergence of a disenchanted modern world where 'narrow specialists without mind, pleasure-seekers without heart' would, in their conceit, come to nullify the conditions that enable life to survive (p 124). In the late twentieth century, the Black feminist scholar, Audre Lorde (2015 [1981], p 90), made a similar claim in a speech to the academy from a different social positionality. Arguing that 'the tools of the master' can only allow for 'the most narrow parameters of change' to become possible, Lorde called for feminists to reorient social research and practice from a model of oppression to one of emancipation (p 94). The feminist science of intersectionality that Lorde participated in founding has sought to replace the either/or framing of rational Western logic with the both/and cognition needed to address complex social challenges (Collins and Bilge, 2016).

More recent decolonial scholarship posits that **epistemic disobedience** is needed to preserve independent thought in a world-system colonized by monocultural science. According to Walter Mignolo (2009), we must figure out how to delink 'from the illusion of the zero point epistemology' that shackles our consciousness to the warring logic of imperial gnosis (p 160). It is only by reconciling the rupture between tradition and modernity that human societies may begin to establish transmodern societies that are able to connect these social forces in culturally creative ways.

There is an urgent need for us to remember that the universal nature of our existence is by no means discrete, but rather fundamentally interconnected with a complex web of biosocial life in both vast and minute ways. In the late twentieth century, particle physicists confirmed the presence of this quantum interconnectedness (Bohm and Hiley, 1977). Finding that subatomic particles are capable of direct connection across the vast terrain of spacetime, the field of physics has had to contend with the 'radically new notion of unbroken wholeness of the entire universe' (p 207). In his articulation of relational philosophy, Gregory Cajete (2022), a Santa Clara Pueblo scholar situated in New Mexico, reminds Western science that the concept of quantum interconnectedness is by no means new to Indigenous societies, whose traditional bodies of knowledge describe our intimate and direct connection to other species on Earth as well as to our more distant relations, the stars. As a relational science, Pueblo philosophy joins other minoritized bodies of knowledge that provide the cognitive means for dismantling authoritarian monocultures that threaten our collective demise.

Authoritarian monocultures

In this section, I return to the three eras of great transformation that I introduced in Chapter 1 to flesh out the concept of authoritarian monocultures. Defined in the Preface as a colonizing mode of existence, this concept advances the pathbreaking scholarship of Vandana Shiva (1993), who inscribed the term 'monocultures of the mind' to explain the relationship between the industrialization of agriculture in India and the agrarian **epistemicide** that occurred in the wake of knowledge homogenization. I posit that authoritarian monocultures are grounded in the imperial logic of categorical separateness, a mode of thinking that likely emerged during the first wave of Western modernization that occurred in the warring city states of ancient Afro-Eurasia. In our current Digital Age, authoritarian monocultures are again expanding their reach into the most remote corners of our planet, colonizing minds and bodies alike. Within academe, technorational systems of control are minoritizing the humanities, cultures and arts (Santos, 2014), and in agriculture, robotic technologies are driving the formation of mega farms that are sacrificing human and animal welfare to achieve hyper-standardized economies of scale (Emel and Neo, 2010).

Yet the world's earliest agrarian civilizations did not develop in homogenous or linear ways. In *The Dawn of Everything*, David Graeber and David Wengrow (2021) examine an emerging body of anthropological and archaeological evidence, arriving at the conclusion that prehistoric agrarian societies were wildly divergent in their modes of social organization. It would appear that, in this heady mix of social experimentation, a mode of hierarchical existence arose, planting the seeds for what would become an authoritarian and monocultural way of life. While imperial societies did form around the world, it was in the ancient Afro-Eurasian realm that the first movement toward Western modernization occurred, and a reading of the physical and philosophical record provides some insight as to how.

Anatomically modern humans first emerged in Africa during the Middle Pleistocene period, approximately 300,000 years ago and subsequently spread across the world during the Late Pleistocene, mixing with other archaic humans who had evolved elsewhere (Eswaran et al, 2005). At the dawn of this Great Human Trek, societies had begun to produce a sophisticated array of Stone Age technologies, engendering a human naissance in artistic, cultural and linguistic centres of knowledge, production and trade. This Palaeolithic naissance gave rise to Neolithic innovation, marked by the revolutionary development of metallurgy during the Bronze Age, which began in Western Asia and the Near East around 3300 BCE (Graeber and Wengrow 2021). If some Neolithic societies chose to harness human innovation to develop peaceful urban collectives based upon a small-scale mode of horticultural production, other cultural complexes began shifting to the more invasive technology of agriculture, which involved the mass production of crops in open fields. According to Christopher Chase-Dunn and Bruce Lerro (2016), these early transitions to agriculture occurred in patriarchal societies, where elites rationalized the production of food to accumulate capital and grow in power and prestige.

These patriarchal formations produced a succession of warring city states whose hierarchical mode of existence expanded in all directions through the colonization of new territories and the enslavement of conquered peoples. Accumulating capital through dispossessed and displaced labour, elites funded the development of technologies and rationalized management systems in pursuit of yet more wealth. The violent means by which these ancient states functioned inevitably resulted in social and ecological devastation, political and economic decline and cultural collapse, with few empires surviving more than a few hundred years (Diamond, 2011). What is missing from most analyses of these historical events, however, is an inquiry into the worldsense of people who inhabited the temporal borderlands between an ancient and egalitarian mode of existence and a proto-modern and patriarchal way of life. A reading of what some scholars believe to be the oldest book in the world provides further insight into the cognitive negotiation that occurred at such pivotal moments of social transformation.

During the Fifth Dynasty of Egypt, circa 2388 BCE, a bureaucratic functionary wrote *The Teachings of Ptah Hotep*. This ancient book elucidated a set of proverbs to produce an ethic for social development that arguably shaped the broader formation of African and Western moral philosophies during later ages (Hilliard et al, 1987; Sesanti, 2018). In my reading of this book, I find Hotep's articulation of social ethics to be paradoxically wise and cruel. In one breath, this Egyptian vizier claims that right conduct is 'more hidden than emeralds, yet it may be found among maids of the grindstones', his adulation of low-ranking women directly challenging the patriarchal and stratified world in which he lived (Hilliard et al, 1987, p 17). Yet in another breath, Hotep proclaims, 'God will hate him who crosses you. His guilt was determined in the womb', suggesting lived experience with self-other rupture (p 22). In following passages, Hotep sows the imperial seeds of authoritarian monoculture by commanding the reader to 'accept the authority of your leaders' (p 29) and to 'punish firmly and chastise soundly' those who transgress the law (p 31).

Given the gulf in spacetime that stands between Hotep's existence and that of my own, it is unclear whether the contradictory nature of his proverbial teachings was a product of his cognition or an effect of translation. Nevertheless, I remain struck by the paradox of an ancient book that proclaims the values of generosity and humility alongside those of rigidity and hate. Considering the temporal borderlands in which Hotep lived, it is entirely plausible that his cognitive development had been dualistically informed by an archaic set of Nile River Valley values – handed down by his horticultural and art-loving ancestors who had lived in egalitarian social units in a time before pharaohs – and a proto-modernizing logic of patriarchal hierarchy that was coming into being during the early dynasties of ancient Egypt, when an emerging body of rulers were busy establishing the foundation for a highly stratified civilization that would enable pharaohs to be mummified and entombed in opulence while the poorest among them slaved and starved.

Moving ahead in the longue durée sweep of time to the onset of the Industrial Revolution, the authoritarian monoculture of European feudalism had morphed into a colonial slave system in the wake of mercantilist renaissance (Brook, 2008). During the late medieval era, the revitalization of ancient Greco-Roman knowledge challenged the authority of Rome, and the concurrent rise of a mercantilist bourgeoisie disrupted the power of kings. In the late eighteenth and early nineteenth centuries, European mercantilists – who had been enriched by the capital produced by slaves on their colonial plantations – started building factories in Great Britain, sparking the Industrial Revolution (Polanyi, 1957). Harnessed to this modernizing movement, rational Western science demonstrated its capacity to achieve rapid innovation, delivering a marvellous array of technologies that enabled Western Europe to transform from a rural, religious, and agrarian condition into a secular, urban, and industrial one in the space of one century (Rostow, 1960).

Yet these achievements occurred at great cost to European societies and their far-flung colonial territories. European serfs – who had been displaced through the privatization of land, and who were persecuted for their involvement in religious movements that challenged the power structures of their day – emigrated en masse to colonies in search of freedom. Once in these new territories, however, they reproduced the authoritarian monocultures that they had sought to escape, this time proclaiming themselves to be the masters of colonized subjects.

A reading into the first geographical site of modern-colonial conquest provides further insight into the cognition undergirding this shift. In 1493, the Genoese explorer Christopher Columbus landed upon the shores of the Caribbean Island of Hispaniola, having been funded by the Spanish monarchy to seek spices, gold and wealth. The subsequent Spanish conquest of **Abya Yala**[1] initially was justified in accordance with an authoritarian monocultural interpretation of Christianity, which European empires previously had deployed to rationalize wealth-generating Crusades against Islamic infidels and Baltic pagans. In the wake of the European Enlightenment, the instrumental reasoning undergirding fundamentalist Christianity was reformed in a secular guise. According to Kaye and Stråth (2000), scientific rationalism provided modernizing states with the means for justifying ecological and cultural genocide as the unfortunate, but necessary, cost of development.

As a decolonial feminist scholar, María Lugones (2010) clarifies the patriarchal dynamics undergirding these colonial formations. In her research on the Conquest of the Americas, Lugones finds that the European system of compulsory heteronormativity provided colonizers with the dichotomous logic needed to develop a racialized social system that would serve colonial interests. Segregating people into two discrete sexes, the heteronormative dictate ascribed gender hierarchy, in part by identifying female sexuality as evil and male sexuality as divine.

In colonial Latin America, the European bourgeois man was centred in public leadership, not for his abilities, but rather for his ethnicity and sex, as colonizing forces assumed him to be the sole lifeform capable of rational reason. In contrast, the colonial role of the European bourgeois woman was to reproduce 'race and capital through her sexual purity, passivity, and being homebound in the service of the white, European, bourgeois man' (Lugones, 2010, p 743). Like the European woman, Indigenous peoples and enslaved Africans of all sexes were presumed to be 'uncontrollably sexual and wild' if not under the constant surveillance of the master; and, in accordance with the system of compulsory heterosexuality, Indigenous and Black expressions of gender and sexual diversity served as evidence for such claims (p 743). Whether in religious or scientific guise, the authoritarian monocultural logic of categorical separation enabled European colonizers to justify the sexual violation of racialized women's bodies and the terror inflicted upon gender divergent Indigenous peoples – whose bodies were fed alive to dogs and whose vaginas were turned into hats – as a necessary act; indeed, a civilizing mission.

In her work on patriarchal territoriality, Rita Segato (2016) has advanced the decolonial feminist discourse by defining the collective mood of the Industrial Revolution in terms of hysteria. According to Segato, early capitalist formations replaced the reciprocal relations of village life with the categorical relations of the modern public sphere. Not only did this sphere move patriarchy from the traditional margins to the modern-colonial centre of existence, but the public sphere was shallow and combative, sundering the more intimate relationships that had shaped life in earlier times.

The formation of these modernizing forces served to relegate women's spaces, knowledges and roles to a minoritized private sphere, causing women to experience collective trauma. Expressed in the form of anxiety and agitation, this trauma was interpreted by a modernizing body of elite male European knowledge as hysteria. In the late nineteenth and early twentieth centuries, continental psychoanalysts developed a host of theories to explain the neurosis of the times. Rather than listening to patients like 'Dora' who expressed their lived experiences with gender inequity and the toll that it took on their mental health, the modern rational psychoanalyst, Sigmund Freud deduced that hysteria was a result of oedipal complex. For

Freud, women who did not conform to European dictate of compulsory heteronormativity by developing an appropriately passive female sexuality had failed in childhood to put aside their sexual desire for father and form a more appropriate attachment to mother (Bernheimer, 1990).

The post-Second World War era witnessed the emergence of a modern-industrial development regime, ruled by International Governance Organizations (IGOs). Having emerged from the war as the most powerful nations in the First World, the United States and the United Kingdom established a rationalized and economistic approach to global development, instituting the World Bank and International Monetary Fund (IMF) during the United Nations Bretton Woods Conference in 1944. Accompanying this political development, a generation of mid-century modernization scholars rebranded coloniality in accordance with the prevailing ideology, redefining the former imperial nations of the global North as 'developed' and the former colonized nations of the global South as 'developing'.

Trained in elite British and US universities, this cadre of White male scholars theorized development as a linear and universal project. In *The Stages of Economic Growth*, the American economist Walt Rostow (1960) used the metaphor of airplanes to describe a superior Euro-American world whose planes had reached cruise control and an inferior developing world comprised of agrarian societies that had yet to get off the ground. From his privileged position at Harvard, Alex Inkeles (1969) deployed the same monocultural logic in *Making Men Modern*, where he called for developing states to school their 'men in modern attitudes' so as to eradicate the traditional 'attitudes, values, and ways of acting' that hindered 'economic modernization' (p 208).

Like Ptah Hotep, Alex Inkeles' consciousness was shaped by the modern-colonial spacetime in which he resided. The cognitive underpinnings of *Making Men Modern* echoes the North American 'kill the Indian, save the man' doctrine that had led to the formation of Indian boarding schools as part of the ongoing occupation of Turtle Island (Alejandro et al, 2020). According to Paulo Freire (1970), a Brazilian pedagogical scholar who examined these trends from an anticolonial lens, these modernist policies were part of the colonial 'banking system of education'. Designed to ensure a ready supply of compliant labour, this banking system has been operationalized through the deployment of credentialed educators who are tasked with depositing approved knowledge into the minds of morally dead students whose only role lie in 'receiving, filing, and storing the deposits' (p 58).

If the banking system developed during the violent conquest and colonization of the Americas, the silencing of divergent ecologies of knowledge has severed people around the world from their rich cultural, linguistic and philosophical heritage (Santos, 2014). The systemic nature of epistemicide has been so widespread that critical scholars – who themselves have been trained in accordance with banking system precepts – have found it nearly impossible to educate students or conduct research in non-colonizing ways (Chilisa, 2009).

In the 300 centuries since the European Enlightenment, disciplines such as physics, biology and sociology have advanced, with increasingly sophisticated tools uncovering evidence of interconnected systems (Curtin, 2005). Yet the ideal logic governing scientific research has yet to evolve in connection with these advances in empirical understanding. Not only have scholars failed to revisit the assumptions undergirding Enlightenment concepts such as the individualistic notion of 'human rights', but scientific protocols continue to assume the discrete and superior existence of the expert, whose disembodied mind has been trained to be morally detached in pursuit of the ultimate truth. Consequently, modern rational science has become the new global religion: corrupted by power, its high priests have been morally absolved from the devastating consequences of the technologies they produce for their political and economic masters, whether in the form of forever chemicals or nuclear warheads.

The military industrial complex that emerged during the Eisenhower administration of the mid-twentieth century generates revenue for a select power elite through treadmills of production and destruction. Defined by Hooks and Smith (2013) as the co-constituted processes of endless accumulation and warfare, these treadmills are generating a convergence in social, economic and environmental catastrophes. Returning to Segato's work on the patriarchal territoriality of capitalist empire (2016), the deepening commodification of all aspects of social existence has caused the world-system to transition from the Industrial zeitgeist of hysteria to the Late Modern curse of psychopathy. The existential question facing the world today is whether we can turn away from authoritarian monocultural pathways in time to save ourselves, our species and our planet from needless suffering and mass extinction. Given the failure of modern rational logic to solve the problems that it has caused, what other knowledges may help us find our way, as we seek to heal our fractured selves, societies and planet?

Egalitarian ecocultures

Let us return to the Axial Age, but from the differing perspective of societies that had not yet been colonized. Precolonial Latvia and South Africa may have existed at distance from the core of the Afro-Eurasian world-system, but long-distance trade networks likely served as conduits for information exchange. Assuming ancient Latvians and South Africans possessed some knowledge of the distant empires with whom they traded, why didn't these tribes seek power and prestige by modernizing in the same way? In the same vein as Jared Diamond (2011), I posit that the free societies of the Axial Age actively chose to avoid the violence and cyclical collapses occurring at the core of the world-system by retaining an egalitarian set of values and practices that enabled them to live in peace. Defined in the Preface as an emancipatory mode of existence, egalitarian ecocultures are rooted in Indigenous cosmovisions that recognize the interconnected nature of reality.

An inquiry into the social organization of precolonial civilizations suggests that societies have more agency to determine the course of their development than Western science has assumed. Recent archaeological evidence has found that ancient societies sometimes chose to change course in response to systemic crises, rather than falling into the predictable pattern of imperial growth and collapse. In precolonial Mesoamerica, for example, Teotihuacan evolved as an egalitarian city similar in size to ancient Rome. It formed around the year 0, when people across the region were fleeing a series of volcanic eruptions in their homelands (Graeber and Wengrow, 2021). To establish a unified civic society, the leaders of Teotihuacan invested in monument building. This required the sacrifice of natural resources, human labour and human life, which occurred through ritualized killings. However, instead of becoming stratified as other Mesoamerican societies had done, the citizens of Teotihuacan chose a different path. Around 300 CE, people looted, desecrated and burned down the temple-based power structure, permanently halting pyramid construction and ritualized killings. Instead, what entered into the archaeological record was a vital era of city-state democracy, brought about through 'an extraordinary flow of urban resources into the provision of excellent stone-build housing, not just for the wealthy or privileged, but for the great majority of Teotihuacan's population' (Graeber and Wengrow, 2021, p 342).

On the other side of the world, in Afro-Eurasian empires, a similar wave of rebellion occurred, with revolutionary philosophers emerging across the continent in response to the violence of imperial rule. According to Karen Armstrong (2006), these counterhegemonic movements drew from vastly different cultural traditions to articulate an ethic of reciprocity that opened space for social healing. The Golden Rule not only has been found in the teachings of all the world's major religions, from Judaism and Christianity to Buddhism, Hinduism, and beyond, but it also was articulated in the counterhegemonic secular philosophy of the Axial Age. If proto-Hindu philosophers taught the Golden Rule as *ahimsa*, or a collective praxis of nonviolence, secular Greek philosophy taught the avoidance of doing what one would blame others for doing.

The Golden Rule was by no means limited to Afro-Eurasia, for Mesoamerican Olmec philosophy likewise recognized that 'every "thing" is potential kin' given that all things exist in relatedness (Astor-Aguilera, 2017). In the shamanic tradition of the Unangan,[2] who have long lived along the shores of the Bering Sea, the Golden Rule is expressed as 'living from the heart' (Jamail, 2022a, p 30). Ilarion Merculieff, an Unangan elder raised in the traditional way, states that this philosophy of the heart was 'the way of the original human beings throughout the entire world' (p 32).[3] Sharing insight from neighbouring Yupik elders, Merculieff posits that humans have 'reversed the laws for living ... because one of the most salient laws is that the heart used to tell the mind what to do, and the mind's job is to figure out how to implement what the heart is telling you' (Jamail, 2022a, p 33). If my analysis locates the problem as a self-other conflict wrought by the imperial assumption of categorical separateness, Native Alaskan epistemology identifies it as a desertion of the heart and thus, the wholeness of oneself.

The Daina ethic

1. Padoms

Discussed in Chapter 3, the Latvian concept of *padoms* translates into wise knowing, or the form of deep consciousness accrued through centuries of knowledge acquisition, integration and transmission. If the production of *padoms* is a cyclical and multi-generational affair, it also is an embodied and interdisciplinary praxis, for *padoms* can neither be achieved through the detachment of mind and body nor through the study of any one discipline alone. Given the socially embedded and physically embodied nature of *padoms*, it also is a relational affair, developed through mindful presence and multi-sensual connection with the differently situated *padoms* of other peoples and species.

At an interrelational level, *padoms* is cultivated through a position of humility. Within Latvian moral existence, it is not appropriate to interrupt or boast, for one should never seek the sensation of empowerment by either purposely or inadvertently placing oneself above another, as this generates psychosocial wounds that hinder mutual learning and growth. Neither should one abase oneself before another for, as President Vaira Vīķe Freiberga reminded her people during the opening speech of the 2001 song and dance festival, the other side of humility is the possession of self-respect. In times of great inequity, the colonizing master may wrest control over your body and attempt to seize control of your mind through subjugation and force; but it is important to remember that the mind cannot be given to the master without one's free will. In her translation of Dainas that relate the misery of serfdom, Auziņa Szentivanyi (2018, p 118) describes the Latvian perception of the master-servant relationship thusly:

> Latvians obviously did not consider their masters their superiors in any way except power ... the comparison of the two kinds of people, their cultures and wisdom is clear. The word 'padoms,' which I have chosen to represent with 'wise thinking' includes the ideas of wisdom, common sense, and experience that was accrued over generations.

2. *Inner freedom*

When considering the development of modernity over the longue durée, as I have done in this book, it becomes clear that the global power elite of today are but a modernized version of the colonial and feudal overlords of yesteryear, who themselves were but a modernized version of the imperial masters of antiquity, whose mode of existence originated in the patriarchal mindset of proto-ancient peoples, who chose to elevate mind over heart by assuming a linear ontology and hierarchical mode of social organization that brought great suffering to their people and lands.

On the surface of things, the Baltic German bourgeoisie who had colonized Latvia were free, and the Latvian serfs who were forced to toil for their overlords were enslaved. Yet a reading of the Dainas tells a different story. While colonial-era Dainas do evoke feelings of anger, bitterness, loss and despair, these songs also quite witfully describe the ignorance of colonial masters who, like young children, have not yet learned how to reason, and thus are the prisoners of their own unruly whims and desires.

In contrast to Latvian serfs, who learned from their elders how to produce the foods, arts, crafts and seasonal celebrations that made life enjoyable, the Baltic German masters owned land that they did not know how to farm and were wholly dependent upon those they enslaved for their bodily wellbeing. Not knowing how to spend their time during the slow winter months, these masters whipped up wars for excitement, sending their serfs into battle and killing off their labour supply. Unable to satisfy their voracious hunger for power, these masters sealed themselves off from their own humanity, raping women, beating children and living all together unhappy and miserable lives. When seeking to answer the question of who, among these two groups, understood the nature and meaning of freedom, I posit that Latvians – who managed to keep their language, ecology and culture alive across nearly 800 centuries of foreign occupation and systemic attempts at cultural genocide – were in the collective possession of a deep fire of inner freedom.

3. *Feminine divine*

As the guardian of knowledge, tradition and culture, the ideal Latvian mother teaches both boys and girls how to harness the receptive force of yin energy. Like the Birch, the deeply grounded and receptive energy of the feminine divine is what has enabled Latvians to remain resilient in strong winds. This does not mean that the masculine divine does not exist: although it has not been my focus in this book, there are many Dainas about the father, who symbolizes the yang force of Oak energy, stalwart in the face of light wind; and Latvia's pantheon of gods includes as many male deities as those inscribed in female form. However, the active and upward force of yang energy can overwhelm the receptive and grounded yin energy in everyday life, particularly during moments of crisis when emotions run high. Thus, by centring the mother and all of her material and ideal forms in its teachings, Latvian moral philosophy maintains a thoughtful balance between these receptive and active lifeforces that it describes in feminine and masculine ways.

The Latvian mother of the Daina always acts out of kindness, and even the most frightening faces of Latvia's goddesses, such as that of Veļu Māte (Mother Reaper), who comes to collect the souls of the dying is motivated not by cruelty, but rather by loving kindness. As an aspect of the feminine divine, the Latvian conceptualization of kindness is akin to the feminist ethic of care, defined by Fisher and Tronto (1990, p 40) as an activity that involves the maintenance and repair of life so that all may live well. The Latvian mother plays an equal, if not greater role, in transmitting the *padoms* of her family, clan and land to the next generation, and perhaps for this reason, the teachings of the Dainas assume a gentle and encouraging tone. Unlike patriarchal Indo-European traditions, where social values have been encoded as commandments, Latvian values are transmitted through witty, playful, and mournful poems that, when sung, socialize children into the grace of *wise knowing*. Moreover, these learning activities occur in celebratory settings and in close connection with the natural world: thus, one obtains *padoms* not through formal education, but rather by singing along with elders around the bonfire, and by creating crafts around the cosy hearth in winter.

During the four years that I lived in Latvia, people often told me that they felt a sense of kinship with the Indigenous people of Turtle Island, a land that my own ancestors helped to colonize. Gently reminding me that the Indigenous people of my homeland are continuing to suffer what Indigenous Balts have endured for so many centuries, my Latvian comrades shared specific examples of cultural interconnection. I discovered, for example, that ethnic Latvian names typically derive from nature in a similar vein as Native American traditions, and that the matriarchal impulse in Latvian gnosis has sprung from the same ancient source of knowledge as that of the people of Turtle Island. Consider the connection between the teachings of the Dainas and the Cree[4] teaching of the sacred feminine and sacred masculine, as shared by Terri Delahanty in *We Are the Middle of Forever* (Jamail, 2022b, pp 100–101):

'The Sun Dance is about praying up to the universe, to the Star Nation and Creator, it's all about upward and outward. But when a woman is on her moon, it is literally inward and downward. She's literally flowing downward and receiving that nurturing and the nourishment from the Earth ...'

In sum, the Daina ethic teaches us to: (1) live in tune with rather than against the chaotic forces of nature by knowing when to bend like the birch and when to stand strong like the oak; (2) take the time to develop direct relationships with ourselves and other species by spending time together and communicating our feelings; (3) reconnect with the knowledge of our ancestors and learn from our past; (4) learn the languages of other peoples and other species and shift our voices to harmonize with their difference; and (5) use rhythmic modalities such as song and dance to heal our sorrows and rediscover the joy of living.

The Ubuntu ethic

1. Truth

Ubuntu teaches a similar and yet complementary set of lessons on the development of caring and wise communities. First and foremost, Ubuntu reminds us that peace cannot flourish in secretive realms of existence, where people are taught to present a stiff upper lip to the world by locking away the pain in their hearts. On a superficial level, such detached forms of relationality may provide a semblance of peace, enabling people who hate one another to continue living together, but as South Africa's TRC hearings have taught us, it is precisely this culture of silence that causes hurt to fester and harm to continue. By breaking this culture of silence and speaking honestly to one another, we may begin to heal the wounds of our past and start living freer lives. Consider Nelson Mandela's answer to the following question put to him by US President Bill Clinton (2013) and shared in his foreword to *Long Walk to Freedom* (p ix):

> 'Tell me the truth. When you were leaving prison after twenty-seven years and walking down that road to freedom, didn't you hate them all over again?' And he said, 'Absolutely I did, because they'd imprisoned me for so long. I was abused. I didn't get to see my children grow up. I lost my marriage and the best years of my life. I was angry. And I was afraid, because I had not been free in so long. But as I got closer to the car that would take me away, I realized that when I went through that gate, if I still hated them, they would still have me. I wanted to be free. And so I let it go.'

Steve Biko's voice is far angrier, but no less grounded in the Ubuntu teaching on truth. Murdered by state security officers who arrested him for daring to speak out against the apartheid state in 1977, Biko (1978b, p 75) reminds us that it is okay to be angry in the face of injustice; indeed, that one should harness one's anger to challenge abusers who refuse to acknowledge the truth of their conduct, in an attempt to stop the harm:

Aimée Cesaire once said: 'When I turn on my radio; when I hear that Negroes have been lynched in America, I say that we have been lied to: Hitler is not dead: when I turn on my radio and hear that in Africa, forced labour has been inaugurated and legislated, I say that we certainly have been lied to: Hitler is not dead' – Perhaps one need add only the following in order to make the picture complete: – 'When I turn on my radio, when I hear that someone in the Pondoland forest was beaten and tortured, I say that we have been lied to: Hitler is not dead, when I turn on my radio, when I hear that someone in jail slipped off a piece of soap, fell and died I say that we have been lied to: Hitler is not dead, he is likely to be found in Pretoria.'

2. Forgiveness

In *No Future Without Forgiveness* (1999), Desmond Tutu teaches the Ubuntu value of forgiving, noting that this is an important step in the healing process. Yet he also recognizes that forgiveness is a matter of the heart, and not something that can be forced. For practitioners and educators who engage in peace and reconciliation, it also must be remembered that the process is difficult for all of those involved. In the following passage, Tutu offers an intimate description of the trauma that he experienced during the TRC hearings. His voice illustrates the paradoxical nature of this Ubuntu praxis, for it is at once costly and rewarding; traumatic and uplifting; harmful and healing.

At the beginning of our work on the commission our mental health worker on the staff gave us a briefing about coping with what was to be a gruelling and demanding task. We were advised to make sure that we had a soul mate or some such friend or counsellor to whom we could go to unburden ourselves. ... We thought we had been reasonably prepared for the traumatic experience.

Despite all this we were shattered at what we heard and we did frequently break down or were on the verge of it ...

... I learned that I had prostate cancer. It probably would have happened whatever I had been doing. But it just seemed to demonstrate that we were engaging in something that was costly. Forgiveness and reconciliation were not something to be entered into lightly, facilely ...

It has given a new intensity to life, for I realize that there is much that I used to take very much for granted – the love and devotion of my wife Leah, the laughter and playfulness of my grandchildren, the glory of a splendid sunset, the dedication of colleagues, the beauty of a bedewed rose ...

> Yes, I have been greatly privileged to engage in the work of helping to heal our nation. But ... I have come to realize that perhaps we were effective only to the extent that we were ... 'wounded healers'.

During my own exposure to the ugly reality of White supremacy, apartheid and poverty, I too have experienced the paradoxical set of emotions that Tutu describes. When I returned from South Africa, I spent more than a year in therapy trying to learn how to let go of the fear of a sudden attack and to work through the deep sadness that had lodged in my heart. At the same time, my memories of South Africa are filled with a richness of life and joy that I have rarely had the privilege to experience, and the lessons that I learned have made me into a more resilient and more thoughtful person. Through my Buddhist praxis, I have come to understand that pleasure and pain are two sides of one coin. We may seek out the first because pleasure feels good, and we may try to avoid the second because pain hurts, but we cannot truly appreciate pleasure without having first experienced pain, in the same way that truth opens the door to forgiveness.

3. Unity

Given the above lessons on truth and forgiveness, the cultivation of unity is no saccharine affair, and the experience of it is far from black or white. The hegemonic Western discourse on human rights fails to recognize the co-constructed relationship between individual and collective rights because the assumption of categorical separateness causes it to place the individual and the collective into either/or opposition. As modern rational philosophy has come to situate existence in the individual mind, it can only view the collective as a negation of individual identity and something to be feared; yet in so doing, the teaches the individual to become separated from the web of life, resulting in anomie. Consider, for example, the French philosophy of existentialism, which illustrates the cosmic purposelessness of a life lived without loyalty to anyone or anything. The following quote from *The Stranger*, a novel written by Albert Camus' (1988 [1942], p 121) gives us the voice of an indifferent French colonial protagonist, Meursault, who is on trial for the murder of an Arab man:

> Nothing, nothing mattered, and I knew why. So did he. Throughout the whole absurd life I'd lived, a dark wind had been rising toward me from somewhere deep in my future, across the years that were still to come, and as it passed, this wind levelled whatever was offered to me at the time, in years no more real than the ones I was living. What did other people's deaths or a mother's love matter to me; what did his God or the lives people choose or the fate they think they elect

matter to me when we're all elected by the same fate, me and billions of privileged people like him who also called themselves my brothers?

Now consider Fatima Meer's (2017) description of her life during the 1956 Treason Trial, when her husband was one of the 156 people imprisoned for his involvement in the anti-apartheid movement:

> Ismail and I wrote to each other at least once a day and sometimes twice. We had been married just over five years and the letters depict the very strong bond we had developed and that we were more in love than ever before. They also reveal that our married life was not without its stresses and strains but that we recognized these and committed ourselves to overcoming them.
>
> My life, at age 28 was suddenly full of newfound responsibilities which included caring for the children, running the home, looking after Ismail's office (or at least keeping an eye on it), working out ways to curb household expense, looking for some employment, and over and above this, supervising the building of our new home.
>
> I had the support of my family – my mothers, my sisters and the cousins who lived with them. Leila and Sharda Maharaj looked after the children and Phoowa kept the house and cooked.

On the surface of things, Meursault is privileged in relation to Meer. As a White French colonial subject with a girlfriend and a leisurely life, he could do whatever he wished. In contrast, Meer had been racially classified by the apartheid state, lacked basic freedoms due to her designated race and was burdened by the responsibility of managing affairs while her husband was in prison. Trapped in the melancholy of his detached mind, Meursault's voice is bored, isolated and indifferent. Although this fictional character derides the hypocrisy of French colonial society, his nihilistic sensibility causes him to reproduce coloniality by carelessly killing an innocent Algerian man. Embodied and connected to people, Meer's voice is filled with love and engaged with the business of everyday life. Although this anti-apartheid activist experiences tremendous burdens, her compassionate sensibility causes her to triumph over oppression. If the French existentialists are right, and the only meaning in life is that which we give it, I ask: which one of these voices is most free, and which one of these lives would you prefer to live?

Decolonizing praxis

My dialectical framing of development and its alternatives has brought two odd couple cases into conversation, showing how Latvian and South African cosmovisions share numerous values in common, including deep relationality with difference and the imperative to heal our relations with one another and with the Earth. To enact the wisdom of the cultural lessons I have learned, I have written a book that crosses many borders, from the disciplinary, theoretical and methodological, to the cultural, geographic and temporal. This act of epistemic disobedience also is grounded in the teachings of a broader set of decolonial, Indigenous, and Black philosophies that challenge us to shift our consciousness by awakening to the power of plurality. I have employed dialectical method to deconstruct the divergent bodies of knowledge and empirical data that this book engages, not to reproduce the binary modality of either/or logic, but to demonstrate that seemingly oppositional forces are neither inherently different nor discrete. While we may categorize the forces that shape our societies as 'good' or 'bad' and 'right' or 'wrong', these concepts are co-constructed, meaning that they merely describe two parts of one whole, in the same way that there can be no light without dark.

If we are to decolonize development, we must begin by acknowledging that oppositional ideologies simply inter-are. If neither tradition nor modernity are inherently superior, then the same may be said about religion and science, rationalism and humanism, capitalism and communism, and so forth. We may go to war over such ideologies, with the firm conviction that one way is right and the other wrong; however, in the grander scheme of things, these ideological forces co-arise, co-exist and co-adapt in relation to one another. Thus, what matters is not the ideology, which is a product of the mind, but the practice, which is the produce of the heart. By returning to a heart-based practice – one grounded in the cultivation of love for ourselves and for all the lives around us that are suffering – we may begin cultivating the emotional maturity needed to transcend our ideological divisions and heal our Earth in crisis.

For the modern rational reader who may chafe at my embrace of an activist voice and the critique I have made of rationalism, I want you to know the writing of this book also been guided by my training in modern rational thought. There is no value that I hold greater – in my own work as a humanist social scientist – as that of the foundational meaning of scientific method. Well before Galileo Galilei's seventeenth-century contribution to modern Italian philosophy, Ibn al Haytham taught scientific method to his pupils during the Islamic Golden Age of the tenth and eleventh centuries. As a mathematician and physicist, al Haytham studied the physical properties of optics and visual perception (Laurence, 1995). He obtained his knowledge by ruthlessly questioning his own assumptions regarding the nature of reality, rather than focusing on the assumptions of others. If the critically reflexive orientation that al Haytham taught helped his students learn how to shed the veil of their assumptions and develop a more accurate understanding of the nature of reality, in our current era this modality of ruthless self-questioning provides us with a framework for investing in multicultural and interdisciplinary approaches to sustainable development.

Given the interwoven complexities of the challenges facing humanity in the Age of the Anthropocene, we must bring all of our bodies of knowledge to bear to effectively address the ecological and social challenges of our times. However, we cannot embark upon such a collaborative journey with a hegemonic body of knowledge that views itself to be the only correct way of knowing. In this vein, I assume a similar position as Roothaan (2019, p 142) who concedes that there is room for modern science to negotiate knowledge with other cultures, but only when it is 'ready to concede that its rationality is not unique, but that its boundaries are blurred' with the critical and Indigenous sciences with whom it has so long warred.

Around the world, a consortium of Indigenous elders has convened to discuss the problem of our time. Having received the transmission of the knowledge of the ancients through their elders, who received it from their elders, all the way back in time to the spoken record of the first wave of modernization that assaulted our Earth, the global Indigenous elders of today have determined that there is no more time to wait: the time to act falls upon us who are alive today. Ilarion Merculieff, the president of the Global Centre for Indigenous Leadership and Lifeways, the first Alaska Native commissioner of Alaska's Department of Commerce and Economic Development and the founder of several environmental organizations, discusses this decision, which was made at a global Indigenous conference in Kuai in 2017 (Jamail, 2022a, pp 46–47):

> He went on to speak to how, according to one of the stories he carries, roughly six thousand years ago there was a shift in the balance of Mother Earth into the masculine imbalance that we're still in today. Elders during that time sought a solution to this, given their sacred teachings were feminine-based.
>
> Ilarion compared this occurrence to a piece of paper being torn into small pieces. If the pieces during that time weren't put together, if they weren't practiced for two generations, they would be completely lost to their people ...
>
> But no culture forgot the same thing as another, so we had this tapestry of pieces around the world. And the only time people would be able to get that back would be if they open up their hearts and trust each other around the world.
>
> ... Thus, according to Ilarion, for the last thirty years elders have been traveling the world, sharing what they know, in the prayer that the hoop of the sacred teachings be made whole once again and during our lifetime.

And that means trust, trust in life, trust in your life. Trust in Mother Earth, trust in the universe, trust in what we call 'the Maker' or the Great Spirit[5] that lives in all things. And that we have no more time to hide these teachings, we've got to share them.

... The template was set by elders and they said we must be at peace. We must be love.

And the rest will take care of itself. Don't worry about what's going to happen. ... No meeting happens by accident.

In terms of my own development praxis, I have found a home in the Plum Village tradition of socially engaged Buddhism where the Vietnamese Zen insight of interbeing has helped me to begin cultivating greater compassion for myself in relation to others (Nhất Hạnh, 2013). If the natural simplicity of Zen invokes, for me, the inward teachings of the Latvian Dainas, the radically open spirit of Nhất Hạnh's mindfulness teachings also strengthens my connection to the outward lessons of African Ubuntu. In a study on the psychosocial dimension of social-ecological transformation, Walsh (2017, p 1) describes engaged Buddhism as 'a post-secular synthesis of ethics and mindfulness ... informed by a non-binary understanding of religion and secularism'. Like Walsh, I recognize that this post-secular movement offers scope for reconciling the false division between religion and science. However, it is important to remember that engaged Buddhism is but one stream within transnational currents of social consciousness that espouse similar values. In short, Zen teachings are not the only path to truth, any more than modern rational science is the only right way.

Just as the false dichotomy of science and religion serves to disconnect the ecologies of knowledge that human societies have developed to explain the manifold experiences of our existence, the segregation of humans into Indigenous and foreign categories is yet another false dichotomy. Not only do these identities overlap in historically colonized societies around the world, but the ancient historical record suggests that some Indigenous peoples chose to become colonizers and others did not (Graeber and Wengrow, 2021). In ideal form, categorical concepts offer explanatory power by breaking down complexities into more manageable components, but it is important to remember that pure ideological forms do not exist on the material plane, as the nature and meaning of existence is paradoxically mixed.

However complex the story of human development may be, those of us who are alive today are faced with a clear choice. Fevered by COVID, burning from climate change and ravaged by authoritarian discourses of fear and hate, Earth has arrived at a pivotal crossroads in geological time. Given the Anthropogenic foundation that undergirds this crossroads, it falls to our species to determine a course of action. In one direction flows existential pathways of love, freedom and intergenerational life, entangled together.

This ideal form represents the wise ways of the original Peoples of Earth, with whom we all are interrelated. In the other direction lies fear, oppression and mass species extinction. This is the authoritarian speedway of the self-segregated Master, whether in the form of person or social institution, an entity that cannot abide life. The structural conditions that we confront are beyond the scope of individual actions, but in psychosocial terms and with critical consciousness, even the least among us can choose to think, act and relate to one another in colonizing or non-colonizing ways.

The cases of Latvia and South Africa remind us that transformative societies are capable of pivoting in response to the winds of change, however paradoxical these winds may be. In the summer of 2023, Edgars Rinkēvičs became the first openly gay president of the Republic of Latvia. Although he presides over a nation that has a poor track record on gay and lesbian rights, Rinkēvičs nevertheless is one of only seven out LGBTQ+ heads of state in the world today (Pannett, 2023). Recognizing that everyone and everything are interconnected in ways that are hard to fathom, I conclude this book by posing three questions for reflection and discussion:

1. How can societies transcend the systemic trauma of our collective past if even our most liberatory languages and movements contain, within them, the warring spark of imperial cognition?
2. What traditions, values and knowledges do you bring to the development global justice table, and how might you shift your social-ecological relations and practices in ways that open room for healing?
3. How are you situated? In what ways do you have the power and influence to enact the changes you wish to see? Where is your agency? How might you wield the powers that you have more wisely in your development praxis? What are the heterotopian spaces in of your world, and how are those collectives putting ideas into collective action?

As you wander the entangled pathways of creation and destruction that manifest in your praxis, you may wish to ponder such deeper questions as:

1. *What Kind of Ancestor Do You Want to Be?*, a topic recently queried by John Hausdoerffer and colleagues (2021);
2. What is the Indigenous practice of *Becoming Kin*, an Anishinaabe-Ukrainian perspective on social change transmitted by Patty Krawec (2022);
3. What is the multiracial and multicultural praxis of *Healing Justice,* as identified by Loretta Pyles (2018), a social justice scholar and grassroots development practitioner; and
4. How is sovereignty described in *Food Sovereignty the Navajo Way* by Charlotte J. Frisbie, Tall Woman, and Augusta Sandoval (2018)?

Notes

Chapter 1

[1]   I capitalize Black, Indigenous and White as an invitation to the reader to think deeply about the meaning of race and its relationship to identity. I do not capitalize the term 'coloured' for the same reason. While the term is considered derogatory in many countries, it remains in use as an official racial category in South Africa. Within coloured community, some South Africans embrace the term, and others reject it.

[2]   According to Armstrong (2006), these parallel traditions ranged from biblical monotheism and Greek rationalism in the Mediterranean to Hinduism and Buddhism in South Asia and Confucianism and Taoism in the Far East.

[3]   In addition to the ecology and feminism movement, the French economy and humanism movement established by Louis-Joseph Lebret espoused an integral development approach grounded in the ethic of social justice. This movement was in dialogue with liberation theology in the global South. Given Lebret's dual role as a French Dominican priest and sociologist, he conducted field surveys with impoverished communities in Europe, Latin America, Africa and the Middle East (Villas Boas and Folloni, 2021).

[4]   This Spanish term translates to 'Way of the Peasant'.

[5]   Like Besten (2009), I employ the linguistically representative spelling of 'Khoe' rather than the Westernized 'Khoi'.

[6]   Vaira Vīķes-Freibergs, the Latvian-Canadian scholar and Vaira Vīķe-Freiberga, the former president of Latvia are the same person. In Latvia, the 's' ending is masculine while 'e' and 'a' endings are feminine. After World War II, Latvian refugees acculturated into receiving nations by standardizing the 's' ending for both genders; thus Vaira's Canadian identity is Vīķes-Freibergs, but in Latvia, she is known by her linguistically correct name.

[7]   This chapter draws from material presented in the following published article, although the book chapter has been substantially revised: Keahey, J. (2009) 'Regional economic integration and local food: The case of Latvia during European Union accession', *International Journal of Sustainable Society*, 1(3): 292–304.

[8]   This chapter draws from material presented in the following published article, although the book chapter has been substantially revised: Keahey, J. (2019) 'Sustainable heritage development in the South African Cederberg', *Geoforum*, 104: 36–45.

Chapter 2

[1]   A few forest brothers remained in hiding. According to a news article authored by Māra Grīnberga (1995), the last to emerge was Jānis Pīnups, a Latvian man who had deserted the Red Army in 1944. Fearing execution, Pīnups remained in the forest throughout the Soviet occupation, only returning to society in 1994 when Russian troops fully departed the Baltics.

[2]   Based on 1993 prices, the lower bound poverty rate denoted a per capita income of ZAR198 (USD58) or less per month.

3   This includes the United States Peace Corps, for whom I worked as an English teacher trainer.

4   Latvians from the Second World War diaspora returned in the 1990s to visit family, reclaim their property and in many cases remain. Skultans (1998) writes hauntingly of the atmosphere in the Rīga airport when families separated by war met for the first time in 50 years.

Chapter 3

1   In 2021, Latvia ranked 20 of 156 countries on the World Economic Forum's Global Gender Gap Index, and in 2019, it ranked 39 of 189 countries on the UNDP Gender Inequality Index.

2   While this sounds plausible, I have been unable to locate published research on the connection.

3   *Puzuri* are cultural objects that one hangs on trees and around the home. Brunner (2012) attributes the invention of the Christmas tree to Baltic German merchants who placed a lighted tree in their guild house in 1510. If this is accurate, Rīga's merchant class may have appropriated an older ethnic Latvian tradition.

4   Zemes Māte and Dievs are Mother Earth and Father Sky.

5   See, for example, Ausma Spalviņa's (2017) video tutorial on the subject.

6   Unless otherwise noted, I employ pseudonyms based on Latvian mythology to protect individual identities, given the personal nature of these stories.

7   Given the low cost of health care and the prevalence of alternative healing modalities, Latvia's working class could afford such therapies.

8   Humility toward self-others is a key cultural value. Whatever one's gender, it is not culturally appropriate to boast or brag as these actions place one above the other. Nor is it appropriate to place oneself below the other, even if the other in question has misplaced you. The Latvian conception of humility plays a critical role in helping families and communities reconcile differences and remain resilient in the face of hardship.

9   Latvian variant of my name.

10   Real names.

11   The aggressive atmosphere surrounding Bush's 2005 visit stood in stark contrast to that of another presidential visit. In 2001, the French president, Jacques Chirac, visited Rīga and Old Town remained open. I have a photograph of Chirac strolling through the park with Vīķe-Freiberga. Only a few guards accompanied the two presidents and, in typical Latvian fashion, the public accorded them privacy by ignoring them.

Chapter 4

1   The ANC has proposed renaming this pejoratively named mountain Mandelaberg. The local Khoekhoe have countered this with a request to change the name to Autshumato mountain range. Mandela had no cultural ties to the mountain, but South Africa's first freedom fighter, Chief Autshumato, had gazed upon it daily. Living in the seventeenth century, he was the first prisoner sent to Robben Island for mounting resistance against invading Dutch forces.

2   As I write this in 2022, South Africa is the most unequal country in the word.

3   Afrikaans term for defensive encampment.

4   Lieutenant Johannes Jakobus Viktor, a Special Branch interrogator who alternately threatened and flirted with First during her final month in confinement.

5   Derogatory South African term for homosexuals with probable etymological roots in Afrikaans.

6   Noleen was astonished when I brought this cake home. She told me she had never been able to get any shop in Stellenbosch to write her name correctly. When I asked why, she said that her name was spelled in the coloured way, and that Whites insisted on spelling it the 'proper' White way.

Chapter 5

[1] Between November 1990 and January 1994, would-be farmers raced to purchase newly available plots of land, increasing the ownership of individual farms by ninefold.

[2] As a consequence of land reform, nearly all land in Latvia has been privatized.

[3] This size is large in relation to average Latvian farm size, but 100 hectares is the average farm size in Latgale, which is why Ruta purchased more land.

[4] The brown bottles aided in delivering a quality unpasteurized product, as I was told that it prevented sunlight from entering the product and breaking down milk proteins.

[5] Slow Food Manifesto. https://slowfood.com/filemanager/Convivium%20Leader%20Area/Manifesto_ENG.pdf

[6] Courtesans.

[7] Nāves Māte also is known as Veļu Māte (Mother Reaper), a white-robed goddess who collects the souls of the dead and accompanies them on their journey to the behind-the-sun underworld of Vinsaule. This journey is depicted in the midsummer solstice song 'Līgo' (Sway). Sung around the bonfire, this song is comprised of a series of Daina stanzas that invoke the cyclical force of life and death. Called by Māra, one's broken golden reed (lifeforce) walks over a mist-shrouded lake to arrive at the shores of Vinsaule, where wreath-crowned maidens invoke the regenerative force of līgo to heal the spirit and prepare one for rebirth in a new material form.

[8] In the differing knowledge realm of Western physical science, particle physicists have recorded the existence of the Higgs-Bosen particle, a sub-atomic element that theoretically is capable of moving through all places and times simultaneously.

Chapter 6

[1] Sarah Baartman was born into a Khoekhoe family in 1789. She was taken to Europe in 1810 where she was put on exhibit. After her death in 1815, her remains were displayed in a French natural history museum. South Africa demanded her return in 1994, and she was brought home in 2002. See Tessa McWatt (2020) for the full story of Baartman's life and afterlife.

[2] For more information regarding the broader project and its outcomes, see Keahey et al (2016).

[3] To ensure mission-wide access, elections occurred in Kleinvlei, Heuningvlei, Suurrug, Wupperthal, and Eselbank.

[4] Mission women demanded inclusion resulting in community elections for male–female leadership teams.

[5] Farmer interviews were conducted in Afrikaans and translated on the spot by farmer leaders who spoke English. Higher level interviews occurred in English.

[6] Raynolds and Ngcwangu (2010) offer an analysis on the inception of the Fairpackers partnership, and Keahey (2015) provides an in-depth analysis of its demise.

[7] Pseudonym.

[8] Wet tonnage. When dried, rooibos tea decreases two to three times in volume. This figure also includes small volumes of wild rooibos, though access to wild rooibos is strictly controlled.

[9] Pseudonym.

[10] A few years after I left Wupperthal, a farmer leader contacted me to say that the mission had finally gotten wireless service. Most people had cheap mobile phones with a pay-as-you-go service, enabling them to remain in occasional contact with the outside world, although computers and a regular internet service remained out of reach for most.

[11] For in-depth coverage of gender relations, see Keahey (2018).

[12] Pseudonym.

[13] Pseudonym.

14 Old fashioned term used to describe the Indigenous peoples of southern Africa.
15 My project partner and I responded by seeking funding for a second project cycle, but we failed to secure the funds needed to move forward with this plan.

Chapter 7

1 The Global Indigenous term for the Americas. It derives from the Kuna language spoken by Guna people whose homeland is located at the borderlands of North and South America, in the Darién Gap of what is now southern Panama and northern Colombia.
2 Decolonized term for Aleut.
3 The Unangan trace their heritage to ancient Egypt, with oral record describing a trek through Outer Mongolia and Kamchatka then across the Bering Sea in skin boats.
4 A Canadian First Nation.
5 For the secular reader, the Great Spirit who moves through all things may be interpreted in a figurative way.

References

Adhikari, M. (2006) *Not White Enough, Not Black Enough: Racial Identity in the South African Coloured Community.* Cape Town: Double Storey Books.

Adhikari, M. (2009) *Burdened by Race: Coloured Identities in Southern Africa.* Cape Town: UCT Press.

Adhikari, M. (ed) (2015) *Genocide on Settler Frontiers: When Hunter-Gatherers and Commercial Stock Farmers Clash.* New York: Berghahn Books.

Aistara, G.A. (2018) *Organic Sovereignties: Struggles over Farming in an Age of Free Trade.* Seattle, WA: University of Washington Press.

Alejandro, A.J., Fong, C.J. and De La Rosa, Y.M. (2020) 'Indigenous graduate and professional students decolonizing, reconciling, and Indigenizing belongingness in higher education', *Journal of College Student Development*, 61(6): 679–696.

Alexander, N. (2003) *An Ordinary Country: Issues in the Transition from Apartheid to Democracy in South Africa.* New York: Berghahn Books.

Aliber, M. and Cousins, B. (2013) 'Livelihoods after land reform in South Africa', *Journal of Agrarian Change*, 13(1): 140–165.

Alschuler, L.R. (2006) *The Psychopolitics of Liberation Political Consciousness from a Jungian Perspective.* 1st edition. New York: Palgrave Macmillan.

Altieri, M.A. and Nicholls, C. (2020) 'Agroecology: challenges and opportunities for farming in the Anthropocene', *International Journal of Agriculture and Natural Resources*, 47(3): 204–215.

Andrews, P.E. (1998) 'Violence against women in South Africa: the role of culture and the limitations of the law', *Temple Political & Civil Rights Law Review*, 8: 425.

Arendse, D.E. (2020) ' "Coloured" consciousness: reflecting on how decoloniality facilitates belonging', *Alternation*, 33: 267–289.

Armstrong, K. (2006) *The Great Transformation: The Beginning of our Religious Traditions.* New York: Knopf.

Astor-Aguilera, M. (2017) 'Latin America: Indigenous cosmovision', in W. Jenkins, M.E. Tucker and J. Grim (eds) *Routledge Handbook of Religion and Ecology.* London: Routledge, pp 158–167.

Auers, D. (2012) 'The curious case of the Latvian Greens', *Environmental Politics*, 21(3): 522–527.

August, K.T. (2005) 'Reconciliation in the South African political context: a challenge to the church for community building', *Scriptura*, 88: 14–29.

Auziņa, A. (2011) 'Our mothers' in I. Lešinska (ed) *Six Latvian Poets*. Todmorden: Arc Publications, pp. 446–447.

Auziņa Szentivanyi, I. (2018) *Dainas: Wit and Wisdom of Ancient Latvian Poetry*. Rīga: Apgāds Mansards.

Baatjes, I. (2003) 'The new knowledge-rich society: perpetuating marginalization and exclusion', *Journal of Education*, 29: 179–204.

Bagger, H. (1993) 'The role of the Baltic in Russian foreign policy, 1721–1773', in H. Ragsdale (ed) *Imperial Russian Foreign Policy*. Cambridge: Cambridge University Press, pp. 36–74.

Baltic News Network (2019) 'Latvian Green Party excluded from European Green Party', Baltic News Network. Available at: https://bnn-news. com/latvian-green-party-excluded-from-european-green-party-207229 (Accessed on 2 January 2023).

Bankovska, A. (2020) 'Patchworks of care: ethics and practice of care in the organic food movement in Latvia'. PhD thesis, University of Helsinki, Helsinki.

Barchiesi, F. (2011) *Precarious Liberation: Workers, the State, and Contested Social Citizenship in Postapartheid South Africa*. Albany, NY: State University of New York Press.

Barnard, A. (2008) 'Ethnographic analogy and the reconstruction of early Khoekhoe society', *Southern African Humanities*, 20(1): 61–75.

Barnard, A. (2019) *Bushmen: Kalahari Hunter-Gatherers and their Descendants*. Cambridge: Cambridge University Press.

Barry, M. (2004) 'Now another thing must happen: Richtersveld and the dilemmas of land reform in post-apartheid South Africa', *South African Journal on Human Rights*, 20(3): 355–382.

Barry, R. G. (2020) 'Climate change: polar regions', in Y. Wang (ed) *Atmosphere and Climate*. Boca Raton, FL: CRC Press, pp 309–316.

Barry, S., Ndlovu, M. and Khan, D. (eds) (2002) *ink@boiling point: A Selection of Twenty-First Century Black Women's Writing from the Southern Tip of Africa*. Revised edition. Cape Town: WEAVE.

Battiste, M. and Youngblood Henderson, J.S.k.j. (2000) *Protecting Indigenous Knowledge and Heritage: A Global Challenge*. Saskatoon: Purich Publishing.

Beck, U. (1992) *Risk Society: Towards a New Modernity. Theory, Culture & Society*. London: Sage Publications.

Beldavs, A.V. (1977) 'Goddesses in a man's world: Latvian matricentricity in culture and spheres of influence in society', *Journal of Baltic Studies*, 8(2): 105–129.

Belkin, A. and Canaday, M. (2010) 'Assessing the integration of gays and lesbians into the South African National Defence Force', *Scientia Militaria: South African Journal of Military Studies*, 38(2): 1–21.

Bellah, R.N. and Joas, H. (2012) *The Axial Age and Its Consequences*. Cambridge: Harvard University Press.

Bernheimer, C. (1990) *In Dora's Case: Freud–Hysteria–Feminism*. New York: Columbia University Press.

Besky, S. (2013) 'The labor of terroir and the terroir of labor: geographical indication and Darjeeling tea plantations', *Agriculture and Human Values*, 31(1): 83–96.

Besky, S. (2014) *The Darjeeling Distinction: Labor and Justice on Fair-Trade Tea Plantations in India*. Berkeley, CA: University of California Press.

Besten, M. (2009) '"We are the original inhabitants of this land": Khoe-San identity in post-apartheid South Africa', in M. Adhikari (ed) *Burdened by Race: Coloured Identities in Southern Africa*. Cape Town: UCT Press, pp 134–155.

Bialostocka, O. (2022) 'Transmodern heritage as radical delinking from modernity', *Curator: The Museum Journal*, 65(3): 509–522.

Bickford-Smith, V. (2002) *Ethnic Pride and Racial Prejudice in Victorian Cape Town: Group Identity and Social Practice, 1875–1902*. Cambridge: Cambridge University Press.

Biénabe, E. and Marie-Vivien, D. (2017) 'Institutionalizing geographical indications in southern countries: lessons learned from Basmati and Rooibos', *World Development*, 98: 58–67.

Biko, S. (1978a) 'Black consciousness & the quest for a true humanity', *Ufahamu: A Journal of African Studies*, 8(3): 10–20.

Biko, S. (1978b) *I Write What I Like*. San Francisco: CA: Harper & Row, Publishers.

Bilbe, M.C. (1999) 'Wupperthal: listening to the past'. Honours/Master's degree thesis, University of Cape Town, Cape Town.

Bilbe, M.C. (2009) *Wupperthal: The Formation of a Community in South Africa, 1830–1965*. Cologne: Rüdiger Köppe Verlag.

Bissen, S. (2020) 'Yes, U.S. farmer suicide is significantly higher than the national average', *Organisms. Journal of Biological Sciences*, 4(1): 17–25.

Blumberg, R. (2009) 'Mothers of invention? The myth-breaking history and planetary promise of women's key roles in subsistence technology', in Y. Amichai-Hamburger (ed) *Technology and Psychological Well-Being*. Cambridge: Cambridge University Press, pp 227–259.

Boehmer, E. (2011) 'Where we belong: South Africa as a settler colony and the calibration of African and Afrikaner Indigeneity', in F. Bateman and L. Pilkington (eds) *Studies in Settler Colonialism: Politics, Identity and Culture*. London: Palgrave Macmillan, pp 257–271.

Bohm, D. and Hiley, B. (1977) 'On the intuitive understanding of non-locality as implied by quantum theory', in J. Lopes and M. Paty (eds) *Quantum Mechanics, A Half Century Later*. Dordrecht: D. Reidel Publishing Company, pp 207–226.

Bojtár, E. (2000) *Forward to the Past: A Cultural History of the Baltic People*. Translated by S. Redey and M. Webb. Budapest: Central European University Press.

Bowen, S. and De Master, K. (2011) 'New rural livelihoods or museums of production? Quality food initiatives in practice', *Journal of Rural Studies*, 27(1): 73–82.

Brook, T. (2008) *Vermeer's Hat: The Seventeenth Century and the Dawn of the Global World*. New York: Bloomsbury Press.

Brunner, B. (2012) *Inventing the Christmas Tree*. Haven, CT: Yale University Press.

Buceniece, E. (1997) 'Latvians: models of self-awareness', *Anthropological Journal on European Cultures*, 6(1): 61–72.

Bula, D. (2017) 'A complete edition of an oral tradition: text selection practices in the history of publishing Latvian folk songs', *Folklore*, 128(1): 37–56.

Buttel, F.H. (2000) 'Ecological modernization as social theory', *Geoforum*, 31(1): 57–65.

Cajete, G. (2022) 'Relational philosophy: the stars are our relatives', in N. Lushetich and I. Campbell (eds) *Distributed Perception: Resonances and Axiologies*. New York: Routledge, pp 17–30.

Cameron, E. (2006) *Pride: Protest and Celebration*. Johannesburg: Jacana Media.

Camus, A. (1988 [1942]) *The Stranger*. Translated by M. Ward. New York: Knopf.

Cape Nature (2019) 'Greater Cederberg Biodiversity Corridor'. Available at: www.capenature.co.za/care-for-nature/conservation-in-action/landsc ape-scale-conservation/corridors/the-greater-cederberg-biodiversity-corri dor/ (Accessed on 21 May 2019).

Carolan, M.S. (2008) 'More-than-representational knowledge/s of the countryside: how we think as bodies', *Sociologia Ruralis*, 48(4): 408–422.

Carolan, M.S. (2011) *Embodied Food Politics*. Burlington: Ashgate.

Carpenter, I.G. (1996) 'Festival as reconciliation: Latvian exile homecoming in 1990', *Journal of Folklore Research*, 33(2): 93–124.

Carrigan, A. (2011) *Postcolonial Tourism: Literature, Culture, and Environment*. New York: Routledge.

Chambers, W.S., Hopkins, J.G. and Richards, S.M. (2021) 'A review of per- and polyfluorinated alkyl substance impairment of reproduction', *Frontiers in Toxicology*, 3: 1–9.

Chaplin, G. (2020) 'Settler-colonialism, nationalism and geopolitical politics: an overview of the mobilization of race in South Africa in the context of lost turning points', in N.G. Jablonski (ed) *Persistence of Race*. Cape Town: Sun Press, pp 43–78.

Chase-Dunn, C. (2013) 'Five linked crises in the contemporary world-system', *Journal of World-Systems Research*, 19(2): 175–180.

Chase-Dunn, C., Fenelon, J., Hall, T.D., Breckenridge-Jackson, I. and Herrera, J. (2020) 'Global indigenism and the web of transnational social movements', in I. Rossi (ed) *Challenges of Globalization and Prospects for an Inter-Civilizational World Order*. Springer, pp 411–434.

Chase-Dunn, C. and Lerro, B. (2016) *Social Change: Globalization from the Stone Age to the Present*. New York: Routledge.

Chatterji, S.K. (1968) *Balts and the Aryans in Their Indo-European Background*. Simla: Indian Institute of Advanced Study.

Chilisa, B. (2009) 'Indigenous African-centered ethics: contesting and complementing dominant models', in D.M. Mertens and P.E. Ginsberg (eds) *The Handbook of Social Research Ethics*. Thousand Oaks, CA: Sage Publications, pp 407–425.

Chilisa, B. (2020) *Indigenous Research Methodologies*. Second edition. Thousand Oaks, CA: Sage Publications.

Chopra, M. and Sanders, D. (2004) 'From apartheid to globalization: health and social change in South Africa', *Hygiea Internationalis*, 4(1): 153–174.

Cimdiņa, A. (2003) *In the Name of Freedom: President of Latvia Vaira Viķe Freiberga*. Rīga: Trimdadimd Books.

Claeys, P. (2015) 'Food sovereignty and the recognition of new rights for peasants at the UN: a critical overview of La Via Campesina's rights claims over the last 20 years', *Globalizations*, 12(4): 452–465.

Clinton, B. (2013) 'Foreword', in N. Mandela, *Long Walk to Freedom*. New York: Back Bay Books, pp ix–x.

Cock, J. and Bernstein, A. (2001) 'Gender differences: struggles around "needs" and "rights" in South Africa', *NWSA Journal*, 13(3): 138–152.

Coetzer, O. (2000) *Fire in the Sky: The Destruction of the Orange Free State*. Weltevreden Park: Covos-Day Books.

Collins, P.H. and Bilge, S. (2016) *Intersectionality*. Malden: Polity Press.

Conroy, M. (2007) *Branded: How the Certification Revolution is Transforming Global Corporations*. Gabriola Island, BC: New Society Publishers.

Coombe, R.J., Ives, S. and Huizenga, D. (2014) 'The social imaginary of geographical indicators in contested environments: politicized heritage and the racialized landscapes of South African Rooibos TEA', in M. David and D. Halbert (eds) *The Sage Handbook on Intellectual Property*. Thousand Oaks, CA: Sage Publications, pp 224–237.

Cradle of Humankind World Heritage Site (2020) 'The Cradle of Humankind World Heritage Site', Maropeng Visitor Centre. Available at: www.maropeng.co.za/content/page/introduction-to-your-visit-to-the-cradle-of-humankind-world-heritage-site (Accessed on 25 June 2020).

Cropley, E. (2018) 'Winnie Mandela, Tarnished 'Mother' of Post-Apartheid South Africa', Reuters, Johannesburg. Available at: www.reuters.com/article/uk-safrica-winniemandela-obit/winnie-mandela-tarnished-mother-of-post-apartheid-south-africa-idUKKCN1H91OR (Accessed on 5 December 2022).

Curtin, D. (2005) *Environmental Ethics for a Postcolonial World*. Lanham, MA: Rowman and Littlefield.

d'Eaubonne, F. (1974) *Le féminisme ou la mort*. Paris: Pierre Horay Ed.

d'Eaubonne, F. and Paisain, J. (1999) 'What could an ecofeminist society be?', *Ethics & the Environment*, 4(2): 179–184.

DAC (2018) 'National Heritage Council: Department of Arts and Culture', Republic of South Africa. Available at: www.dac.gov.za/national-herit age-council (Accessed on 19 June 2018).

Daniels, E. (1998) *There & Back: Robben Island 1964–1979*. Bellville: Mayibuye Books, University of the Western Cape.

Darst, R.G. (2001) *Smokestack Diplomacy: Cooperation and Conflict in East-West Environmental Politics. Global Environmental Accord*. Cambridge, MA: MIT Press.

David-Fox, M. (2015) *Crossing Borders: Modernity, Ideology, and Culture in Russia and the Soviet Union*. Pittsburgh: University of Pittsburgh Press.

Daviron, B. and Vagneron, I. (2011) 'From commoditisation to de-commoditisation … and back again: discussing the role of sustainability standards for agricultural products', *Development Policy Review*, 29: 91–113.

De France, M. (1983) *Les lais de Marie de France. Les Classiques français du Moyen Age*. Paris: H. Champion.

de Gruchy, J.W. and de Gruchy, S. (2005) *The Church Struggle in South Africa*. Minneapolis: Fortress Press.

de Navarre, M. (1982) *Heptameron*. Paris: Flammarion.

Diamond, J. (2011) *Collapse: How Societies Choose to Fail or Succeed*. Revised edition. New York: Penguin.

Diamond, J.M. (2005) *Guns, Germs, and Steel: The Fates of Human Societies*. New York: Norton.

Dikgang, J. and Muchapondwa, E. (2016) 'The effect of land restitution on poverty reduction among the Khomani San "Bushmen" in South Africa', *South African Journal of Economics*, 84(1): 63–80.

Dini, P.U. (2014) *Prelude to Baltic Linguistics*. New York: Brill.

Donato, D. (2018) 'Agrotowns, a brief history and review of resources', *International Critical Thought*, 8(3): 501–506.

Dubow, S. (2014) *Apartheid: 1948–1994*. Oxford: Oxford University Press.

Ducastel, A. and Anseeuw, W. (2018) 'Facing financialization: the divergent mutations of agricultural cooperatives in postapartheid South Africa', *Journal of Agrarian Change*, 18(3): 555–570.

Durkheim, E. (2002 [1897]) *Suicide: A Study in Sociology*. New York: Routledge.

Earth Charter (2000) 'The Earth Charter'. Available at: https://earthchar ter.org/about-the-earth-charter/ (Accessed on 22 October 2021).

Edelman, M. and Wolford, W. (2017) 'Introduction: critical agrarian studies in theory and practice', *Antipode*, 49(4): 959–976.

Eglitis, D. S. and Ardava, L. (2017) 'Challenges of a post-Communist presidency: Vaira Vike-Freiberga and the leadership of Latvia', in V. Montecinos (ed) *Women Presidents and Prime Ministers in Post-Transition Democracies*. London: Palgrave Macmillan, pp 259–276.

Einbinder, N. and Morales, H. (2020) 'Development from within: agroecology and the Quest FOR Utziil K'asleem in the Maya-Achí territory of Guatemala', *Journal of Latin American Geography*, 19(3): 133–158.

Elbourne, E. and Ross, R. (1997) 'Combating spiritual and social bondage: early missions in the Cape Colony', in R. Elphick and T.R.H. Davenport (eds) *Christianity in South Africa: A Political, Social, and Cultural History*. Berkeley, CA: University of California Press, pp 31–50.

Ellis, S. and Tsepo, S. (1992) *Comrades against Apartheid: The ANC and the South African Communist Party in Exile*. Bloomington, IN: Indiana University Press.

Emel, J. and Neo, H. (2010) 'Killing for profit: global livestock industries and their socio-ecological implications', in R. Peet, P. Robbins and M.J. Watts (eds) *Global Political Ecology*. New York: Routledge, pp 81–97.

Eswaran, V., Harpending, H. and Rogers, A.R. (2005) 'Genomics refutes an exclusively African origin of humans', *Journal of Human Evolution*, 49(1): 1–18.

Eurostat (2008) 'Archive: Farm structure in Latvia: 2007 results', Eurostat, Luxembourg. Available at: https://ec.europa.eu/eurostat/statistics-explai ned/index.php?title=Archive:Farm_structure_in_Latvia_-_2007_results (Accessed on 2 January 2013).

Evans, D.M. and Mylan, J. (2019) 'Market coordination and the making of conventions: qualities, consumption and sustainability in the agro-food industry', *Economy and Society*, 48(3): 426–449.

Everingham, M. and Jannecke, C. (2006) 'Land restitution and democratic citizenship in South Africa', *Journal of Southern African Studies*, 32(3): 545–562.

Ezergailis, A. (1996) *The Holocaust in Latvia 1941–1944*. Rīga: Historical Institute of Latvia.

Fabricius, C. and de Wet, C. (2002) 'The influence of forced removals and land restitution on conservation in South Africa', in D. Chatty and M. Colchester (eds) *Conservation and Mobile Indigenous Peoples: Displacement, Forced Settlement, and Sustainable Development*. New York: Berghahn Books, pp 142–157.

Fanon, F. (1967) *Black Skin, White Masks*. New York: Grove Press.

Feder, S. (2012) 'Inspiring for liberation – legitimizing for occupation: interpretations of the exodus from Southern Africa', in M.R. Gunda and J. Kügler (eds) *The Bible and Politics in Africa*. Bamberg: University of Bamberg Press, pp 236–250.

Feldmanis, A.E. (2002) *Maslenku traģēdija: Latvijas traģēdija [Tragedy of Maslenki: Latvia's tragedy]*. Rīga: Latvijas 50 gadu okupācijas muzeja fonds.

Fenelon, J.V. (2021) *Migration, Racism and Labour Exploitation in the World-System*. New York: Routledge.

Ferguson, J. (2010) 'The uses of neoliberalism', *Antipode*, 41(s1): 166–184.

Fester, G. (2000) 'A plea to poetry', in S. Barry, M. Ndlovu and D. Khan (eds) *ink@boiling point: A Selection of 21st Century Black Women's Writing from the Southern Tip of Africa*. Cape Town: WEAVE, pp 82–83.

First, R. (2010 [1965]) *117 Days: An Account of Confinement and Interrogation under the South African 90-Day Detention Law*. London: Hachette UK.

Fisher, B. and Tronto, J.C. (1990) 'Toward a feminist theory of caring', in E. Abel and M. Nelson (eds) *Circles of Care: Work and Identity in Women's Lives*. Albany, NY: State University of New York Press, pp 36–54.

Fletcher, W.A. (1976) 'The British navy in the Baltic, 1918–1920: Its contribution to the independence of the Baltic nations', *Journal of Baltic Studies*, 7(2): 134–144.

Fokkens, A.M. (2012) 'Afrikaner unrest within South Africa during the Second World War and the measures taken to suppress it', *Journal for Contemporary History*, 37(2): 123–142.

Fontefrancesco, M.F. and Corvo, P. (2020) 'Slow Food: History and activity of a global food movement toward SDG2', in W. Leal Filho, A.M. Azul, L. Brandli, P. Özuyar and T. Wall (eds) *Zero Hunger. Encyclopedia of the UN Sustainable Development Goals*. Cham: Springer, pp 766–774.

Fortson, B.W. (2010) *Indo-European Language and Culture: An Introduction*. Second edition. Malden, MA: Wiley-Blackwell.

Foucault, M. and Miskowiec, J. (1986) 'Of other spaces', *Diacritics*, 16(1): 22–27.

Fourie, J. (2013) 'Slaves as capital investment in the Dutch Cape Colony, 1652–1795', in E. Hillbom and P. Svensson (eds) *Agricultural Transformation in a Global History Perspective*. New York: Routledge, pp 136–159.

Fredrickson, G.M. (1981) *White Supremacy: A Comparative Study in American and South African History*. New York: Oxford University Press.

Freire, P. (1970) *Pedagogy of the Oppressed*. New York: Herder and Herder.

Frisbie, C., Woman, T. and Sandoval, A. (2018) *Food Sovereignty the Navajo Way: Cooking with Tall Woman*. Albuquerque: University of New Mexico Press.

Gereffi, G. (1994) 'The Organization of Buyer-driven global commodity chains', in G. Gereffi and M. Korzeniewicz (eds) *Commodity Chains and Global Capitalism*. Westport, CT: Praeger, pp 95–122.

Giblin, J. (2015) 'Critical approaches to post-colonial (post-conflict) heritage', in E. Waterton and S. Watson (eds) *The Palgrave Handbook of Contemporary Heritage Research*. New York: Palgrave Macmillan, pp 313–328.

Gibson, J.L. (2002) 'Truth, justice, and reconciliation: judging the fairness of amnesty in South Africa', *American Journal of Political Science*, 46(3): 540–556.

Gimbutas, M. (1963) *The Balts: Ancient Peoples and Places*. New York: Frederick Praeger Press.

Gimbutas, M. (1985) 'Pre-Indo-European goddess in Baltic mythology', *Mankind Quarterly*, 26(1): 19–25.

Gimbutas, M. (1991) *Civilization of the Goddesses: The World of Old Europe*. San Francisco: Harper.

Ginkel, J. (2018) 'Identity construction in Latvia's "Singing Revolution": why inter-ethnic conflict failed to occur', *Nationalities Papers*, 30(2): 403–433.

Gomez, M. and Brown, V. (2020) 'Contemplations of the Five Mindfulness Trainings: New Paradigm for Racial Justice and the Global Pandemic', ARIZE Sangha. Available at: https://arizesangha.org/contemplations-on-the-five-mindfulness-trainings/ (Accessed on 19 January 2022).

Gonzalez, C.G. (2021) 'Food Sovereignty and Food Justice', in M. Valverde, K.M. Clarke, E. Darian Smith and P. Kotiswaran (eds) *Routledge Handbook of Law and Society*. New York: Routledge, pp 132–137.

Goodman, D. (1999) 'Agro-food studies in the "age of ecology": nature, corporeality, bio-politics', *Sociologia Ruralis*, 39(1): 17–38.

Goodman, D., DuPuis, E.M. and Goodman, M.K. (2012) *Alternative Food Networks: Knowledge, Practice, and Politics*. New York: Routledge.

Gorbachev, M. (2006) *Manifesto for the Earth: Action Now for Peace, Global Justice, and a Sustainable Future*. East Sussex: Clariview Books.

Gorelik, B. (2017) *Rooibos: an Ethnographic Perspective*. Pniel: Rooibos Council.

Gradín, C. (2012) 'Race, poverty and deprivation in South Africa', *Journal of African Economies*, 22(2): 187–238.

Graeber, D. and Wengrow, D. (2021) *The Dawn of Everything: A New History of Humanity*. New York: Penguin.

Grant, C. (2007) 'Geographical Indications and Agricultural products: investigating their relevance in a South African context', Master's thesis, University of Pretoria, Pretoria.

Greenberg, S. (2015) 'Agrarian reform and South Africa's agro-food system', *The Journal of Peasant Studies*, 42: 1–23.

Grīnberga, M. (1995) 'Pēdējā pasaules kara pēdējais mežabrālis [The final forest brother of the last World War]', *Diena*, 18 May 1995.

Grudule, M. (2013) '*The Dawn of Latvian Poetics* (1697) and its resonance in 19th century literature', in E. Wåghäll Nivre, B. Schirrmacher and C. Egerer (eds) *(Re-)Contextualizing Literary and Cultural History: The Representation of the Past in Literary and Material Culture*. Stockholm: Stockholm University, pp 149–168.

Guenther, M. (2020) *Human-Animal Relationships in San and Hunter-Gatherer Cosmology, Volume 1: Therianthropes and Transformation*. Cham, Switzerland: Palgrave Macmillan.

Gutto, S. (2001) *Equality and Non-Discrimination in South Africa: The Political Economy of Law and Law Making.* Cape Town: New Africa Books.

Haak, W., Lazaridis, I., Patterson, N., Rohland, N., Mallick, S., Llamas, B., Brandt, G., Nordenfelt, S., Harney, E. and Stewardson, K. (2015) 'Massive migration from the steppe was a source for Indo-European languages in Europe', *Nature,* 522(7555): 207–211.

Hạnh, T.N. (2008) 'History of engaged Buddhism: A Dharma talk by Thich Nhat Hanh-Hanoi, Vietnam, May 6–7, 2008', *Human Architecture: Journal of the Sociology of Self-Knowledge,* 6(3): 29.

Hạnh, T.N. (2013) *The Mindfulness Survival Kit: Five Essential Practices.* Parallax Press.

Hanovs, D. and Tēraudkalns, V. (2014) 'Happy Birthday, Mr. Ulmanis! Reflections on the construction of an authoritarian regime in Latvia', *Politics, Religion & Ideology,* 15(1): 64–81.

Hausdoerffer, J., Hecht, B.P. Nelson, M.K. and Cummings, K.K. (eds) (2021) *What Kind of Ancestor Do You Want to Be?* Chicago: University of Chicago Press.

Hawken, P. (1993) *Ecology of Commerce.* New York: HarperBusiness.

Hawken, P. (2007) *Blessed Unrest.* New York: Penguin.

Healey, D. (2002) 'Homosexual existence and existing socialism: new light on the repression of male homosexuality in Stalin's Russia', *GLQ: A Journal of Lesbian and Gay Studies,* 8(3): 349–378.

Held, D., McGrew, A., Goldblatt, D. and Perraton, J. (1999) *Global Transformations: Politics, Economics and Culture.* Stanford, CA: Stanford University Press.

Heller, P. (2020) 'The age of reaction: retrenchment populism in India and Brazil', *International Sociology,* 35(6): 590–609.

Hilliard, A.G., Williams, L. and Damalli, N. (eds) (1987) *The Teachings of Ptah Hotep.* Atlanta, GA: Blackwood Press.

Hochschild, A. (2005) *Bury the Chains: Prophets and Rebels in the Fight to Free an Empire's Slaves.* Boston, MA: Houghton Mifflin.

hooks, b. (1989) 'Choosing the margin as a space of radical openness', *Framework: The Journal of Cinema and Media,* (36): 15–23.

Hooks, G. and Smith, C.L. (2013) 'The treadmill of destruction goes global: anticipating the environmental impact of militarism in the 21st century', in K. Gouliamos and C. Kassimeris (eds) *The Marketing of War in the Age of Neo-Militarism.* New York: Routledge, pp 72–96.

Horlings, L.G. (2015) 'The inner dimension of sustainability: personal and cultural values', *Current Opinion in Environmental Sustainability,* 14: 163–169.

Horne, G. (2018) *The apocalypse of settler colonialism: the roots of slavery, white supremacy, and capitalism in seventeenth-century North America and the Caribbean.* New York: Monthly Review Press.

Hugo, V. (1985) *Les Misérables.* Paris: Le Livre de Poche.

Icaza, R. (2017) 'Decolonial feminism and global politics: border thinking and vulnerability as a knowing otherwize', in M. Woons and S. Weier (eds) *Critical Epistemologies of Global Politics*. Bristol: E-International Relations Publishing, pp 26–45.

Inkeles, A. (1969) 'Making men modern: on the causes and consequences of individual change in six developing countries', *American Journal of Sociology*, 75(2): 208–225.

Innes, A. (2015) 'Hungary's illiberal democracy', *Current History*, 114(770): 95–100.

Ives, S. (2007) 'Mediating the neoliberal nation: television in post-apartheid South Africa', *ACME: An International E-Journal for Critical Geographies*, 6(2): 153–173.

Ives, S. (2014) 'Farming the South African "bush": ecologies of belonging and exclusion in Rooibos tea', *American Ethnologist*, 41(4): 698–713.

Ives, S.F. (2017) *Steeped in Heritage: The Racial Politics of South African Rooibos Tea*. Durham, NC: Duke University Press.

Jaffee, D. and Howard, P.H. (2010) 'Corporate cooptation of organic and fair trade standards', *Agriculture and Human Values*, 27(4): 387–399.

Jamail, D. (2022a) 'Ilarion Merculieff (Unangan): Living from the Heart', in D. Jamail and S. Rushworth (eds) *We are in the Middle of Forever: Indigenous Voices from Turtle Island on the Changing Earth*. New York: The New Press, pp 30–47.

Jamail, D. (2022b) 'Terri Delahanty (Cree): Sacred feminine and sacred masculine', in D. Jamail and S. Rushworth (eds) *We are in the Middle of Forever: Indigenous Voices from Turtle Island on the Changing Earth*. New York: The New Press, pp 96–107.

James, C.L.R. (1989 [1938]) *The Black Jacobins*. New York: Vintage Books.

Jones, P. (2006) 'Introduction: the dilemmas of de-Stalinization', in P. Jones (ed) *The Dilemmas of De-Stalinization: Negotiating Cultural and Social Change in the Khrushchev Era*. New York: Routledge, pp 15–32.

Kalnins, M. (2015) *Latvia: A Short History*. London: Hurst & Company.

Kant, I. (1998 [1781]) *Critique of Pure Reason*. Cambridge: Cambridge University Press.

Kaoma, K.J. (2014) *God's Family, God's Earth: Christian Ecological Ethics of Ubuntu*. Zomba, Malawi: Kachere Series.

Kasekamp, A. (2018) *A History of the Baltic States*. Second edition. London: Palgrave Macmillan.

Kaye, J. and Stråth, B. (eds) (2000) *Enlightenment and Genocide: Contradictions of Modernity*. New York: Peter Lang.

Keahey, J. (2009) 'Regional economic integration and local food: the case of Latvia during European Union accession', *International Journal of Sustainable Society*, 1(3): 292–304.

Keahey, J. (2015) 'Fair trade and racial equity in Africa', in L.T. Raynolds and E.A. Bennett (eds) *Handbook of Research on Fair Trade*. Northampton, MA: Edward Elgar Publishing, pp 441–456.

Keahey, J. (2018) 'Gendered livelihoods and social change in post-apartheid South Africa', *Gender, Place & Culture*, 25(4): 525–546.

Keahey, J. (2019) 'Sustainable heritage development in the South African Cederberg', *Geoforum*, 104: 36–45.

Keahey, J. (2020) 'Ethics for development research', *Sociology of Development*, 6(4): 395–416.

Keahey, J. and Murray, D.L. (2017) 'The Promise and perils of market-based Sustainability', *Sustainable Development*, 3(2): 143–162.

Keahey, Jennifer, Raynolds, L.T., Kruger, S. and du Toit, A. (2016) 'Participatory commodity networking: an integrated framework for Fairtrade research and support', *Action Research*.

Kealiikanakaoleohaililani, K. and Giardina, C.P. (2016) 'Embracing the sacred: an indigenous framework for tomorrow's sustainability science', *Sustainability Science*, 11(1): 57–67.

Kempisty, D.M. and Racz, L. (eds) (2021) *Forever Chemicals: Environmental, Economic, and Social Equity Concerns with PFAS in the Environment*. Boca Raton, FL: CRC Press.

Kenney, H. (2016 [1980]) *Verwoerd: Architect of Apartheid*. Johannesburg: Jonathan Ball Publishers.

King, V.O. (2012) 'Latvia's unique path toward independence: the challenges associated with the transition from a Soviet republic to an independent state', *International Social Science Review*, 87(3/4): 127–154.

Knörr, J. (2010) 'Contemporary Creoleness; or, the world in pidginization?', *Current Anthropology*, 51(6): 731–759.

Kök Arslan, H. and Turhan, Y. (2016) 'Reconciliation-oriented leadership: Nelson Mandela and South Africa', *All Azimuth: A Journal of Foreign Policy and Peace*, 5(2): 29–46.

Koot, S., Hitchcock, R. and Gressier, C. (2019) 'Belonging, indigeneity, land and nature in Southern Africa under neoliberal capitalism: an overview', *Journal of Southern African Studies*, 45(2): 341–355.

Krawec, Patty (2022) *Becoming Kin: An Indigenous Call to Unforgetting the Past and Reimagining Our Future*. Minneapolis: Broadleaf Books.

Krøijer, S., Kolling, M. and Sen, A. (2020) 'Ruins and rhythms of development and life after progress', *Ethnos*: 1–20.

Lashendock, J.H. (2019) 'A race to the stars and beyond: how the Soviet Union's success in the space race helped serve as a projection of Communist power', *The Gettysburg Historical Journal*, 18(1): 10–29.

Latvia 2030 (2010) *Sustainable Development Strategy of Latvia until 2030*. Rīga: Ministry of Regional Development and Local Government.

Laurence, B. (1995) 'Ibn al-Haytham: an answer to multicultural science teaching?', *Physics Education*, 30(4): 247.

Legassick, M. (1974) 'Legislation, ideology and economy in post-1948 South Africa', *Journal of Southern African Studies*, 1(1): 5–35.

Lehohla, P. (1998) *The People of South Africa Population Census, 1996.* Pretoria: Statistics South Africa.

Leitch, A. (2018) 'Slow Food and the politics of "virtuous globalization"', in C. Counihan, P. Van Esterik and A. Julier (eds) *Food and Culture.* New York: Routledge, pp 493–509.

Lettus, H. (2003) *The Chronicle of Henry of Livonia.* Translated by J.A. Brundage, New York: Columbia University Press.

Lorde, A. (2015 [1981]) 'The master's tools will never dismantle the master's house', in C. Moraga and G. Anzaldua (eds) *This Bridge Called my Back: Writings by Radical Women of Color.* New York: Suny Press, pp 90–97.

Lötter, D. and le Maitre, D. (2014) 'Modelling the distribution of Aspalathus linearis (Rooibos tea): implications of climate change for livelihoods dependent on both cultivation and harvesting from the wild', *Ecology and Evolution*, 4: 1209–1221.

Lougheed, J. (2009) 'Subsistence and semi-subsistence farming: a priority for EU rural development policy', *EU Rural Review*, 1: 64–69.

Louw, P.E. (2004) *The Rise, Fall, and Legacy of Apartheid.* Westport: Praeger.

Lugones, M. (2010) 'Toward a decolonial feminism', *Hypatia*, 25(4): 742–759.

Lumans, V.O. (2006) *Latvia in World War II.* New York: Fordham University Press.

Maathai, W. (2003) *The Green Belt Movement: Sharing the Approach and the Experience.* New York: Lantern Books.

MacKinnon, E. (2008) 'Grasping at the whirlwinds of change: transitional leadership in comparative perspective. The case studies of Mikhail Gorbachev and F.W. de Klerk', *Canadian Journal of History*, 43(1): 69–107.

Madikizela-Mandela, W. (2013) *491 Days: Prisoner Number 1323/69.* Athens, OH: Ohio University Press.

Magaziner, D.R. (2010) *The Law and the Prophets: Black Consciousness in South Africa, 1968–1977.* Athens, OH: Ohio University Press.

Mägi, M. (2018) *In Austrvegr: The Role of the Eastern Baltic in Viking Age Communication Across the Baltic Sea.* Leiden: Brill.

Makhaya, G. and Roberts, S. (2013) 'Expectations and outcomes: considering competition and corporate power in South Africa under democracy', *Review of African Political Economy*, 40(138): 556–571.

Malik, K. (2014) *Sustaining Human Progress: Reducing Vulnerabilities and Building Resilience*, New York: United Nations Development Programme.

Mallory, J.P. (2006) 'Indo-European Warfare', *Journal of Conflict Archaeology*, 2(1): 77–98.

Mandela, N. (2008) *Long Walk to Freedom: The Autobiography of Nelson Mandela*. New York: Little, Brown and Company.

Mangulis, V. (1983) *Latvia in the Wars of the 20th Century*. Princeton Junction: Cognition Books.

Martin, D. (2013) *Sounding the Cape: Music, Identity and Politics in South Africa*. Oxford: African Books Collective.

Marx, K. (2019 [1867]) *Capital: A Critique of Political Economy*. New York: Dover Publications.

Mathabane, M. (2018) *The Lessons of Ubuntu*. New York: Skyhorse Publishing.

McFadden, P. (2018) 'Contemporarity: sufficiency in a radical African feminist life', *Meridians*, 17(2): 415–431.

McGrath, M. (2021) 'COP26: Fossil fuel industry has largest delegation at climate summit', BBC News, 8 November. Available at: www.bbc.com/news/science-environment-59199484 (Accessed on 11 November 2021).

McWatt, Tessa (2020) *Shame on Me: An Anatomy of Race and Belonging*. Random House Canada.

Meer, F. (2017) *Fatima Meer: Memories of Love and Struggle*. Cape Town: Kwela.

Melluma, A. (1994) 'Metamorphoses of Latvian landscapes during fifty years of Soviet rule', *GeoJournal*, 33(1): 55–62.

Menchú, R. (2003) 'The Quincentenary Conference and the Earth Summit, 1992', in J. Browdy (ed) *Women Writing Resistance: Essays on Latin America and the Caribbean*. Boston, MA: Beacon Press, pp 109–129.

Menchú, R. (2010) *I, Rigoberta Menchú: An Indian Woman in Guatemala*. Brooklyn: Verso Books.

Meskell, L. (2011) *The Nature of Heritage: The New South Africa*. Chichester: John Wiley & Sons.

Meskell, L. and Scheermeyer, C. (2008) 'Heritage as therapy: set pieces from the New South Africa', *Journal of Material Culture*, 13(2): 153–173.

Michael, L. (2018) 'A Stalinist purge in the Khrushchev Era? The Latvian Communist Party purge, 1959–1963', *The Slavonic and East European Review*, 96(2): 244–282.

Mies, M. and Shiva, V. (2014 [1993]) *Ecofeminism*. London: Zed Books, Limited.

Mignolo, W.D. (2009) 'Epistemic disobedience, independent thought and decolonial freedom', *Theory, Culture & Society*, 26(7–8): 159–181.

Mignolo, W.D. and Walsh, C.E. (2018) *On decoloniality: Concepts, Analytics, Praxis*. Durham, NC: Duke University Press.

Miller, D. (2002) 'Smelter and Smith: iron age metal fabrication technology in Southern Africa', *Journal of Archaeological Science*, 29(10): 1083–1131.

Minins, A. (2015) 'Latvia, 1918–1920: A civil war?', *Journal of Baltic Studies*, 46(1): 49–63.

Mlambo, A. and Parsons, N. (2019) *A History of Southern Africa*. London: Red Globe Press.

Mncube, L. and Grimbeek, S. (2016) 'A history of collusion: the persistence of cartels in South Africa', in F. Jenny and Y. Katsoulacos (eds) *Competition Law Enforcement in the BRICS and in Developing Countries: Legal and Economic Aspects*. Cham, Switzerland: Springer International Publishing, pp 337–347.

Mole, R. (2011) 'Nationality and sexuality: homophobic discourse and the "national threat" in contemporary Latvia', *Nations and Nationalism*, 17(3): 540–560.

Mook, A. and Overdevest, C. (2020) 'Fairtrade credentialism: towards understanding certified producer organizations' perceptions of Fairtrade as a credential', *Globalizations*, 17(1): 110–125.

More, M.P. (2004) 'Philosophy in South Africa under and after apartheid', in K. Wiredu (ed) *A Companion to African Philosophy*. Malden, MA: Blackwell Publishing, pp 149–160.

Mostert, N. (1992) *Frontiers: The Epic of South Africa's Creation and the Tragedy of the Xhosa People*. New York: Alfred A. Knopf.

Mugurēvičs, Ē. (2016) 'The military activity of the Order of the Sword Brethren (1202–1236)', in A.V. Murray (ed) *The North-Eastern Frontiers of Medieval Europe: The Expansion of Latin Christendom in the Baltic Lands*. New York: Routledge, pp 117–122.

Muižniece, L. (1989) 'The poetic 'I' in Latvian folk songs', in V. Vīķe-Freibergs (ed) *Linguistics and Poetics of Latvian Folk Songs*. Kingston and Montréal: McGill-Queens University Press, pp 136–147.

Mullins, D.A., Hoyer, D., Collins, C., Currie, T., Feeney, K., François, P., Savage, P. E., Whitehouse, H. and Turchin, P. (2018) 'A systematic assessment of "Axial Age" proposals using global comparative historical evidence', *American Sociological Review*, 83(3): 596–626.

Murray, A.V. (ed) (2001) *Crusade and Conversion on the Baltic Frontier 1150–1500*. London: Routledge.

Mutere, M. (2012) 'Towards an Africa-centered and pan-African theory of communication: Ubuntu and the oral-aesthetic perspective', *Communicatio*, 38(2): 147–163.

Mwaba, K. (2009) 'Attitudes and beliefs about homosexuality and same-sex marriage among a sample of South African students', *Social Behavior and Personality: an international journal*, 37(6): 801–804.

Nabhan, G.P. (2002) *Coming Home to Eat: The Pleasures and Politics of Local Foods*. 1st edition. New York: Norton.

Nadesan, M.H. and Keahey, J. (2022) 'Energy neomercantilism and regenerative alternatives', in J. Simões, F. Leandro, R. Oberoi and E. Caetano de Sousa (eds) *Changing the Paradigm of Energy Geopolitics: Resources and Pathways in the Light of Global Climate Challenges*. New York: Peter Lang Publishing.

Nagar, R. and Geiger, S. (2007) 'Reflexivity and positionality in feminist fieldwork revisited', in A. Tickell, E. Sheppard, J. Peck and T. Barnes (eds) *Politics and Practice in Economic Geography*. Thousand Oaks, CA: Sage Publications, pp 267–278.

Narayanan, V. (2001) 'Water, wood, and wisdom: ecological perspectives from the Hindu traditions', *Daedalus*, 130(4): 179–206.

National Planning Commission (2015) *Our Future: Make it Work*. Pretoria: Republic of South Africa.

Nietzsche, F. (2021) *God is Dead: God Remains Dead. And We Have Killed Him*. New York, NY: Penguin.

Nissinen, M. (1999) *Latvia's Transition to a Market Economy: Political Determinants of Economic Reform Policy*. London: Palgrave Macmillian.

Norgaard, K.M. and Fenelon, J. (2021) 'Towards an Indigenous Environmental sociology', in C.B. Schaefer, A. Jorgenson, S.A. Malin and L. Peek (eds) *Handbook of Environmental Sociology*. Cham, Switzerland: Springer, pp 477–494.

Norkus, Z. (2018) 'First calculations of the total output of Latvia and Lithuania in the 1920s: a comparison', *Journal of Baltic Studies*, 49(2): 241–261.

Norkus, Z., Morkevičius, V. and Markevičiūtė, J. (2020) 'From warfare to welfare states? Social and military spending in the Baltic States 1918–1940', *Scandinavian Economic History Review*, 69: 1–21.

Ntsebeza, L. (2011) 'The land question: exploring obstacles to land redistribution in South Africa', in I. Shapiro and K. Tebeau (eds) *After Apartheid: Reinventing South Africa?* Charlottesville, VA: University of Virginia Press, pp 294–308.

O'Connor, K.C. (2019) *The House of Hemp and Butter: A History of Old Riga*. Dekalb, IL: Northern Illinois University Press.

Okereke, C. (2008) *Global Justice and Neoliberal Environmental Governance*. New York: Routledge.

Okoro, N.K. (2015) 'Ubuntu ideality: the foundation of African compassionate and humane living', *Journal of Scientific Research and Reports*, 8(1): 1–9.

Olivier, E. (2009) 'Afrikaner spirituality: a complex mixture', *HTS Teologiese Studies/Theological Studies*, 62(4): a405.

Orr, D.W. (1996) 'Slow knowledge', *Conservation Biology*, 10(3): 699–702.

Otieno, S.A. (2020) 'Ethical thought of Archbishop Desmond Tutu: Ubuntu and Tutu's moral modeling as transformation and renewal', in N. Wariboko and T. Falola (eds) *The Palgrave Handbook of African Social Ethics*. Cham, Switzerland: Palgrave Macmillan, pp 589–604.

Ozola, S. (2021) 'Generative creating of sacral space: mythology, cosmology and places for cult rituals', *Society. Integration. Education. Proceedings of the International Scientific Conference May 28th–29th, 2021*, IV: 626–652.

Ozoliṇa, L. (2019) *Politics of Waiting: Workfare, Post-Soviet Austerity and the Ethics of Freedom*. Manchester: Manchester University Press.

Pabriks, A. and Purs, A. (2001) *Latvia: The Challenges of Change*. London: Routledge.

Page, S.W. (2018) 'Social and national currents in Latvia, 1860–1917', *American Slavic and East European Review*, 8(1): 25–36.

Pannett, Rachel. (2023) 'LGBTQ groups celebrate Latvia electing E.U.'s first openly gay president.' Washington Post, 1 June. Available at: https://www.washingtonpost.com/world/2023/06/01/latvia-president-gay-edgars-rinkevics/ (Accessed on 3 September 2023).

Parker, P. and Mokhesi-Parker, J. (1998) *In the Shadow of Sharpeville: Apartheid and Criminal Justice*. London: Macmillan Press.

Patel, R. (2009) 'Food sovereignty', *The Journal of Peasant Studies*, 36(3): 663–706.

Patrickson, S., Malgas, R. and Oettle, N. (2008) 'Rooibos tea: environmental threat or conservation opportunity?', *Veld & Flora*, 94(1): 8–11.

Penikis, A. (1996) 'The third awakening begins: the birth of the Latvian popular front, June 1988 to August 1988', *Journal of Baltic Studies*, 27(4): 261–290.

Penn, N. (2005) *The Forgotten Frontier: Colonist & Khoisan on the Cape's Northern Frontier in the 18th Century*. Cape Town: Double Storey Books.

Penn, N. G. (1986) 'Pastoralists and pastoralism in the Northern Cape frontier zone during the eighteenth century', *Goodwin Series*, 5: 62–68.

Pichler, M. (2013) '"People, planet & profit": consumer-oriented hegemony and power relations in palm oil and agrofuel certification', *The Journal of Environment & Development*, 22(4): 370–390.

Plakans, A. (1995) *The Latvians: A Short History*. Stanford, CA: Hoover Institution Press.

Polanyi, K. (1957) *The Great Transformation: The Political and Economic Origins of Our Time*. Boston, MA: Beacon Press.

Posel, D. (2009) 'The assassination of Hendrik Verwoerd: The spectre of apartheid's corpse', *African Studies*, 68(3): 331–350.

Pretorius-Heuchert, J. (1992) 'Familicide from a clinical-community psychology perspective', *Koers-Bulletin for Christian Scholarship*, 57(4): 397–412.

Pruitt, W. (2010) 'The progress of democratic policing in South Africa', *African Journal of Criminology and Justice Studies*, 4(1): 116–140.

Purs, A. (2013) *Baltic Facades: Estonia, Latvia and Lithuania since 1945*. London: Reaktion Books.

Purs, A. and Plakans, A. (2017) *Historical Dictionary of Latvia*. Third edition. New York: Rowman & Littlefield.

Pyles, L. (2018) *Healing Justice: Holistic Self-Care For Change Makers*. Oxford: Oxford University Press.

Randle, S. and Barnes, J. (2018) 'Liquid futures: water management systems and anticipated environments', *WIREs Water*, 5(2): e1274.

Rao, M. (2012) 'Ecofeminism at the crossroads in India: a review', *DEP*, 20(12): 124–142.

Raphael-Hernandez, H. (2017) 'The right to freedom: eighteenth-century slave resistance and early Moravian missions in the Danish West Indies and Dutch Suriname', *Atlantic Studies*, 14(4): 457–475.

Ray, M.L. (2003) 'Recovering the voice of the oppressed: master, slave, and serf in the Baltic provinces', *Journal of Baltic Studies*, 34(1): 1–21.

Raynolds, L.T. (2004) 'The globalization of organic agro-food networks', *World Development*, 32(5): 725–743.

Raynolds, L.T. and Bennett, E.A. (2015) 'Introduction to research on fair trade', in L.T. Raynolds and E.A Bennett (eds) *Handbook of Research on Fair Trade*. Northampton, MA: Edward Elgar, pp 3–23.

Raynolds, L.T. and Greenfield, N. (2015) 'Fair trade: movement and markets', in L.T. Raynolds and E.A Bennett (eds) *Handbook of Research on Fair Trade*. Northampton, MA: Edward Elgar, pp 24–41.

Raynolds, L.T. and Ngcwangu, S.U. (2010) 'Fair trade rooibos tea: connecting South African producers and American consumer markets', *Geoforum*, 41: 74–83.

Reed, M. (2010) *Rebels for the Soil: The Rise of the Global Organic Food and Farming Movement*. New York: Routledge.

Reinsone, S. (2016) 'Forbidden and sublime forest landscapes: narrated experiences of Latvian national partisan women after World War II', *Cold War History*, 16(4): 395–416.

Relethford, J.H. (2008) 'Genetic evidence and the modern human origins debate', *Heredity*, 100(6): 555–563.

Richardson, E. (2018) *NATO, the Warsaw Pact, and the Iron Curtain*. New York: Cavendish Square.

Roothaan, A. (2019) *Indigenous, Modern and Postcolonial Relations to Nature: Negotiating the Environment*. New York: Routledge.

Rose, D. and Allen, R. (2018) *Ancient Civilizations of the World*. London: Ed-Tech Press.

Rostow, W.W. (1960) *The Stages of Economic Growth: A Non-Communist Manifesto*. Cambridge: Cambridge University Press.

Rowell, S.C. (1994) *Lithuania Ascending: A Pagan Empire within East-Central Europe, 1295–1345*. Cambridge: Cambridge University Press.

Ruether, R.R. (2000) *Women Healing Earth: Third World Women on Ecology, Feminism, and Religion*. Maryknoll, NY: Orbis Books.

Sahan, E. (2019) 'Greed does not have to drive business: the role of Fair Trade Enterprises as proof of concept', *Journal of Fair Trade*, 1(2): 14–23.

Santos, B.d.S. (2014) *Epistemologies of the South: Justice Against Epistemicide*. New York: Routledge.

Sarmiento, E.R. (2017) 'Synergies in alternative food network research: embodiment, diverse economies, and more-than-human food geographies', *Agriculture and Human Values*, 34(2): 485–497.

Schwartz, K.Z.S. (2006) *Nature and National Identity After Communism: Globalizing the Ethnoscape*. Pitt Series in Russian and East European Studies. Pittsburgh, PA: University of Pittsburgh Press.

Schwartz, K.Z.S. (2007) '"The occupation of beauty": imagining nature and nation in Latvia', *East European Politics and Societies*, 21(2): 259–293.

Seekings, J. (2007) '"Not a single white person should be allowed to go under": swartgevaar and the origins of South Africa's welfare state, 1924–1929', *The Journal of African History*, 48(3): 375–394.

Seekings, J. (2011) 'Poverty and Inequality in South Africa, 1994–2007', in I. Shapiro and K. Tebeau (eds) *After Apartheid: Reinventing South Africa?* Charlottesville, VI: University of Virginia Press, pp 21–51.

Segato, R. (2016) 'Patriarchy from margin to center: discipline, territoriality, and cruelty in the apocalyptic phase of capital', *South Atlantic Quarterly*, 115(3): 615–624.

Seidman, G. (2001) 'Guerrillas in their midst: armed struggle in the South African anti-apartheid movement', *Mobilization: An International Quarterly*, 6(2): 111–127.

Sesanti, S. (2018) 'Teaching ancient Egyptian philosophy (ethics) and history: fulfilling a quest for a decolonized and Afrocentric education', *Educational Research for Social Change*, 7(SPE): 1–15.

Shiva, V. (1993) *Monocultures of the Mind: Perspectives on Biodiversity and Biotechnology*. London, UK: Zed Books.

Shiva, V. (2003) 'The Chipko women's concept of freedom', in R.S. Gottlieb (ed) *This Sacred Earth: Religion, Nature, Environment*. New York: Routledge.

Shiva, V. and Jafri, A.H. (2002) 'Seeds of suicide: the ecological and human costs of globalization of agriculture', in V. Shiva and G. Bedi (eds) *Sustainable Agriculture and Food Security: The Impact of Globalization*. New Delhi: Sage Publications.

Silova, I. (2006) *From Sites of Occupation to Symbols of Multiculturalism: Reconceptualizing Minority Education in Post-Soviet Latvia*. Greenwich, CT: Information Age Publishing.

Skultans, V. (1998) *The Testimony of Lives: Narrative and Memory in Post-Soviet Latvia*. London: Psychology Press.

Šmidchens, G. (2014) *The Power of Song: Nonviolent National Culture in the Baltic Singing Revolution*. Seattle, WA: University of Washington Press.

Smith, A. B. (2009) 'Pastoralism in the Western Cape Province, South Africa: a retrospective review', *Journal of African Archaeology*, 7(2): 239.

Smith, C. (1991) *The Emergence of Liberation Theology: Radical Religion and Social Movement Theory*. Chicago, IL: University of Chicago Press.

Smith, D.J., Pabriks, A., Purs, A. and Lane, T. (2002) *The Baltic States: Estonia, Latvia, and Lithuania*. London: Routledge.

Smith, Jackie, Gemici, B., Plummer, S. and. Hughes, M.M. (2018) 'Transnational social movement organizations and counter-hegemonic struggles today', *Journal of World-Systems Research*, 24: 372-403.

Smuts, D. and Westcott, S. (1991) *The Purple Shall Govern: A South African A to Z of Nonviolent Action*. Oxford: Oxford University Press.

Šnē, A. (2006) 'The economy and social power in the late prehistoric chiefdoms of ancient Latvia', *Archaeologia Baltica*, 6: 68–78.

Sniķere, V. (2019) *Dainas: Translated from Latvian*. Rīga: Apgāds Mansards.

Sommers, J. (2009) 'The Anglo-American model of economic organization and governance: entropy and the fragmentation of social solidarity in twenty-first century Latvia', *Debatte: Journal of Contemporary Central and Eastern Europe*, 17(2): 127–142.

Spalviņa, A. (2017) 'Latvian Puzuris Mastery' [video], Investment and Development Agency of Latvia (LIAA). Available at: www.facebook.com/watch/?v=2226792714004891 (Accessed on 5 June 2022).

Spechler, M.C., Ahrens, J. and Hoen, H.W. (2017) *State Capitalism in Eurasia*. London: World Scientific.

Springer, E. (2020) 'Bureaucratic tools in (gendered) organizations: performance metrics and gender advisors in international development', *Gender & Society*, 34(1): 56–80.

Stepanova, F. and Stepanova, E. (2011) 'Alliteration in (Balto-) Finnic languages', in J. Roper (ed), *Alliteration in Culture*. New York: Springer.

Stinchcombe, A. (1995) *Sugar Island Slavery in the Age of Enlightenment: The Political Economy of the Caribbean World*. Princeton, NJ: Princeton University Press.

Strambach, S. and Surmelier, A. (2013) 'Knowledge dynamics in setting sustainable standards in tourism: the case of "Fair Trade in Tourism South Africa"', *Current Issues in Tourism*, 16(7–8): 736–752.

Strange, S. (2015) *Casino Capitalism*. Manchester: Manchester University Press.

Strods, H. (2005) 'Sovietization of Latvia 1944–1991', in V. Nollendorfs and E. Oberländer (eds) *The Hidden and Forbidden History of Latvia Under Soviet and Nazi Occupations 1940–1991*. Rīga: Institute of the History of Latvia, pp 209–227.

Strods, H. and Kott, M. (2002) 'The file on operation "Priboi": A re-assessment of the mass deportations of 1949', *Journal of Baltic Studies*, 33(1): 1–36.

Sullivan, M. and Arat, A. (2018) 'Postsecular charisma: Thich Nhat Hanh and the ethics of mindfulness', in S. Stanley, R.E. Puser and N.N. Singh (eds) *Handbook of Ethical Foundations of Mindfulness*. Cham, Switzerland: Springer, pp 339–354.

Switzer, L. (2000) 'Introduction: South Africa's Resistance Press in Perspective', in L. Switzer and M. Adhikari (eds) *South Africa's Resistance Press: Alternative Voices in the Last Generation under Apartheid*. Athens: Ohio University Center for International Studies, pp 1–53.

Symons, S. (2020) '"Casting shadows": Militarized boyhoods in apartheid South Africa during the 1980s', *Childhood*, OnlineFirst.

Taagepera, R. (2011) 'Albert, Martin, and Peter too: their roles in creating the Estonian and Latvian Nations', *Journal of Baltic Studies*, 42(2): 125–141.

Thompson, L. (2014) *A History of South Africa*. Fourth edition. New Haven, CT: Yale University Press.

Tinker, G.E. (2004) *Spirit and Resistance: Political Theology and American Indian Liberation*. Philadelphia: Fortress Press.

Tinker, G.E. (2020) *American Indian Liberation: A Theology of Sovereignty*. Maryknoll, NY: Orbis Books.

Tombs, D. (2021) *Latin American Liberation Theology*. Boston, MA: Brill.

Triegaardt, J.D. (2005) 'The Child Support Grant in South Africa: a social policy for poverty alleviation?', *International Journal of Social Welfare*, 14(4): 249–255.

Tucker, S.C. (2015) *Wars That Changed History: 50 of the World's Greatest Conflicts*. Santa Barbara: ABC=CLIO.

Turnbull, S. (2004) *Crusader Castles of the Teutonic Knights (2): The Stone Castles of Latvia and Estonia 1185–1560*. Oxford: Osprey Publishing.

Tutu, D.M. (1999) *No Future without Forgiveness*. New York: Doubleday.

Tutu, D. and Tutu, M. (2014) *The Book of Forgiving: The Fourfold Path for Healing Ourselves and Our World*. New York: Harper One.

UNDP (2019) *Gender Inequality Index*. New York: United Nations Development Programme.

UNESCO (1999) 'Fossil Hominid Sites of South Africa', United Nations Educational, Scientific, and Cultural Organization. Available at: https://whc.unesco.org/en/list/915/ (Accessed on 5 June 2020).

Uysal, H.H., Plakans, L. and Dembovskaya, S. (2007) 'English language spread in local contexts: Turkey, Latvia and France', *Current Issues in Language Planning*, 8(2): 192–207.

Vallance, S., Perkins, H.C. and Dixon, J.E. (2011) 'What is social sustainability? A clarification of concepts', *Geoforum*, 42(3): 342–348.

Vallie, I. (2019) 'Beyond the skyline', in S. Gunn and S. Haricharan (eds) *Voices from the Underground*. Cape Town: Penguin Random House, pp 201–218.

Van den Bercken, W. (1989) *Ideology and Atheism in the Soviet Union*. Berlin: Mouton de Gruyter.

van der Waal, C.S. (2012) 'Creolization and purity: Afrikaans language politics in post-apartheid times', *African Studies*, 71(3): 446–463.

Van Vuuren, H. (2018) *Apartheid Guns and Money: A Tale of Profit.* London: C. Hurst & Co.

Via Campesina (2007) 'Nyéléni declaration. Sélingué, Mali: Forum for Food Sovereignty', Forum for Food Sovereignty. Available at: https://viacampes ina.org/en/declaration-of-nyi/ (Accessed on 17 May 2022).

Vīķe-Freiberga, V. (1997) *Trejādas saules I. Kosmoloģiskā saule.* Rīga: Karogs.

Vīķe-Freiberga, V. (1999) *Trejādas saules II. Hronoloģiskā saule.* Rīga: Karogs.

Vīķe-Freiberga, V. (2001) Runa Dziesmu svētku noslēguma koncertā Mežaparka Lielajā estrādē 2001.gada 29.jūlijā. Available at: https://www.vestnesis.lv/ta/id/27917 (Accessed on 15 August 2023).

Vīķe-Freiberga, V. (2002) *Trejādas saules III. Meteoroloģiskā saule.* Rīga: Karogs.

Vīķe-Freibergs, V. (ed) (1989) *Linguistics and Poetics of Latvian Folk Songs.* Montréal: McGill-Queens University Press.

Vīķis-Freibergs, V. (1997) 'Sink or swim: on associative structuring in longer Latvian folksongs', *Oral Tradition,* 12(2): 279–307.

Vīķis-Freibergs, V. (1999) 'Similarity and contrast as structuring principles in the Latvian Daina Quatrain', *Journal of Baltic Studies,* 30(3): 201–226.

Villas Boas, A. and Folloni, A. (2021) 'The "common good" spirituality of Louis-Joseph Lebret and his influence in the Constitution and development thinking in Brazil', *Journal of Global Ethics,* 17(2): 185–203.

Viswanathan, P.K. (2014) 'The rationalization of agriculture in Kerala: implications for the natural environment, agro-ecosystems and livelihoods', *Agrarian South: Journal of Political Economy,* 3(1): 63–107.

Waetjen, T. (2004) *Workers and Warriors: Masculinity and the Struggle for Nation in South Africa.* Urbana, IL: University of Illinois Press.

Waitt, G. (2005) 'Sexual citizenship in Latvia: geographies of the Latvian closet', *Social & Cultural Geography,* 6(2): 161–181.

Walsh, Zack (2017) 'Contemplative praxis for social-ecological transformation', *The Arrow,* 4: 1–19.

Warburton, D.A. (2009) 'Egypt and Mesopotamia', in G. Leick (ed) *The Babylonian World.* Abingdon: Routledge, pp 496–511.

Ward, L. (2020) *America's Racial Karma: An Invitation to Heal.* Berkeley, CA: Parallax Press.

Watene, K. and Yap, M. (2015) 'Culture and sustainable development: indigenous contributions', *Journal of Global Ethics,* 11(1): 51–55.

Waterton, E. (2014) 'A more-than-representational understanding of heritage? The 'past' and the politics of affect', *Geography Compass,* 8(11): 823–833.

World Commission on Environment and Development (WCED) (1987) *Our Common Future.* Available at: https://sustainabledevelopment.un.org/cont ent/documents/5987our-common-future.pdf (Accessed on 12 June 2023).

Weber, H. and Weber, M. (2020) 'When means of implementation meet Ecological Modernization Theory: a critical frame for thinking about the Sustainable Development Goals initiative', *World Development*, 136: 105129.

Weber, M. (1978 [1922]) *Economy and Society: An Outline of Interpretive Sociology*. Berkeley, CA: University of California Press.

Weber, M. (2012 [1920]) *The Protestant Ethic and the Spirit of Capitalism*. London: Routledge.

Wilson, N.L.W. (2005) 'Cape natural tea products and the US market: Rooibos rebels ready to raid', *Review of Agricultural Economics*, 27(1): 139–148.

Winter, T. (2013) 'Clarifying the critical in critical heritage studies', *International Journal of Heritage Studies*, 19(6): 532–545.

World Economic Forum (2021) *Global Gender Gap Report 2021*, Geneva: Switzerland.

Zafirovksi, M. (2010) *The Enlightenment and Its Effects on Modern Society*. New York: Springer.

Zagorska, I. (2019) 'The Early Mesolithic bone and antler industry in Latvia, Eastern Baltic', in D. Groß, H. Lübke, J. Meadows and D. Jantzen (eds) *Working at the Sharp End: From Bone and Antler to Early Mesolithic life in Northern Europe*. Kiel/Hamburg: Wachholtz Verlag, pp 305–318.

Žakevičiūtė, R. (2016) 'Socio-economic differentiation in the post-communist rural Baltics: the case of three kolkhozes', *Journal of Baltic Studies*, 47(3): 349–368.

Zinkina, J., Christian, D., Grinin, L., Ilyin, I., Andreev, A., Aleshkovski, I., et al (2019) *A Big History of Globalization: The Emergence of a Global World System*. Cham, Switzerland: Springer.

Zobena, A. (1998) 'Organic farming in the Baltic countries social aspects of development', in A. Vlavianos-Arvanitis and J. Morovic (eds) *Biopolitics, Volume VI*.

Index

References to figures are in *italics*. References to endnotes show
both the page number and the note number (158n1).